The Small Isles

The Small Isles

John Hunter

Published in 2016 by
Historic Environment Scotland

Historic Environment Scotland
Longmore House
Salisbury Place
Edinburgh EH9 1SH

telephone +44 (0) 131 662 1456

Historic Environment Scotland
Scottish Charity SC045925

British Library Cataloguing-in-Publication Data.
A catalogue record for this book is available from
the British Library.

ISBN 978 1 902419 92 3

Typeset in Garamond, Brunel and Gill Sans
Printed in Poland by Pozkal

Front Cover

The Small Isles.
HES DP031342

Back Cover

The ground floor hall in Kinloch Castle.
HES DP039613

Endpapers

Herring curing on Canna, c1900.
© National Trust for Scotland. Licensor Scran
Cows in the Bay of Laig, Eigg overlooking the mountains of Rum.
© Gareth Wyn Jones. Licensor Scran

Frontispiece

Eigg, Muck, Rum, Canna and Sanday.
HES DP221659

Contents

Preface

At the turn of the 18th and 19th centuries the Small Isles were visited by a lady called Sarah Murray, one of the few female visitors at that time. She described them as 'emerging from legend' – a particularly apposite phrase which, in archaeological terms, encapsulates the end of those centuries of which we know little, and the beginning of those years of which we know more. It was the time when the cultures of island communities were brought into the realities of an economic world in which the kelp industry and intensive sheep farming provided massive social change. In researching this volume it soon became clear that the traditions and customs developed over hundreds of years in these four islands had become either depleted or erased in the first part of the 19th century. This was the result of eviction and emigration, enforced or otherwise, which saw the wholesale exodus of family units and social groups. These movements occurred throughout the Highlands, but their effects were most pronounced among the islands where the physical constraints of insularity shaped culture on a local scale. Reduced populations lived under new controls, former communal enterprises were no longer possible with a depleted population, social structures changed, and the way of life was fundamentally altered. Incomers arrived and within a few generations local cultural memories had faded and a new order developed. Place-names had become obsolete or

altered, buildings and structures abandoned, and traditions forgotten. In most respects the Small Isles had become islands without memories. Their traditions and customs over the centuries now lie embedded in a landscape of grass-grown foundations, field systems and obscure earthworks. Landscapes were created by people, and this is a book about the footprints they left behind.

In considering how this volume should be structured, I was torn between several conflicting options: whether it should be configured on an island-by-island basis, on a thematic basis, or according to accepted chronological periods. There were arguments in favour of each, but it soon became clear that the character and landscape histories of the individual islands, the nature of the archaeological sites on each and, not least, the effects of their ownership through time, were so distinctive that it was impossible to discuss the four islands as a single entity. Hence, each is treated individually, but in a broad chronological way that allows a degree of cross-island comparison, and with an over-riding introductory chapter. Structuring the volume in this manner also allows visitors to each island to have a dedicated text on that island's general character, an understanding of particular sites worthy of note, and a map of suggested sites which might be visited. In writing it I have tried to find a compromise between the serious tenor of an academic publication and the accessibility of a popular guidebook. I have also tried to introduce human elements to the historic landscape wherever I could.

Galmisdale, Eigg, photographed by Erskine Beveridge in 1883.
HES SC743154

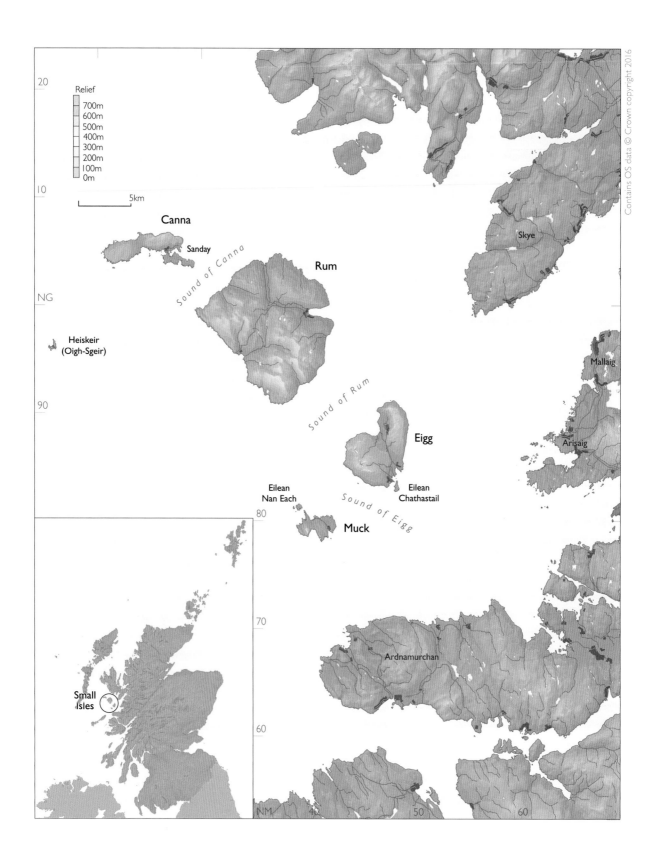

Relief

700m
600m
500m
400m
300m
200m
100m
0m

5km

Canna

Sanday

Sound of Canna

Rum

Skye

NG

Heiskeir
(Oigh-Sgeir)

Sound of Rum

90

Mallaig

Eigg

Arisaig

Eilean
Nan Each

Eilean
Chathastail

80

Sound of Eigg

Muck

Small
Isles

70

Ardnamurchan

60

NM   40   50   60

Chapter One
The Small Isles

The Natural Environment

The Small Isles comprise four main inhabited islands – Canna, Eigg, Muck and Rum – and a tiny outlier, Heiskeir (otherwise known as Oigh-Sgeir), which is little more than a rock outcrop in the sea surmounted by an automated lighthouse. Rum is by far the largest (10,400ha), bleak and recognised by its towering mountains; the other three are smaller, greener and look friendlier. Canna (1,130ha) and Muck (560ha) are both relatively low-lying, but Eigg (3,050ha) is characterised by the sombre silhouette of the Sgurr, a huge jutting stump of pitchstone eagerly climbed by day-trippers. Canna, Eigg and Muck each include an associated smaller island. The largest of these is Sanday, which is inhabited, connected to the south-east of Canna by a modern road bridge, but formerly by a narrow footbridge which was washed away in 2005. The small island of Eilean Chathastail (Castle Island) sits off the south-east coast of Eigg, and Eilean nan Each (Horse Island) lies off the north-west of Muck. Both of these are generally accessible only by boat, although Eilean Chathastail can be reached by foot during certain low tides. The whole group lies to the south of Skye, adjacent to the sea routes that run up the west coast of the mainland or across to the Western Isles.

Fig 1.1 The Small Isles and their location. HES GV006082

This chapter sketches a brief settlement history through time, focusing on archaeology and landscape development. Subsequent chapters take an island-by-island view – on Canna, Eigg, Muck and Rum respectively – each one detailing those sites which are either unique, good examples of their type, or sites which are representative of their period. Although this is a book predominantly about archaeology, there is inevitably a thread of history that runs through it. In evaluating and interpreting landscape features from historic periods, archaeology and history become woven together.

All four islands have unique topographies, and different stories to tell; each has its own idiosyncratic visual character and merits individual attention in its own right. The islands are all very different too in their expressions of past human activity, not so much as a result of human impact on the local environment, but as a result of the limitations of individual island landscapes. Furthermore, the various interests, ambitions and whims of the island owners over the last two centuries have played no small part in determining the levels of archaeological survival in each. Between them the four islands present a palimpsest of human settlement and activity from earliest times through to the present day – from the lithic workings of itinerant Mesolithic peoples almost ten thousand years ago to the management of Victorian sporting estates,

Fig 1.2 The small uninhabited island of Heiskeir lies to the west of Rum and is dominated by its lighthouse, engineered by the Stevenson family. HES DP109421

conservation and community buy-outs. But no single island exhibits all of them.

The geology of all four islands is well documented: providing the full details is unnecessary here and the interested reader is directed towards geological texts.[1] In short, the islands are volcanic, mostly composed of igneous rocks formed during a period of intense volcanic activity beginning about 60 million years ago, well beyond the timescale of human occupation covered in this book. Torridonian sandstones dominate the northern part of Rum, and small areas of Jurassic sandstones, mudstones and limestones are visible around sections of its coast, as well as around parts of Eigg and Muck. Muck, with mostly basalt derived soils, has enormous variety in the microgeography of its fertile areas adjacent to bogs and peat (often marked by bracken). The three smaller islands have unusual terrace-like surfaces – the result of lava flows, chiefly of basalt and mugearite, which have weathered into a series of gently sloping ledges. Being relatively soft, these ledges have developed fertile soils which make them well suited to cultivation and grazing. As a result all three have become attractive propositions for settlement throughout the centuries. That said, Eigg's heather-covered upland has been shattered by the Sgurr which looms over the island, its presence resulting from a lava flow that once filled a river valley cut deeply into the basalt, but is now left standing proud as the softer valley sides have eroded away.

Rum is different altogether: its igneous rocks have a distinctive origin. These are mostly intrusive rocks formed from magma that failed to break the surface but cooled deep within an enormous volcano, now eroded down to its roots. Neither these rocks nor the hard-wearing Torridonian sandstones of the northern half of the island provided the nutrients necessary for the development of fertile soils. Instead, combined with Rum's high rainfall, the landscape is dominated by wet heathland. Settlement and cultivation is limited to a few blotches of green where the valleys meet the coast.

The Small Isles sit within the Atlantic fringe of Scotland, to some extent sheltered by the Outer Hebrides, at approximate latitude 57° N. Put in a wider context, this places them on roughly the same latitude as Hudson Bay, Canada, to the west, and slightly north of Moscow to the east. Proximity to Atlantic weather systems and water circulation makes them relatively sensitive to any change in climatic conditions. It also presents some limitations on vegetation and

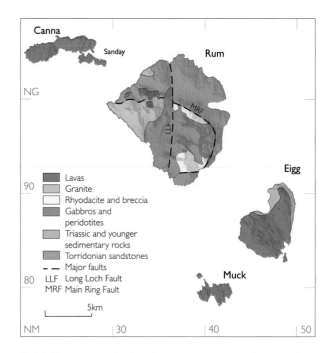

Fig 1.3 The intense volcanic activity which created the Small Isles has left an arresting mark on the islands' geology. Rum's principal rock types differ from the other islands, and as a consequence the island has a unique character. HES GV006083

tree cover and, in turn, in what would have been possible in terms of land use and in the nature of a farming cycle. Little work has been carried out on the palaeoecology of the islands themselves, but there is enough information from pollen cores and from similar research in the surrounding areas, notably in the Outer Hebrides, Skye and Mull where conditions are comparable, to be able to understand their likely climatic and vegetation conditions over time.

We know, for example, that in the earlier part of prehistory, in the mid 8th millennium BC, much of the terrain was likely to have been covered by scrub woodland of hazel (*Corylus avellana*) and willow (*Salix*), with some birch (*Betula*).[2] These species flourished, especially in the more sheltered areas away from Atlantic exposure, and would have presented a landscape very different from the predominantly

Fig 1.4 The craggy peak of Askival on Rum demonstrates the continuing weathering process which has shaped the islands over the millennia since their volcanic beginnings. HES DP094990

treeless environment seen today. Such species require relatively long periods of stable warmth in order to prosper, and are often used as proxy indicators of earlier climate. The same periods of stable warmth would also encourage settlement. Alder (*Alnus*), a species preferring wetter conditions as well as being salt-tolerant, appears on the scene in the later 5th millennium BC and, as a result, has often been taken to suggest a period of climatic deterioration. However, the eventual decline of the alder in the pollen record together with that of hazel and willow by the mid 4th millennium BC is more likely to have been attributable to the effects of human interference on the landscape than to significant climatic change.

The prehistory of Rum and Canna can be further explored through insights gained from pollen analysis. The Rum data, which has the benefit of associated radiocarbon dates, demonstrates a relatively sudden and sustained shift in the pollen record at around the mid 4th millennium BC. Woodland reduction, in harness with the emergence of grasses, cereal pollen and charcoal, points heavily to human involvement.[3] Soil erosion, evidenced from the presence of hillwash in the pollen record, points to a similar conclusion – namely the gradual deforestation of the island in

Fig 1.5 Eigg (foreground) and Muck, from the north-east.
HES DP095087

favour of agriculture during the early part of the Neolithic, probably around 3500 BC. Rum contains only small areas of fertile land, but the processes that took place there almost certainly occurred in a more ubiquitous way than on its neighbours Canna, Eigg and Muck. The Canna data, without radiocarbon dating, mirrors similar pollen events, also supporting the interpretation of early human impact on the islands.[4]

The formation of peat can result from a combination of environmental factors such as saturated ground, a consistently high water table and limited evaporation. However, peat formation can also be brought about by specific human activities which lead to changes in soil hydrology. Research suggests that in many parts of the Scottish uplands persistent woodland clearance caused the newly exposed heathland to foster conditions amenable to peat formation. Moreover, over-cultivation and the denuding of soils, combined with climatic deterioration, may have also caused upland settlement

Fig 1.6 Canna (right) and Sanday (left) from the north-east.
HES DP094967

to be abandoned. This may then have resulted in population movement to lower levels with blanket peat eventually burying many early prehistoric houses and field systems. This is well attested in both the Outer Hebrides and Shetland,[5] and we see it too on Canna where hut-circles and their attendant field systems are only partly visible in the peat-bogs at the west end. Although little pollen analysis has been carried out on the Small Isles, there is sufficient evidence to suggest that the creation of peat there was at least in part caused by the deliberate removal of woodland. Today, Rum is particularly rich in peat, partly through its relative size, but also partly due to its denuded upland landscape. Its wealth in this respect was noted in the *Statistical Account* in the late 18th century which records it supplying fuel to both Canna and Muck.[6]

Areas of the islands may have been wooded well into the Middle Ages and the probable extent of original forestation on Rum has been postulated to have covered much of the north and north-east parts of the island.[7] However, by the end of the 18th century

one learned visitor recorded that Canna was 'destitute of even a gooseberry-bush',[8] and from the later 19th century successive owners of Rum busied themselves creating plantations, suggesting that the ancient superstitious name for the island *Riogachd na Forraiste Fiadhaich* (Kingdom of the Wild Forest) was pretty much irrelevant.[9]

Prehistory
In the 1980s Rum achieved fame as the home of 'Scotland's First Settlers' following the excavation of Mesolithic nomadic activity at Kinloch Fields at the head of Loch Scresort, to the north of Kinloch Castle. Radiocarbon dates from the site indicated occupation at about 7500 BC and, until recently, these were the earliest dates for a human settlement anywhere in Scotland. Current work on Applecross and the east coast of Skye suggests widespread Mesolithic activity there too, but no other material confirmed to this period has so far been recorded on the Small Isles. Eigg, however, offers some potential here among the many rock shelters concealed in the boulder screes beneath the cliffs on the east coast of the island, some of which have substantial shell middens spreading out from their entrances. There are further rock shelters on

Muck and on Rum, but neither these nor those on Eigg have been fully investigated.

The pollen record suggests that by the middle of the 4th century BC nomadic activity of this nature was waning, and that woodland clearances were occurring in order to enable agriculture to take place. The Small Isles were already becoming home to resident settlers as part of a wider Neolithic society (c4000–2500 BC) whose traces are more visible than those of their predecessors. During the Canna survey large quantities of pottery of this period, including Unstan Ware and Early Bronze Age Beaker sherds, were discovered in the upcast from rabbit burrows dug into a series of large earthen mounds. These were probably the remains of settlements, although this will only be proven by excavation. Earthen mounds have also been recorded on Eigg and Muck, but burrow spoil on Eigg has produced only post-medieval (ie post c AD 1500) pottery. On Rum, the excavations at Kinloch demonstrated that activity continued through the Neolithic period, while stray finds on Eigg include two stone axes, a flint spearhead and two leaf-shaped arrowheads. Thumbnail scrapers, probably of this period, were also picked up on ploughed fields during the Eigg and Muck surveys. What is lacking, however, are any intact examples of burial or ritual monuments of this period. Three are known, but all have been heavily robbed: a cairn on Canna; the site of a 'long cairn' at Laig on Eigg, removed in the early 1850s to provide packing for field drains (two stone cists within the cairn were said to contain 'articles of stone and bone'), and a flattened cairn with associated Neolithic pottery discovered during excavations at Kildonnan, Eigg. One final site that may belong to this period is an unusual oval structure near Galmisdale on Eigg, whose closest parallels are to be found amongst prehistoric houses on Shetland.

About three dozen round cairns, presumably of Bronze Age date (c2500–800 BC), are distributed across the four islands. Most of these survive as simple circular stony mounds, though some have visible traces of a kerb. A cairn at Kildonnan on Eigg is the only one to have been formally excavated, but in 1875. The finds from the Kildonnan excavation belong to a Viking burial, but this had been placed in a ruined cist that is probably prehistoric; recent excavation in the same area has confirmed multi-period activity. Three other cists, each within a cairn,

were discovered on Eigg during land improvements in the early 1860s, but there are no records of any finds being recovered from them.

The vast majority of hut-circles in the Small Isles are on Eigg and Canna which between them have around 40 possible examples, the best preserved ones being on Canna. By contrast, only two possible hut-circles have been identified on Muck and there is a small, if unconvincing, group on Rum. Exploratory excavations of a hut-circle at Galmisdale on Eigg by the National Museums Scotland in the spring of 2002 produced Bronze Age pottery, though the tradition of building circular structures probably spans most or all of the last two millennia BC. Nearly all of the Eigg and Canna huts are situated in heather moorland or other rough pasture, well above the limits of post-medieval cultivation. Very few survive within the areas of improved ground. This distribution explains their absence from the other two islands: there is very little unimproved or uncultivated ground on Muck, while on Rum locations suitable for settlement have presumably always been restricted to the same few niches around the coast which eventually became saturated. Thereafter there was only limited cultivation at Kinloch, with the other settlement sites not being occupied during the 19/20th century crofting phase, hence the survival of the lazy beds there. Only on Canna can the settlement sites be seen to lie in association with prehistoric field systems, although there are possibly also traces on the moorland in north-west Eigg. At the west end of Canna hut-circles are spaced out among a network of fields and enclosures defined by edge-set stones. It may be that a mixed agricultural economy can be detected here, with smaller fields defining arable plots, while longer boundaries, disappearing into the moorland peat, may have divided up areas of pasture.

One of the more remarkable discoveries to emerge during the survey of Eigg also dates from the Bronze Age. In May 2001 Commission staff were shown a collection of metalworking debris discovered by an islander while digging a hole to bury his cat. Dating to the Late Bronze Age, the collection included fragments of clay crucible in which bronze was smelted and clay moulds for the casting of socketed axes, a knife and a pointed tool. Finds of Bronze Age metalwork are relatively common in Scotland, but there are no more than a handful of sites with evidence for the process of metalworking itself. Alerted to the discovery, the

Fig 1.7 The great brooding presence of the Sgurr on Eigg.
Compare the 1883 photograph Fig 3.14 HES SC729680

National Museums Scotland immediately began
excavating the site, and work continued into 2002.
It is now thought to be the temporary workshop
of a Late Bronze Age smith, possibly an itinerant
craftsperson.[10]

There are at least fourteen forts and duns scattered
across the islands – four on Canna, three on Rum,
one on Muck and at least six on Eigg. They belong
to the earlier and middle parts of the Iron Age (c800
BC – AD 100); nearly all of them are sited on small
coastal stacks and promontories, needing no more
fortification than a thick stone wall barring the line of
easiest access. The term 'fort' may well be a misnomer.
While their defensive capabilities may have been
overt, they were hardly practical for this purpose.
It is equally possible they were visible expressions of
power more than anything else. Several are dramatic
in appearance. The interiors of most of them are either
featureless, or contain footings of buildings that are
demonstrably later than the defences; only one fort,

on the west side of Laig Bay, Eigg, has visible remains
of circular house-platforms that may be contemporary
with its original use. One Eigg fort, however, on the
Sgurr, is quite different. A stone wall, almost 2m high
in places, cuts off the only approach to the summit and
encloses about 4ha, most of it bare rock with hardly
any level ground. It is inconceivable that this was
ever permanently occupied, and it should perhaps be
seen either as a temporary retreat or as a focal point
for the local community, perhaps used for gatherings
or festivals at particular times of the year. Given the
Sgurr's great brooding shape, it is not difficult to
imagine it holding some symbolic importance.

Another site on Eigg is of similar vein. This stands
among a jumble of boulders beneath the cliffs on the
north-east coast, the most remote corner of the island.
Here, a substantial platform has been constructed
supporting the remains of a circular enclosure, and
below it is a large boulder cave, modified by walling
and containing midden. The most impressive factor,
however, is the natural rock formation of vertical
basalt columns in the cliffs above it: this gives the site
a dramatic visual impact and the notion of it somehow
being a special place.

Early Christian and Viking

Canna and Eigg were both sites of important monasteries in the early medieval period, the former recorded as being the place where Columba had a chapel built at A'Chill in the later 6th century, and the latter where Donnan was martyred in AD 617. Both sites have been partly identified through excavation, and both islands, Canna in particular, have examples of early medieval sculpture probably dated between the 7th and 9th centuries. These appear to belong to both standing and recumbent grave markers. Some of these are simple incised crosses,

Fig 1.8 (below) Canna's prominent role in the early church can be seen through the remnants of stone crosses found on the island. This cross at A'Chill, Canna, is reproduced at 1:15 (see also Fig 2.21). HES SC373294, SC373295

Fig 1.9 (right) Certain places on the islands were significant for early monasticism. The circular setting at Sgorr nam Ban-Naomha (Cliff of the Holy Women) on Canna typifies the remoteness and difficulty of access of many of these early Christian sites. HES DP109405

others more ornately decorated; three show strong signs of Pictish influence in the animals and figures portrayed. Canna also has the remains of an unusual monastic enclosure lying at the foot of a steep cliff on the remote south-west coast, known as Sgorr nam Ban-Naomha (Cliff of the Holy Women), which may have been a hermitage or nunnery subordinate to the monastery at A'Chill. The presence of the early church on Muck (Kiel) and Rum (Kilmory) is attested by two cross-slabs from each, and also by the place-name Papadil (Norse 'Priests' valley') at the southern tip of Rum. 'Papa' place-names have been the subject of special study and appear to represent defined locations of Christian monasticism in Norse times.[11] In contrast to these overtly Christian sites and monuments, the square cairn cemetery at Laig on Eigg may be regarded as pagan, quite possibly Pictish, and serves as a reminder that this part of Scotland was very much a cultural frontier in the mid 1st millennium AD.

Norse seafarers were travelling through the Western Isles during the 8th century. Although there is no evidence to say that they may have settled at that time, it would be equally surprising if they were not attracted by the fertile landscapes later on. Norse place-names are common in the Small Isles and throughout the Hebrides, but many pertain to locational features such as mountains or valleys which may simply represent markers seen from the sea during passage to and from Norway and Ireland. Nor are there any '*Thing*' or *-ting* (assembly) place-names in the Small Isles which might suggest a substantial Norse occupation and infrastructure. That said, there is some archaeological evidence to support a Norse presence. It is limited to a small, albeit important, group of artefacts, chiefly from Eigg, and a possible building discovered during the Muck survey. In Eigg, the Laig boat stems and the Kildonnan sword are among the best known Viking artefacts from the Hebrides. The stems were discovered in the 19th century during the draining of a bog. The sword was found, together with a whetstone for sharpening knives and fragments of other artefacts, around 1830, while levelling a 'hillock' (likely to be a burial mound) to the north-east of Kildonnan farmsteading. Two other Viking burials, this time to the south-west of Kildonnan, each containing a sword and other artefacts, are also recorded. Otherwise, the only Norse artefacts from the Small Isles are a bone or ivory gaming piece discovered in a cave on the east coast of Rum and a ring-headed bronze pin found on Canna. In the 1928 *Inventory* Canna is also credited with several Viking burials, including one known locally as the grave of the King of Norway, but these have since been argued to be kelp kilns or bases for agricultural buildings. The remains of a possible Norse house identified on Muck lies on the north coast of the island. Its shape is bow-sided and is a very different style of building compared with those of the 18th and 19th century settlements on the island. From the surface evidence it seems reasonable to suggest a Norse date although, given our patchy understanding of rural vernacular building styles in the Highlands before 1700, a later date is also possible. Only excavation will show.

Medieval and Post-Medieval Landscapes

In the medieval period (which has a customary end-date of around AD 1500), and in the immediate centuries following, the islands confusingly changed hands several times. In the 13th century Eigg and Rum were held by the MacRuaris of Garmoran, from whom they descended to the MacDonalds of Clanranald – a name which reoccurs throughout the island histories. The Clanranalds retained Eigg until 1827, but in the 15th century Rum passed to the Macleans of Coll, whose ownership lasted until 1845 (although in the 1590s it was recorded as again being in the hands of Clanranald). Canna belonged to the Benedictine Abbey of Iona in 1203, and may well have been in Church hands earlier. By the 1590s, it too appears to have been in Clanranald hands and, although the Earl of Argyll was granted the island in 1628, Clanranald may have retained possession, leasing the island in 1672, before finally selling it in 1827. Muck first appears on record in 1549, when it was the property of the Bishop of the Isles, but it had passed to the Macleans of Coll by 1626. In 1799 Muck also passed to the Clanranalds, though fourteen years later it returned to the Macleans. Given the part played by the Church and clan feuding in this, it is interesting to see the slow erosion of religious connection over time, particularly in Canna and Muck, during a gradual process of secularisation.[12] Of course, change of ownership may have been irrelevant to those who lived there: proprietors came and went, and rents were paid irrespectively. Changes to the landscape occurred when the proprietors' income could be maximised in novel ways, and these came later in the form of kelping, sheep farming and sporting estates. Before then, other than perhaps with the effects of deer hunting on Rum, there is little to suggest that the landscape was other than a slowly evolving dynamic of small farming communities regardless of changing ownership.

There are few visible remains on the islands that can be confidently ascribed to the medieval period. Eigg has the remains of a church and some medieval carved stones, and there is a possible chapel on Muck. There are no visible remains either of the medieval parish church on Canna, or the chapel that probably stood at Kilmory on Rum, though the wall-footings of the former were identified by excavation in 1994. As far as secular monuments are concerned, the only 'castle' on the islands, Coroghon on Canna, is probably of 17th century date and sometimes denoted as a 'prison'. Many of the numerous shieling-huts on the islands are likely to be medieval (or at least have medieval origins), but the most interesting monuments that have been tentatively assigned to this period are the vast deer traps on Rum. The best preserved of these, and first identified by Love,[13] comprise a high-walled oval enclosure into which deer were funnelled down the mountainside over a distance of several hundred metres through the scree for slaughter.

Several of the townships on the islands are probably medieval in origin, though none of the visible foundations need be any earlier than the 18th century.

Even though documentary sources no doubt help in analysing the pattern of medieval settlement, there will always be difficulties in matching a recorded settlement with a particular group of archaeological remains. Moreover, likely organic building materials from the Middle Ages, such as turf and timber, are poor archaeological survivors, and any stone walling may have been robbed for later buildings. Many dwelling sites, chosen for proximity to good land, shelter and fresh water, will have been used and reused over the centuries. What you see on the landscape is what you get. Only archaeological intervention can allow us to look into processes of continuity, for example in some of the later townships where traces of earlier buildings might be found buried. The best-preserved townships are at Kiel on Muck, Harris on Rum and Five Pennies, Lower Grulin and Upper Grulin on Eigg; there are also substantial remains at several other sites on Eigg. The earliest buildings within them are typically constructed with a turf core, faced inside and out with stone. In most cases the surrounding fields have been obliterated by later improvement and cultivation, though a substantial field system survives at Five Pennies, while Harris is set within a remarkable landscape of lazy beds enclosed by a head dyke.

Fig 1.10 Rum's deer traps probably had their origins in the medieval period. Here, high in the mountains at Ard Nev, the deer could be funnelled between walling to an enclosure for slaughter. HES DPI65381

Shieling

The use of high pastures during the summer months was an important and integral part of the farming calendar throughout Highland Scotland. It involved moving livestock into fresh grazing land and the construction of small temporary shelters (shieling-huts) where any dairy produce was stored, and which acted as temporary accommodation for family members, often the young, during herding and shepherding duties. In many cases the huts were incorporated into existing rock outcrops or located where there was a ready stone supply, possibly from an earlier monument. Small groups of huts are to be found in the more remote areas of all of the Small Isles – almost 400 structures have been recorded on Rum and there are probably over 100 on Eigg. John Love identified three types of hut on Rum: small circular or oval stone-walled huts with corbelled roofs; huts with two or more chambers, and rectangular huts, usually built largely of turf.[14] These types also occur on the other islands, particularly the chambered and rectangular forms. While the rectangular huts are the most common, and are similar to shieling-huts found throughout the Highlands, the chambered forms are probably the most interesting. Most of the Eigg examples had a figure-of-eight plan: the entrance led into the larger compartment from which a narrow passage, often roofed with stone lintels, gave access to the smaller chamber. The latter was invariably constructed of stone with a turf embankment against its outer face, probably intended to keep the interior cool for the storage of butter and cheese, the traditional products of the shieling months. This type of hut is also well known on Skye where several examples have been excavated. After the Clearances many of the huts, especially the larger ones, appear to have been deliberately damaged in order to make them unsuitable for more permanent settlement. Dating, however, remains a problem, although at least some of these huts may be medieval. Some were certainly still active during Hugh Miller's visit to Eigg in 1845 – his exploration took him to the remote area

Fig 1.12 A surviving covered shieling. This rare example is on Harris, Western Isles, and demonstrates how roofing may have been constructed. John Hunter

Fig 1.11 The township of Upper Grulin, Eigg, was devastated by the Clearances. A single bothy remains standing today among the ruins of other dwellings and enclosures. This pattern of depopulation was repeated across the islands. HES DPI09440

of Struidh on the eastern cliffs and his description of what he categorises as a 'shieling' is frequently cited:

Save the lonely shieling, not a human dwelling was in sight. An island girl of eighteen, more than merely good-looking, though much embrowned by the sun, had come to the door to see who the unwonted visitors might be … There was a turf fire at the one end, at which there sat two little girls, engaged in keeping up the blaze under a large pot, but sadly diverted from their work by our entrance; while the other end was occupied by a bed of dry straw, spread on the floor from wall to wall, and fenced off at the foot by a line of stones. The middle space was occupied by the utensils and produce of the dairy – flat wooden vessels of milk, a butter-churn, and a tub half-filled with curd; while a few cheeses, soft from the press, lay on a shelf above. The little girls were but occasional visitors, who had come, out of a juvenile frolic, to pass the night in the place; but I was informed by John that the shieling had two other inmates, young women, like the one so hospitably engaged in our behalf, who were out at the milking, and that they lived here all alone for several months every year, when the pasturage was at its best, employed in making butter and cheese.[15]

Kelp, the Clearances and Crofting

The late 18th and early 19th centuries saw rapid change throughout the Highlands as chiefs and landowners sought to maximise income from their possessions. In the 1780s and 1790s, rising rents and a rising population prompted a wave of emigrations, despite the opposition of landowners who needed the workforce. By then the price of kelp, a soda ash produced by burning seaweed, which was important as a bleaching agent and in the manufacture of soap, glass and gunpowder, had begun to soar. Kelp production

took place on all the islands (although less fruitfully on Rum), the parish shores producing some 50 tons annually in a good year.[16] Much work has been done in identifying the remains and significance of the kelp industry in parts of Ireland,[17] but in Scotland it was an industry that left remarkably little in the way of

Fig 1.13 This 2003 photograph of Cleadale, Eigg, shows the 19th century crofting divisions (marked by long parallel wall lines) overlying earlier, more irregular field systems. HES SC875772

archaeological evidence (or evidence that has yet to be been recognised) in spite of its intensity. Kilns, drying areas, storehouses and even slipways would have been required. Only a few kelp kilns have been identified and a contemporary description may explain why:

> *The usual mode is to cut a portion of kelp annually from the rocks, taking it from the same place only once in three years. After the kelp has been dried, it is placed in a kiln prepared for the purpose, of stones loosely piled together, and burned. After it is consumed, and the fire is to be extinguished, a long pole pointed with iron is plunged into it and it is stirred about; the result of the burning being, by this time, a thick glutinous liquid, which runs from the kelp in burning. As soon as this liquid cools, it hardens and the operation is at an end. It is then shipped off to market.*[18]

These kilns of 'stones loosely piled together' are likely to have been dismantled after each burning and the only traces that survive appear to be rectangular flagged platforms, often stone-edged, on the ground surface near the shore.

To accommodate the growing population needed to harvest the seaweed, the Clanranald estate, which included Canna, Eigg and (from 1799 to 1813) Muck, reorganised the holdings of its tenants, converting the existing multiple-tenant farms into crofting townships. In 1809 plans were made to divide Muck into 47 holdings, and on Eigg in the same year the neighbouring farms of Cleadale and Knockeiltach were converted into 28 crofts. Cleadale remains a crofting township today, and the straight stone-walled boundaries of its narrow plots stand in marked contrast to the irregular enclosures of the earlier farms that are still visible beneath. The construction of the buildings themselves may also have changed at this time. The walls of most of the houses in the crofting settlements have a core of stone rather than turf and a striking number have an internal length of over 9m. This uniformity of length is most noticeable on Eigg, and suggests a degree of control by the estate over the size of crofters' dwellings.

The kelp boom collapsed at the end of the Napoleonic Wars as peacetime allowed the import of cheaper sources of alkali from Spain. Faced with a rising population increasingly unable to pay rents, proprietors became more interested in the concept of emigration. Moreover, before the kelp boom, seaweed had been traditionally used to enrich the agricultural soils, which had now become less fertile. In 1826, some 300 people were cleared from Rum, which was converted into a farm for 8,000 sheep, and 50 more followed in 1828 leaving, according to some sources, only one indigenous family on the whole island. In the same year 150 people emigrated from Muck. The population of Canna was greatly reduced after its sale by Clanranald in 1827, and in 1849 it was halved again. On Eigg, 140 people elected to emigrate in 1843 and, ten years later, Laig and Grulin (roughly the western half of the island) were let for sheep and the Grulin tenants were evicted. A population of sheep, as opposed to humans, brought with it a new set of landscape features – fanks, pens, shelters and stone dykes.[19] On Canna the sheep dykes were built by using the stone pulled from the township dwellings at A'Chill and included carved stones from the old graveyard broken up and built into the walling. Population figures for the whole parish, gathered from official census returns and from (less accurate) other accounts and records, show the increasing density of inhabitants with its accompanying pressure on subsistence resources around the end of the 18th century and the beginning of the 19th, and the catastrophic decline after the later Clearances and the introduction of sheep. Individual island tables are shown in the respective chapters.

Year	Population	Source
c1595	436/515	Skene (interpreted, 1577–95)
1764	1,159	McNeill (1764/5)
1768	1,208	Stat Acct (1796)
1796	1,339	Stat Acct (1796)
1803	1,547	Murray (1810)
1821	1,620	Census
1831	1,005	Census
1841	993	Census
1881	541	Census
1991	139	Census

Fig 1.14 Recorded population figures for the Small Isles.[20]

Fig 1.15 The importance of the sea is shown at the sheltered harbour at Galmisdale, Eigg. The two arms of the late 18th century Clanranald jetty can be seen at the top and remains of fish traps sit to the left above the new pier, built in 2003. HES DP109445

Maritime and Military Sites

From earliest times all four islands relied on the sea for communication, trade and fishing, the last being essential for subsistence. All four islands have at least one main landfall, suitably adapted by jetties and quays, which was used as a main harbour. Settlement developed nearby each: at A'Chill on Canna, Galmisdale on Eigg, Port Mor on Muck, and Kinloch on Rum. All are located on the east or south-east coasts, away from the prevailing westerly winds. Harbourage was otherwise limited and the seas were dangerous. Jetties, quays and slipways survive sporadically in suitable sheltered locations, many now only visible at low tide, and there is the occasional kelp kiln, but there is little that reflects the extent of fishing and kelp production that was needed to sustain such a large peak population. Proximity to the fishing grounds was good. The islands were recognised as having the potential for fishing on an industrial as opposed to a domestic scale in the late 18th century, Canna in particular having a fine harbour. Several visitors at the time commented this but also noted the absence of available equipment such as hooks or the provision of salt. The British Fisheries Society was set up by the government in 1786 in order to establish fishing settlements in appropriate locations with the grand title of The British Society for Extending the Fisheries and Improving the Sea Coasts of this Kingdom, identifying Canna as a likely location. However, the opportunity was never taken up owing to disagreement over costs between the Clanranald ownership and the Society, and the fishing remained unexploited.

Two significant modern shipping routes bypass the islands, although in earlier times when water was viewed as an aid to communication and travel rather than an inconvenience, the maritime infrastructure may have been more complex. One route was from mainland Scotland to the Outer Hebrides (from Oban and from Mallaig) especially after the completion of the Fort William–Mallaig railway in 1901 which enabled fresh produce (notably lobster) to be carried rapidly by train to London. The other was the main north–south route passing through the Minch. The completion of the Heiskeir lighthouse in 1904 was intended to safeguard shipping on the latter route from falling foul of the coastlines of Canna, Rum and Heiskeir itself, and to allow smooth passage west of the Small Isles northwards. The light was built by the Stevenson family using contractors from Oban.

	Vessel	Type	Wrecked	Registration	Cargo
1	Lady Betty Balfour	Steam trawler	1922	Aberdeen 1898	-
2	Rona	Wooden yawl	1896	Wick 1876	Ballast
3	?	-	1855	-	-
4	Kingfisher	MFV	1985	Oban 1963	-
5	Bounteous	Drifter	1917	Portnockie 1903	-
6	Midas	Wooden barque	1896	Kragero 1870	Ballast
7	?	-	-	-	-
8	Belmont Castle	Sloop	1800	Greenock 1783	Ballast
9	Kestrel	-	1855	-	-
10	Cabbos d'Or	-	1732	London	Liquor; salt
11	Flora McDougall	Lugsail	1929	Morar	-
12	Auguste	Sloop	1884	Ardrossan 1851	-
13	John & Ann	Smack	1843	Tobermory 1811	-
14	Sisters	-	-	-	-
15	Flora	Brig	1803	Limerick	Ballast
16	Pomona	-	1834	-	-
17	Christian	-	1819	-	-
18	Active	-	1803	-	Sugar; coffee; rum
19	Dispatch	Smack	1847	Inverness 1830	-
20	Choice	Wooden ketch	1908	Stornoway 1861	Fishing stock
21	Edgar	Wooden schooner	1884	-	-
22	Sunshine	Lugsail	1890	Barra	-
23	Scotia	Schooner	1840	Wick 1832	Iron
24	?	-	1819	-	-
25	?	-	1905	-	-
26	Breifond	Steamship	1911	Stavanger 1890	-
27	Garland	Brigantine	1852	Stranraer 1826	-
28	?	3 masts	1868		-
29	Harriet Hamlet	Schooner	1868	-	-
30	Fortitude	-	1815	-	-
31	Gowan	Aux. lugsail	1931	Rosehearty 1903	-
32	Peggy	Sloop	1820	Glasgow 1814	Oats
33	Granfos	Steamship	1912	Norway 1906	Acetylene; timber
34	Anna More	Steamship	1914	Dublin 1890	Coal
35	Doris	Steam trawler	1914	Fleetwood 1907	Ballast
36	Lythe	-	1954	-	-
37	LBF	MFV	1986	Salcombe	-
38	Jennie	Puffer	1954	British 1902	-
39	?	-	1856	-	-
40	Glenelg	Steam yacht	1894	Glasgow 1872	Ballast
41	Sverre	Wooden barque	1890	Moss 1852	Coal
42	Mary	Sloop	1833	Inverness 1824	-
43	Samuel	Brigantine	1799	Liverpool	-
44	Wyre Victory	Motor trawler	1976	Fleetwood 1956	-
45	Caledonia	Steamship	1913	Inverness 1913	Ballast
46	Hermann	Steamship	1904	Preston 1890	Rock salt
47	Southesk	Brigantine	1879	Montrose 1870	-
48	Talifoo	Steam trawler	1894	Hull 1885	Ballast
49	Peggy & Ann	Sloop	1839	Tobermory 1819	-
50	Tartar	Steamship	1895	Glasgow 1885	General
51	Example	Zulu	1901	Whitehills 1899	Ballast
52	Blair	Brig	1871	British	Coal

Fig 1.16 (above and opposite) Distribution of recorded wrecks around the Small Isles where the losses could be specifically located.[22] Fifty-two have been identified, but there are a large number of other losses recorded where the location is unspecific and which are not plotted. Of particular interest is the number of recorded wrecks immediately to the south of Canna: the majority of these date before the construction of the Heiskeir lighthouse and illustrate the light's importance in ensuring that traffic moving northwards steered safely west of the Small Isles. HES GV006084

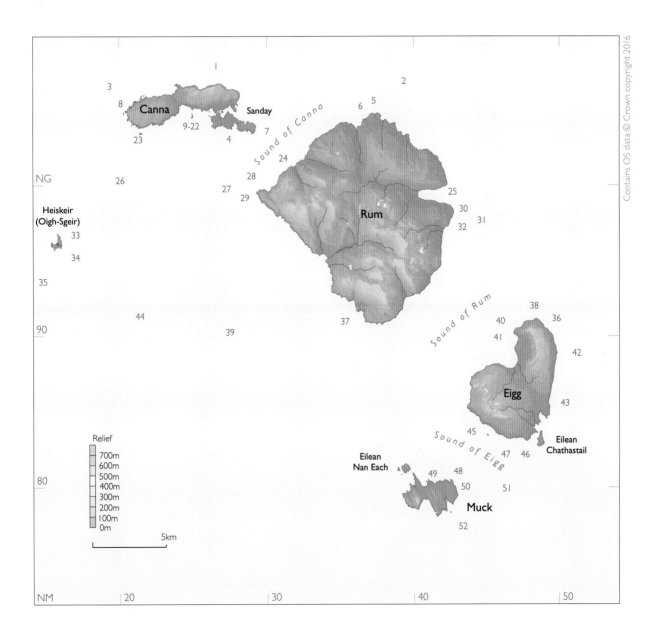

It stands to a height of almost 40m and, until automation in 1997, was one of the last manned lighthouses in Scotland. It is famous for its short golf course constructed by former enthusiastic keepers, and for the published memoirs of another, Peter Hill.[21] There is a further automated light on Canna (Sanday), but otherwise no durable maritime markers elsewhere in the islands, although it seems that the Catholic church on Canna was constructed partly with this in mind.

Fifty-two specific locations of wrecks have been recorded and these are listed and plotted (Fig 1.16)

together with vessel name and type, date of wrecking, date and place of registration and nature of cargo (if known). The earliest recorded here is from 1732 (no. 10), the latest 1986; the majority are wooden vessels falling within the 19th century or early 20th century. Their cargos tend to reflect local traffic, although at least two early wrecks, the *Cabbos d'Or* and *Active* (nos 10 and 18 respectively) carrying liquor and salt, and sugar, coffee and rum respectively are likely to have been involved in international trade. Both foundered off the south coast of Canna on route northwards.

Other recorded cargos were of ballast or coal, although one, the Norwegian steamship *Granfos* (no. 33), was carrying acetylene which exploded during salvage.

None of the recorded losses were military vessels and there is no archaeological or documented evidence of military activity on, or around, any of these islands. This is in sharp contrast to other Scottish islands, notably in Scapa Flow, Orkney, where remains of military installations dominate the landscape and where coastal waters are thick with naval wreckage. Closer, in the Outer Hebrides, there are sporadic military defence positions, but the Small Isles appear to have been almost completely bypassed; they were strategically unimportant during both World Wars, although movement between them was restricted.

Sporting Estates

Since the middle of the 19th century, Eigg, Canna and Muck have each passed through the hands of a series of proprietors. Apart from the crofting areas (now confined to Cleadale on Eigg, Sanday and one croft on Muck), they have been run as sheep and cattle farms, of which there are now three on Eigg and one on each of the other two islands. The existing farm buildings are mostly of late 18th century or 19th century date, the earliest surviving farmhouse being at Howlin on Eigg, built in the 1770s. The Victorian proprietors of Eigg, however, were content to leave the running of the farms largely to their factors, and were more concerned with the sporting opportunities offered by the estate. Norman MacPherson inherited the island from his father in 1854, and his sister Isabella surrounded his house with woodland to encourage pheasants, while Robert Thomson, who bought the island in 1896, considered moving all the tenants to Muck in order to make room for deer. The present Lodge on Eigg, built in 1926–7, was the third proprietor's house built on or near that site, intended, like its predecessors, as a holiday house and base for shooting.

It is Rum which has become most closely identified with the Victorian and Edwardian passion for sporting estates. The sheep farm failed in 1839, and in 1845 the island was bought by the Marquis of Salisbury, who reintroduced deer and made various improvements. The most dramatic changes, however, were introduced by the Bullough family, who held the island from 1888 until Monica, Lady Bullough, sold it to the Nature Conservancy Council (now Scottish Natural Heritage) in 1957. Under John Bullough the deer herd was improved and hunting lodges were built in remote corners of the island. But it is his son, Sir George, who instigated the construction of the most striking monuments of this period, the extravagant Kinloch Castle at the head of Loch Sresort and the Bullough Mausoleum, a Doric-style temple containing the table tombs of Sir George himself, his wife and his father. The Bullough legacy is an eye-opening testimony to 'new money' opulence and egotism.

Fig 1.18 John Lorne Campbell and his wife Margaret Fay Shaw seen here at Canna House, purchased Canna in 1938 and subsequently gifted it to the National Trust for Scotland in 1981. © The Scotsman Publications Ltd. Licensor Scran

Fig 1.17 A hunting photograph taken outside the newly built Kinloch Castle in 1903. As Rum's owner, George Bullough used the island as a personal hunting reserve, discouraging visitors to such an extent that it was referred to as 'The Forbidden Island'. HES SC1081002

Today, the four islands present very different types of ownership and management. Canna is the property of the National Trust for Scotland, Eigg is owned by the islanders themselves as the result of a community buy-out, Muck remains under the private ownership of a family still resident and working on the island, and all but a small part of Rum is owned by Scottish Natural Heritage. Within the melee of ownership and change which preceded this (and in which Eigg probably has the most bizarre history – see Chapter 3), a special comment needs to be made regarding the ownership of Canna. The island was purchased in 1938 by John Lorne Campbell and his wife Margaret Fay Shaw, both dedicated scholars of Gaelic traditions, histories, folklore and music. Their rejection of development on Canna, or any type of cultural interference that was not in the island's interest, has provided a unique level of landscape survival, leaving a number of archaeological sites in a remarkably well preserved state. Their amassed library of Gaelic literature and music, not to mention the assemblage of early Christian carved stones gathered from the island, together with the island itself (including Sanday), was passed over to the National Trust for Scotland in 1981.

Sources and Archaeological Investigation

Sources

In the 18th and 19th centuries the islands were visited and reported upon by government officials and church representatives, the latter mostly with regard to the provision of education, but with particular emphasis on the maintenance of the Catholic faith on Canna and Eigg which both remained substantially 'Popish'. This overt religious schism between Protestant and Catholic which stemmed from the 16th century reformation rears its head throughout the history of the islands and to some extent is still apparent today. The islands also received the attentions of numerous travellers, writers and artists. Some were simply passing through on voyages of curiosity or general scientific interest; others had more focused concerns. These include the geological expeditions of Hugh Miller in 1845 and Edward Clarke in 1797,[23] the research into church history by T S Muir,[24] the broad curiosity of the natural and social worlds shown by Martin Martin,[25] and the interest in flora shown by Sarah Murray. She was one of the few women visitors recorded, she landed on Rum in 1799, and wrote of 'a land still emerging from legend'.[26] Some of

the descriptions are quite extensive, notably Thomas Pennant's 1776 text on Canna, or Edwin Waugh's *Limping Pilgrim* describing his visit to Rum just over a century later, but the majority were more succinct and generalised. Notable absentees to the Small Isles were Johnson and Boswell who, despite attempts in the late 18th century, were thwarted by the poor weather and difficult access; something noted by many others.

These various reports and observations, together with the two Statistical Accounts of 1796 and 1836, which were respectively written by the ministers of the Small Isles parish at the time (the present parish was formed in 1740),[27] both rather confusingly named the Reverend Donald McLean, present a reasonable understanding of island life in those two centuries. In theory the two *Accounts* should be key sources. The earlier *Account* is very detailed and comprehensive, the latter somewhat less so, but its writer appeared to be more interested in secular activities (he was accused of adultery, indecent exposure and drunkenness) and was later dismissed from office for neglect of duty. His text is largely descriptive and only the last three pages make any headway in identifying the major changes in island fortunes during the intervening forty years since the earlier *Account*. The other sources typically embody much generality and literary convention; but there are also occasional glimpses of detail. One highlight is a commissioned census of 1764/5 which lists the names and ages of all the Small Isles' inhabitants and many of the townships in which they lived, together with the religious affiliations of individual families as being either 'protestants' or 'papists'.[28] This detailed census was a 'one-off' commissioned as part of a study of the islands by the Rev. Dr John Walker.[29] It

Fig 1.19 (opposite, top left) A woman on Eigg transports essential supplies of peat on a Highland pony at the start of the 20th century. © National Museums Scotland. Licensor Scran

Fig 1.20 (opposite, top right) Workers on Muck using traditional techniques for grubbing (digging) cabbages in 1962. Eigg can be seen on the distant horizon. Alasdair Alpin MacGregor © National Museums Scotland. Licensor Scran

Fig 1.21 (opposite, below) Erskine Beveridge captured this striking scene of the township of Cleadale, Eigg, in 1883. The house in the foreground was abandoned prior to 1898 and all that remains now are low, grass-grown wall-footings. HES SC743149

KANNAI

Kaming

Bin Moir

Bin Oïr

Loch San:
degory

RVM

Kilmory

Loch Scres
psirc

Ylen na
Aich

Muck

MVCK

EGG

is a remarkable and important document, given that less than a century later the greater part of the island populations had emigrated or were dispersed through the Clearances, many departing to the New World.

There are also a number of unexpected sources, not least being the reports of the British Fisheries Society whose 1788 description of Canna is more informed and detailed than the *Statistical Account* which followed shortly afterwards.[30] Another unexpected source is Joseph L MacDougall, a Canadian historian of Scots descent, whose *History of Inverness County, Nova Scotia*, published in 1922, views the exodus from the Small Isles from the other side of the Atlantic. The book collates the arrival and fortunes of many of the immigrants from the Small Isles, driven by the Clearances in the 1820s. MacDougall records their names, the ships that transported them, their familial relationships, known destinations and where they settled. It would appear that emigration transpired to be a prosperous opportunity for those that survived the crossing. They were, in the words of MacDougall, 'industrious, thrifty and progressive'.[31] Sadly, however, they took with them centuries of tradition and custom, and the links between those times and the present have been mostly severed. To a large extent, these four islands, Rum in particular, have lost their cultural memories, with the transmission of oral tradition and place-names curtailed.

The overview we see from these various glimpses into the past is of an island culture of poverty and hardship, of living conditions barely credible by contemporary standards, and of raw, windswept landscapes. There is much truth in this. Given the constrained island environments in which wind, rain and cool temperatures were (and still are) the norm, methods of subsistence tended to follow well-trodden paths which were known to work. How things were done, when they were done, and why they were done became accepted wisdom. It was a carefully measured recipe for survival, not just subsistence, even if it entailed spending much of the summer preparing for winter. It was a risk-averse society: there was

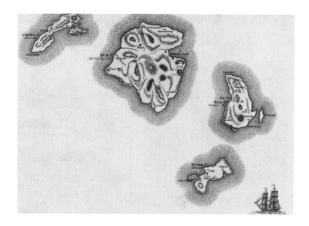

Fig 1.23 George Langlands' 1801 Map of Argyllshire, which includes the Small Isles, is significant for its depiction of key settlements before the major Clearances took place.
© National Library of Scotland. Licensor Scran

little point in changing subsistence methods unless technology intervened to improve them. There is a good case to suggest that the methods of land use and subsistence economics traditionally undertaken in the 19th century had their roots in prehistory, and had altered little since. As a result, one could argue that some of the descriptions given in the travellers' accounts might be little different had their visits been made a thousand years earlier. This is part of the reason why their accounts are so useful, and why they play such an important part in island history. Most of the salient parts of these travellers' tales have been extracted and discussed comprehensively,[32] and there are also many digitised versions of the original texts.

Other useful sources include two early topographical views (Eigg and Rum) drawn by William Daniell in the early 19th century,[33] a small number of photographs taken by Erskine Beveridge in the late 19th century,[34] and the *Edgeworth Diaries* – written on Eigg between 1858 and 1881 presenting the views of Victorian gentry on holiday and accompanied by sketches. A further unusual find is the Pinkieburn Album – the photographic record of a late 19th century family who travelled, among other places, to Egypt, India and Algiers, and Eigg. There is also *Bare Feet and Tackety Boots,* an absorbing account of childhood memories on Rum in the early years of the 20th century, before developments in technology and education had made their mark, which stands as

Fig 1.22 This map of the Small Isles, drawn by Timothy Pont between 1583 and 1596, was first published in Blaeu's *Atlas of Scotland* in 1654. This publication was an important addition to the understanding of Scotland's geography.
© National Library of Scotland. Licensor Scran

a unique piece of social commentary.[35] But before the 18th century the written sources are both few and brief, and our understanding of the islands' social evolution (measurable over around ten millennia) is based largely on what is visible on the landscape, and interpreted through systematic field survey and by occasional archaeological excavation. There is some useful early cartography to complement this, notably Pont's 16th century map of the Small Isles published later by Blaeu (Fig 1.22) and Langlands' 1801 map (Fig 1.23) showing pre-Clearance settlement. But perhaps best of all are William Bald's two maps of Eigg (Fig 3.40) and Canna (Fig 2.37) respectively. Both maps, drawn up in 1805 (Canna, often referred to as the Clanranald map) and in 1806 (Eigg) before the islands were transformed into crofting landscapes, show the early townships and boundaries, individual houses and the extent of cultivated land. Even the 1st edition of the Ordnance Survey (OS) 6-inch to a mile map of the islands surveyed between 1875 and 1877 is helpful in terms of showing place-names which are no longer in existence, or by demonstrating changes to the landscape and the numbers of dwellings between then and the present. The depiction of dwellings as being either roofed or unroofed on the early OS maps is a further guide to abandonment and changing population dynamics.

The place-names depicted on OS maps, particularly on the early editions, predominantly result from the fieldwork of OS surveyors who recorded the names from local evidence and listed them in so-called *Name Books*.[36] Unfortunately, their spellings were not always consistent and the fieldworkers tended to be of a lower military rank (the OS was essentially a military organisation) and not always comfortable with writing down language elements which may have made little sense to them. Some of the names of places or of natural features are Gaelic, some Norse, some an amalgam of both. Some derive from any one of the three. It is unhelpful too that many names have spelling variants in the documentation. A good example are the derivatives from *Cille* (Gaelic 'chapel') which surface as 'Kiel' on Muck, but 'Keil' on Canna. This has inevitably found its way into the National Record of the Historic Environment (hereafter referred to as Canmore) which draws on many sources and provides online access to details, notes and photographs of recorded archaeological sites across Scotland. The overall effect is one of toponymical confusion, which impedes the search for information. One scholar has

Fig 1.24 Michael Pakenham Edgeworth was an Irish botanist who worked mainly in India but visited Eigg in his later years, dying there in 1881. Edgeworth is best known for his extensive diaries, but he also sketched, and this drawing of a mill at Kildonnan, Eigg, is a useful historic record. Eigg Historical Society

produced a list of OS place-name errors on the island of Canna, frustrated at what he perceived as lack of thoroughness on the part of the OS. As one example, he cited the adjacent island of Heiskeir which he saw as an 'obvious' Norse name, now reduced to 'the absurd Gaelic-Norse bastard "Oigh-sgeir"'[37] through the early OS surveying. In this book place-name versions, spellings and capitalisation of letters in place-names are those considered to be in common usage or in Canmore (even if they are linguistically incorrect); these normally pertain to well-attested places and sites allowing for a higher degree of consistency. However some locations, usually those in remote areas which have received less attention, are referred to instead by their designations in the various OS map editions. There is an issue too with respect to locations which are referred to by more than one name, such as the main deserted settlement on Muck. This lies at *Port Mor*, but in some instances the settlement takes the name of the township to which it belongs, *Kiel*, or to the locally used appellation *Sean Bhaile* (Gaelic 'old settlement'). Wherever possible in this book, consistency of a single name is used where it can be cross-referenced back to a main source.

The incorporation of historical documentation and a wider understanding of landscapes has enabled three of the islands to benefit from modern, well-researched and detailed books. John Lorne Campbell's

Fig 1.25 Now a holiday home, this former mill on Eigg still stands with its overshot water-wheel in place. HES SC1499334

book on Canna is an academic synthesis of historical sources (including rentals, charters and leases), especially those of ecclesiastical relevance. He was a former owner of the island and the volume reflects his deep interest in Gaelic tradition, conservation and intellectual purism. The most recent edition has been updated to include an archaeological introduction by staff of the Royal Commission on the Ancient and Historical Monuments of Scotland (now Historic Environment Scotland but in retrospect referred to as the Commission).[38] The island of Eigg has been the subject of a comprehensive narrative by Camille Dressler derived from detailed historical research and folklore sources, complemented by a separate work on the archaeological landscape by Susanna Wade Martins.[39] On Rum, John A Love, a former islander and naturalist, has recorded much of its archaeological past as a result of years of dedicated fieldwalking and recording through mesured sketches and detailed notes. Elements of this appear in his comprehensive history of the island, *Rum: a Landscape without Figures*, which also incorporates a range of sources.[40] All these are superbly researched books and essential reading for anyone wishing to delve more deeply into the complex and intriguing histories of these islands. Additional books, but only tenuously relevant to this volume on the Small Isles, are two other works on Rum, both of which involve human interest events of the 20th century. One, *Eccentric Wealth*, evaluates the social habits and sexual intrigues of the Bullough family in and around Kinloch Castle.[41] The other, *A Rum*

Affair, is a witty analysis of an alleged case of botanical fraud in which a distinguished academic claimed to have discovered on the higher slopes of Rum species of plants which had survived the last ice age. Opinion now suggests he may have planted them there himself. The drama extends to similar doubt regarding a certain species of butterfly on Canna, and water beetles on Barra.[42] The book presents an absorbing account of Rum's botany which can be understood by anyone, like this writer, with no botanical knowledge whatsoever.

In literature terms Muck is perhaps less well served, although the biography of its present owner, Lawrence MacEwen, presents a valuable retrospective view of island life within the parameters of cultural memory.[43] Muck's natural history has also been the subject of a series of short academic papers published between 1985 and 1995,[44] as well as the focus of an independent archaeological sites and monuments survey (below). In addition, there are numerous other publications on various disciplines relevant to individual islands. These are useful to anyone wanting a more specialist background on the Small Isles, for example on place-names,[45] or on the natural environment.[46] Campbell's volume on Canna also contains a set of appendices on topics such as geology, flora and fauna. Key information from these publications has been brought together in works for an interested general readership.[47]

What we know for certain about these islands, from documents, accounts and maps, is heavily skewed towards the last three centuries. The purpose of this volume is to redress the imbalance by exploring the traces of human activity both before and during documented times. It complements what has already been written to make the picture more rounded. It incorporates the results of fieldwork carried out over recent years, as well as aerial photography, geophysical survey and a small element of archaeological investigation. Field survey can only record what is visible on the landscape, or can be seen from the air, and is always open to interpretation. Some features survive better than others, some not at all, and the process is inevitably a selective one: for example, when can the remains of a 'hut' be interpreted as a shieling, or a mound of stones seen as a prehistoric burial as opposed to a 19th century field clearance cairn? Moreover, recent history has shown how archaeologists can change their minds – on Canna the 'Viking graves' recorded in the 1950s are now more likely to be viewed

Fig 1.26 The Shellesder Fort, being surveyed here in 2011, lies adjacent to one of the few areas of fertile ground on Rum. Bloodstone Hill in the background dominates the landscape. HES DP111086

as kelp kilns. Serendipity also plays a part: many grass-covered archaeological features can be partly interpreted as a result of diagnostic pottery fragments being brought to the surface by rabbit burrowing. Muck has no rabbits and hence its archaeological record appears all the poorer by comparison. A major Mesolithic site on Rum was spotted during ploughing, and one of the more important sites in the islands – a Bronze Age metalworking area on Eigg – was discovered not by systematic fieldwork or aerial photography, but by someone burying a dead cat.

Archaeological Investigation

The earliest account of the archaeology of any of the Small Isles is by Norman MacPherson, proprietor of Eigg. His paper of 1878 on the antiquities of the island included a report of an excavation he initiated on the Viking graves at Kildonnan, as well as details of a number of earlier discoveries, mostly made during land improvement operations (Fig 1.30).[48] The islands also came to the attention of several other late Victorian scholars, particularly those attracted by the early medieval crosses on Eigg and Canna, notably T S Muir. Later, in 1924, the distinguished antiquary T C Lethbridge recorded a number of sites on Canna in an unpublished manuscript. This has unfortunately been lost. However, the first attempt at a systematic survey of the islands was the visit of surveyors from the Commission as part of fieldwork for the *Inventory of The Outer Hebrides, Skye and The Small Isles*. Work for the volume commenced in 1914 and the findings were eventually published in 1928;[49] they reflect a rather cursory investigation disrupted by the war and financial stringencies. During a visit to Canna in 1943, a distinguished Scandinavian professor sarcastically remarked that the Commission's investigation could hardly be defined as 'thorough'.[50] He was right. In fact, recording work on the Small Isles was apparently completed during a single week in early July 1925. Fifteen monuments or groups of monuments were recorded, most of them on Canna. On Rum only one site, Kilmory church and burial ground, was described, while on Eigg only the fort on the Sgurr and Kildonnan churchyard appear to have been visited, both on the same day. The number of sites registered for the Small Isles on Canmore now totals well over 1,000 compared to the 15 recorded then. The current figure includes shipwrecks around the island shores, as well as all types of landscape feature and building

remains which were not deemed to be significant in 1925. For example, Kinloch Castle on Rum was excluded in the 1925 survey because it was considered to be too modern.

For the next half century the islands attracted little archaeological attention. The Archaeology Division of the OS spent a month there in the summer of 1972, principally to visit previously known sites, although several new monuments, including hut-circles, were mapped. A study of shielings on Rum by Miller in the 1960s,[51] followed by John Love's more detailed work on the same topic,[52] highlighted the archaeological potential of the island. In 1983 the Commission

Fig 1.27 An early photograph showing the Commission's visit to the fort of Dun Canna, Canna, in 1925. HES SC1470325

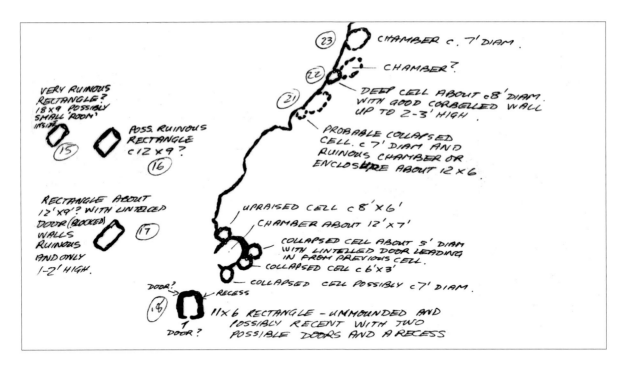

The annotated sketch contains the following handwritten notes:

- CHAMBER c. 7' DIAM. (23)
- CHAMBER? (22)
- DEEP CELL ABOUT c8' DIAM. WITH GOOD CORBELLED WALL UP TO 2-3' HIGH. (21)
- PROBABLE COLLAPSED CELL c 7' DIAM AND RUINOUS CHAMBER OR ENCLOSURE ABOUT 12 × 6.
- VERY RUINOUS RECTANGLE? 18 × 9 POSSIBLY SMALL 'ROOM' INSIDE (15)
- POSS. RUINOUS RECTANGLE c 12 × 9? (16)
- RECTANGLE ABOUT 12' × 9'? WITH LINTELLED DOOR (BLOCKED) WALLS RUINOUS AND ONLY 1-2' HIGH. (17)
- UPRAISED CELL c 8' × 6'
- CHAMBER ABOUT 12' × 7'
- COLLAPSED CELL ABOUT 5' DIAM WITH LINTELLED DOOR LEADING IN FROM PREVIOUS CELL.
- COLLAPSED CELL c 6' × 3'
- COLLAPSED CELL POSSIBLY c 7' DIAM
- DOOR? RECESS
- DOOR? (18)
- 11 × 6 RECTANGLE – UNMOUNDED AND POSSIBLY RECENT WITH TWO POSSIBLE DOORS AND A RECESS

Fig 1.28 Naturalist John A Love recorded details of large numbers of monuments on Rum and his annotated sketches provide a wealth of information. © John Love

returned to Rum and subsequently published a handlist of archaeological sites (under the auspices of the Society of Antiquaries listing programme) which drew heavily on this data. The discovery of Mesolithic flints near Kinloch Castle in the course of that survey prompted a programme of high-profile excavations in the following year.[53] On Eigg, a local team supported by archaeologists from Norfolk completed surveys of a number of sites during the 1980s and 1990s, while in 1986 the Scottish Vernacular Buildings Working Group at Dundee University surveyed farm buildings on both Eigg and Canna. However, it was not until the Commission's survey of Canna commenced in 1994 that the systematic mapping of the archaeology of the Small Isles began and aerial photographs became incorporated. A broadsheet on the Canna survey was published in 1999,[54] and a more detailed archaeological introduction has been incorporated into the fourth edition of Campbell's *Canna: The Story of a Hebridean Island*.[55] The Eigg survey was begun in 2001, also resulting in a published broadsheet (2003),[56] and Muck was surveyed in 2002. Quite independently, a survey

of the historic landscape on Muck by an archaeologist with connections on the island was undertaken in the 1970s–1990s.[57] Meanwhile, the Commission's *Threatened Buildings Survey* completed an in-depth photographic record of Kinloch Castle in 1996 and, in 1998–9, the principal buildings on Eigg were photographed and surveyed. The Commission also undertook further aerial coverage from 2003 followed by additional fieldwork on Rum between 2010 and 2012. By this time the Small Isles Community Council had commissioned an Archaeological Development Plan for the islands covering not only the key sites flagged up by the Commission, but also considering tourism, conservation, access, marketing and commercial activities.[58] Its findings remain highly relevant.

Other archaeological organisations have also been involved in the islands in recent years. The University of Bradford undertook survey and exploratory excavation on Canna in 1994 for the island's owner, the National Trust for Scotland, and further work was carried out by Headland Archaeology recording barns as well as the area of Coroghon Castle. In 2001 Glasgow University Archaeological Research Division (GUARD) conducted an assessment of the archaeology of Rum for Scottish Natural Heritage. In the same year, stimulated by the Commission survey,

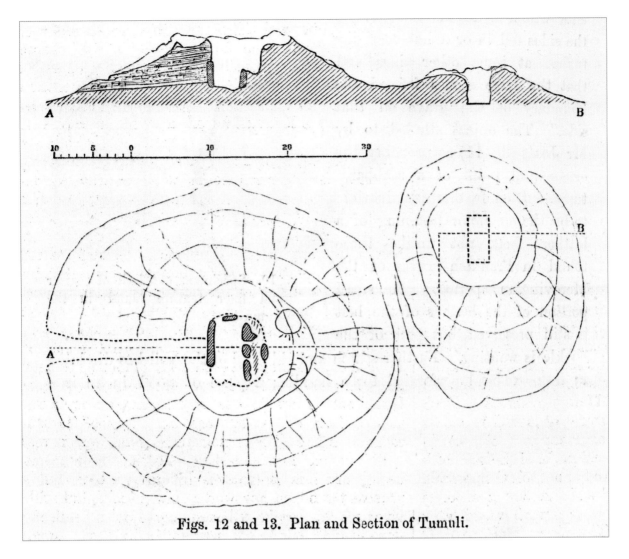

Figs. 12 and 13. Plan and Section of Tumuli.

the National Museums Scotland began excavating a late Bronze Age metalworking site on Eigg, while an assessment has since been made of a wooden boat, possibly 18th century in date, buried in the sand in Galmisdale Bay. Excavations in advance of new pier developments on Eigg and Rum were able to produce quantities of worked flint, and most recently, excavation in 2012 by the University of Birmingham at Kildonnan, Eigg, identified a multi-period site, including the likely remains of an early Christian

Fig 1.30 An early excavation plan and section of a mound at Kildonnan, Eigg, published by the island's owner Norman MacPherson in 1878. HES DP233884

monastery. 'Thistle Camps' – the volunteer work teams for the National Trust for Scotland – as well as professional archaeological groups have been active on a number of small projects on Canna, mostly in response to development needs or erosion. On Eigg a comprehensive archive of old photographs of island life from the 1880s onwards has been collected by the Eigg History Society. Copies can be seen at the Eigg School, Inverness Museum, or the Highland Council Record Office in Fort William.

Fig 1.29 The front steps and covered walkway of Kinloch Castle – a building deemed 'too modern' to be incorporated into the 1925 survey and subsequent *Inventory*. HES DP039596

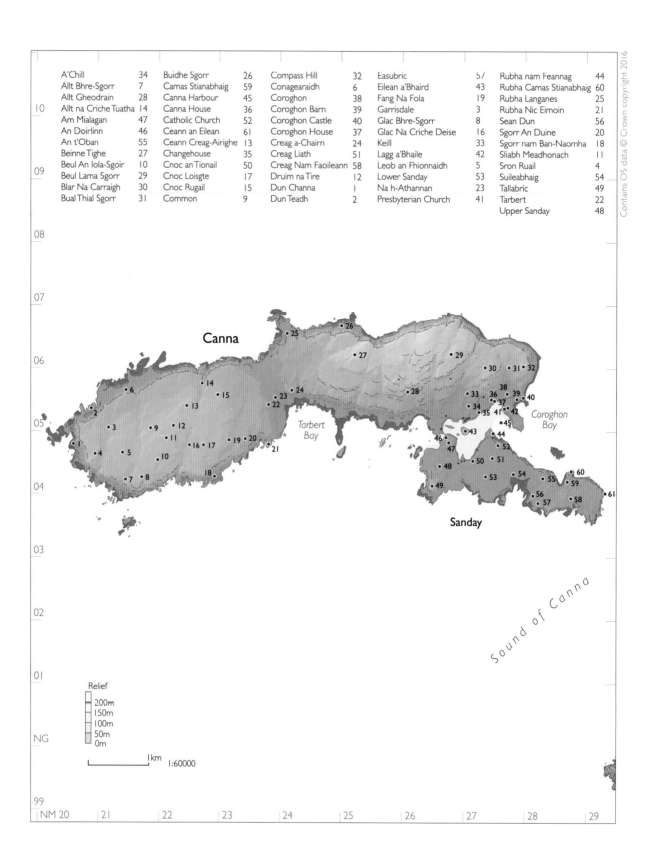

A'Chill	34	Buidhe Sgorr	26	Compass Hill	32	Easubric	57	Rubha nam Feannag	44
Allt Bhre-Sgorr	7	Camas Stianabhaig	59	Conagearaidh	6	Eilean a'Bhaird	43	Rubha Camas Stianabhaig	60
Allt Gheodrain	28	Canna Harbour	45	Coroghon	38	Fang Na Fola	19	Rubha Langanes	25
Allt na Criche Tuatha	14	Canna House	36	Coroghon Barn	39	Garrisdale	3	Rubha Nic Eimoin	21
Am Mialagan	47	Catholic Church	52	Coroghon Castle	40	Glac Bhre-Sgorr	8	Sean Dun	56
An Doirlinn	46	Ceann an Eilean	61	Coroghon House	37	Glac Na Criche Deise	16	Sgorr An Duine	20
An t'Oban	55	Ceann Creag-Airighe	13	Creag a-Chairn	24	Keill	33	Sgorr nam Ban-Naomha	18
Beinne Tighe	27	Changehouse	35	Creag Liath	51	Lagg a'Bhaile	42	Sliabh Meadhonach	11
Beul An Iola-Sgoir	10	Cnoc an Tionail	50	Creag Nam Faoileann	58	Leob an Fhionnaidh	5	Sron Ruail	4
Beul Lama Sgorr	29	Cnoc Loisgte	17	Druim na Tire	12	Lower Sanday	53	Suileabhaig	54
Blar Na Carraigh	30	Cnoc Rugail	15	Dun Channa	1	Na h-Athannan	23	Tallabric	49
Bual Thial Sgorr	31	Common	9	Dun Teadh	2	Presbyterian Church	41	Tarbert	22
								Upper Sanday	48

Canna

Tarbert Bay

Coroghon Bay

Sanday

Sound of Canna

Relief
200m
150m
100m
50m
0m

1km   1:60000

NM 20

Chapter Two
Canna

Canna and its smaller relation Sanday lie at the north-west of the group, relatively small in size (some 1,130ha in total), and relatively low in height compared with neighbouring Rum and Eigg. The highest point is barely 200m above sea level. Straggly in appearance, and with the ancient name of *An t'Eilean Tarsainn* (literally 'the island lying across'),[1] Canna has been described as 'like a bird with outstretched wings' embracing its offspring Sanday.[2] Martin Martin, writing in 1695, additionally records that the natives used the name *Tarsin* when referring to the island from the sea. In common with the other islands and some of their natural features, alternative names were applied from the sea for superstitious reasons.[3] The name Canna itself is probably of Norse origin, the suffix '-ay' (shortened to '-a') indicating 'island', but the remaining element is open to interpretation and has been discussed at length in a wider analysis of the island's place-names.[4] 'Sanday' is simpler to interpret, the name being of Norse origin (Sand Island) and indicative of its lower-lying, sandier character. The two islands are now joined by an elevated track, which replaced a former footbridge across a tidal stream, or can be crossed by foot at low tide. Between them the islands form a natural harbour to the east, well protected from westerly

gales and generally acknowledged as one of the best harbours in the Western Isles. It was 'well sheltered, safe and commodious' according to the Reverend Donald McLean in the *New Statistical Account,*[5] and a welcome haven in seas which claimed numerous wrecks off the south coast of Canna until the construction of the Stevenson lighthouse on Heiskeir in 1904 (Fig 1.2). The Northern Lighthouse Board added a further unmanned light on the east end of Sanday in 1907 as additional protection.

Canna itself can be roughly separated into two parts divided by the isthmus at Tarbert, the narrowest part of the island. Tarbert probably derives from the ancient Gaelic name *tairbeart* (isthmus, or place where two waterways lie adjacent), which suggests that boats may at one time have been carried across land from one coast to the other. On the eastern side the landfall is low-lying along the southern shores by the harbour, and good for cultivation. This is some of the best agricultural land and also where the modern farm is located, but there are steep basalt slopes and cliffs around the northern and eastern sides formed from the volcanic activity of Rum which characterise the landforms of all the Small Isles. Part of this volcanic action produced, at the very eastern tip of Canna, a tall and highly magnetic landform known as Compass Hill, so named because of its effect on compass bearings. This phenomenon, noted by almost every early traveller who landed, was already a visitor attraction in 1695 when Martin Martin wrote that

Fig 2.1 Canna and its small neighbour Sanday, showing locations mentioned in this chapter. HES GV006085

Year	Population	Source
1764/5	253	McNeill (1764/5)
1768	233	Stat Acct (1796)
1772	220	Pennant (1776)
1786	200	Knox (1787)
1788	320	British Fisheries Society
1796	304	Stat Acct (1796)
1821	436	Census
1831	264	Census
1841	255	Census
1851	238	Census
1861	127	Census

Fig 2.3 Combined recorded population figures for Canna and Sanday.

his compass needle 'went round with great swiftness, and instead of settling towards the north, as usual, it settled here due east'.[6] Adjacent on the coastal edge to the south at Coroghon is another landscape feature in the form of a huge stump of basaltic pillars on top of which was built a 'castle' in the 17th or 18th centuries. Here the owner (allegedly) imprisoned his wife because of her great beauty.[7]

The land to the west of Tarbert is more rugged in character and predominantly moorland, but with steep cliffs and terraces dropping down to the shore or sea. The terraces are difficult to access but in times of high population density in the 18th and 19th centuries were extensively cultivated. The lazy bed lines surveyed by the Commission indicate how every conceivable piece of cultivatable land was utilised. The moorland above them contains areas of marshland but little in the way of peat that could be used as fuel, a point noted in the *Statistical Account* when peats were being imported from Rum.[8]

In terms of land use, Canna might be best viewed over two levels. The *Statistical Account* of the late 18th century describes the lower ground as being good for crops, especially oats, and the higher ground good for pasture[9] – a factor reaffirmed in the later *Account*

Fig 2.2 The northern cliffs of Canna looking south to Sanday. The two islands are connected by a bridge. HES DPI09394

of 1845 which additionally alludes to 'great crops of potatoes' and good quality grazing for the rearing of black cattle.[10] One of the earliest descriptions, probably from the 1630s, notes that the islands were 'fertile, both of corn and milk with abundance of all kinds of sea fishing',[11] and Thomas Pennant's description of 1776 was almost utopian: 'each shore appeared pleasing to humanity; verdant, and covered with hundreds of cattle: both sides gave a full idea of plenty, for the verdure was mixed with very little rock.[12] Clearly, whatever Canna may have lacked in mountainous splendour it compensated for in terms of fertility, and this goes a long way to explain its attraction for settlement over the centuries. Sanday is rarely mentioned explicitly in these descriptions, but is presumably included by implication as part of the lower ground. Like Canna, it can be divided into eastern and western parts across a narrow isthmus about 250m wide. The east is mostly moorland surrounded by low cliffs, but the west is more fertile, especially around the southern part of the harbour. Sanday's highest contours are no more than 40m above sea level.

The most fertile areas of the two islands are also those which have inevitably been subject to persistent cultivation over the years, and these are the places where earlier archaeological traces are least likely to survive. Elsewhere, however, even on the cultivated terraces there are sporadic remains of small structures and stretches of walling, many of unknown date, hidden in sheltered locations or utilising the natural rock outcrop faces. Some of these can be interpreted as shieling huts associated with the summer pasturing of cattle, some as prehistoric hut-circles. There is also evidence (uniquely for the Small Isles) of associated prehistoric field systems partly buried in the moorland peat bog running through the western parts of Canna. This itself indicates that the upland slopes were once settled and farmed before a combination of climatic deterioration and soil exhaustion caused settlement to move to the lower contours, with obvious implications for population density in those places. There is also a plethora of other features on the landscape such as mounds and cairns which defy more precise understanding without archaeological intervention. Much of what we know of these monuments stems from recent field survey and aerial reconnaissance carried out by the Commission, and details are housed on the Canmore website. The key sites are shown

Fig 2.4 Canna's gnarled basalt stacks are a testament to the island's volcanic origins and characterise the landform.
HES SC664716

on a broadsheet map of the island (scale of 1:11,500) which shows the advantages of systematic survey and depicts not only areas that have been ploughed, but the individual cultivation ridges within them.[13] Some of the site information has been derived from rabbit activity which has been curiously effective on Canna and Sanday in bringing pottery sherds and other objects to the surface through burrowing. Many of these 'stray' finds have been catalogued: they show a selection of prehistoric pottery types (eg Unstan Ware, Beaker pottery and, less conclusively, Iron Age and medieval styles) which enable some of the sites to be placed in a broadly datable context.[14] Some early fieldwork was carried out by the archaeologist T C Lethbridge, who visited the island in 1924 and recorded a number of sites on a 6-inch map (now unfortunately lost) as well as excavating one of the cairns.[15]

Observations were also made in 1943 by Professor Alf Sommerfelt, a Norwegian historian and linguist, and survey work on putative Norse sites was undertaken by Professor Leslie Alcock in the early 1980s. John Lorne Campbell, owner of Canna

and Sanday from 1938 until 1981, subsequently incorporated all their findings into his book on the island.[16] More recently, in 1994, the University of Bradford undertook further survey work together with an excavation in the vicinity of the standing cross at A'Chill.[17] Excavation and survey work has also been carried out by teams working on behalf of the National Trust for Scotland, the current owner of the two islands, notably in 2006 and 2007, on a Neolithic settlement site at Beinn Tighe[18] and in the graveyard at A'Chill.

The overview of this fieldwork shows an island landscape in a remarkable state of preservation, in no small part due to the conservation efforts of former owner John Lorne Campbell and his wife Margaret Fay Shaw. There is surviving evidence of a prehistoric landscape, settlement sites from the Neolithic, burials,

Fig 2.5 These small terraces on Canna's southern slopes reflect the need to cultivate every useable piece of land.
HES DPI09411

hut-circles and several coastal forts from the Iron Age, not to mention the only souterrain (earth house) known in the Small Isles. The Early Christian period is represented by a series of carved stone crosses, and Canna is the likely location of a lost chapel thought to be associated with Columba's mission in the 6th century AD. Norse place-names are strongly represented on the landscape and, while no Norse sites have yet been verified, there is a strong local tradition of Viking burial. As elsewhere throughout the Highlands, evidence for medieval settlement and land use is difficult to identify, but it seems clear that many of the shieling huts and township dwellings may be of early origin, or stand on earlier sites that were active in the Middle Ages.

By the 18th century the island had evolved into a series of townships, no doubt with much

earlier origins. Kelp burning became a major activity around the end of the 18th and beginning of the 19th centuries and attracted a growing population, leading to a total of 436 recorded souls in the census of 1821 – the current population is just under 20. A number of kelp-burning kilns can still be identified on both Canna and Sanday. Many of the township dwellings were subsequently cleared in order to make way for sheep, their stone buildings dismantled to create sheep dykes. By the time of the estate map produced in 1805 (known as the Clanranald map), there were four main settlements on Canna and two on Sanday; by the middle of the 19th century, after the main Clearances of 1851, these too had become diminished, leaving only 127 inhabitants (Fig 2.3) on the two islands. Many of these dwelling foundations are still visible on the landscape – the problem is in attempting to determine with any degree of certainty, without the benefit of archaeological excavation, whether they relate to medieval, pre-Clearance or post-Clearance times, or indeed whether they illustrate continuity of building tradition in the same location.

Fig 2.6 Today Canna and Sanday look barely populated, but prior to the
Clearances the islands were home to over 400 people. HES DP109398

Early Prehistory

The presence of Mesolithic activity, evident on neighbouring Rum, probably from the 8th millennium BC (see Chapter 5), is not yet attested on Canna. However, it would be surprising if the relative fertility of the island had not been noted by those collecting bloodstone nearby, and efforts made to explore its resources. As owner, John Lorne Campbell's respected insistence on minimising any form of intrusive activity (including archaeology) has guaranteed preservation of the island's historic life story, but at the same time it has served to maintain rather than increase our current level of archaeological knowledge. It is an uncomfortable conundrum. Future work, however, will undoubtedly identify the presence of Mesolithic peoples, particularly in relation to the exploitation of the sea's resources.

Structures

Indications of prehistoric settlement may survive in the form of a series of grass-covered mounds, the majority of which are located inland in the vicinity of Tarbert on Canna. The mounds are typically low, rarely more than 0.5m in surviving height, and amorphous in outline. Most, however, provide the soft soils and structural cavities appreciated by rabbits and are surrounded by piles of burrowing upcast. Their identified distribution around Tarbert is probably misleading: there are mounds elsewhere where the shapes are harder to interpret, or where the rabbits have been less active (for example in the Garrisdale area further west). The few discussed here can be used as a sample to indicate the likely richness of the prehistoric landscape and the quality of its survival. On the basis of pottery fragments found from rabbit burrowing, the earliest of these mounds belong to the period when Unstan Ware was common in northern and western Scotland (arguably from around 4000–2500 BC). Unstan vessels are characterised by being shallow and round-bottomed, often with stabbed or grooved line decoration below the rim, and fragments have been found from an oval mound[19] measuring some 10m by 9m located about 150m north-west of the modern Tarbert farmstead. There are other similar spots in the Tarbert area, including two flattened smaller mounds some 300m north-north-west of the farm, one of which has produced substantial quantities of pottery sherds, also prehistoric, but probably of Late Neolithic or Early Bronze Age date.[20]

Slightly further west at Fang Na Fola there are two low grass-grown mounds on a terrace between two plots of lazy bed cultivation.[21] The larger is oval, approximately 15m by 10m; the smaller some 3.5m in diameter. Both contain evidence for structural stonework, and both have been damaged by rabbit burrowing which has brought pottery fragments to the surface, including a small sherd of Beaker pottery decorated with obliquely incised lines. Another nearby mound with a diameter of some 7m has also yielded early pottery but the date of this find is unclear.[22]

Probably the most interesting site, however, lies on a terrace on the west flank of Beinn Tighe to the east of Tarbert. Here, several potsherds, including a decorated Unstan rim, were found in a rabbit scrape, along with a few flakes and a small scraper of bloodstone. The terrace forms part of the floor of a rocky amphitheatre, and the mound, which is about 20m in diameter, lies towards its leading edge, covered by lazy bed cultivation. On the west fringe of the mound there are two stone features, one of which may be part of the original mound composition. Excavation by the National Trust for Scotland was undertaken in 2006 and 2007 in order to establish the extent of the monument. This additionally succeeded in identifying occupation deposits, which yielded further quantities of Neolithic pottery, and ard marks from ploughing that had cut into the subsoil below the mound, but the original purpose of the site remains unknown.

Fig 2.7 The presence of Neolithic communities on Canna is attested by fragments of Unstan Ware pottery found in grass-covered mounds, particularly in the Tarbert area. HES SC370009

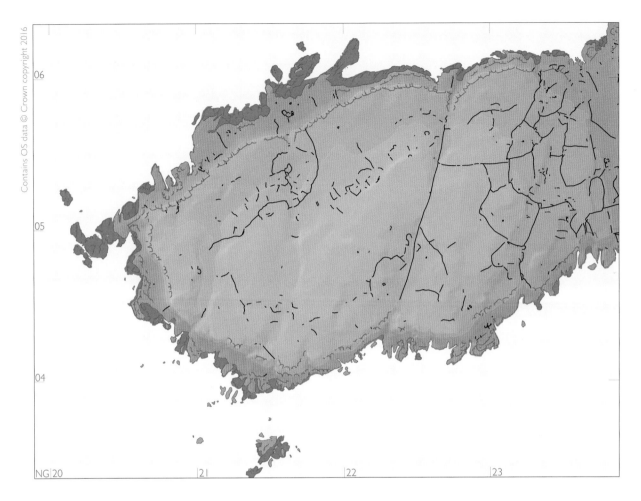

Hut-circles

The term 'hut-circle' is a catch-all term used to describe prehistoric roundhouses, usually in Highland Scotland found on upper moorland slopes. They typically appear as stone foundations, faced on both inner and outer sides, circular or sub-circular in shape, but with no particular consistency of dimension. The Canna examples have diameters ranging from 4.4m to 11.3m, although the majority lie in the upper part of that range. Those which have been excavated elsewhere tend to indicate a Bronze Age date, probably from the second half of the 2nd millennium BC or from the 1st millennium BC, but they can equally well belong to slightly earlier or later periods. Out of all four islands, and probably out of all the Hebrides, Canna has the best preserved examples, not least because several of the hut-circles appear to have associated boundary and field systems. These are defined by lines of earth-fast stones (orthostats, or sometimes known as 'dragon's

Fig 2.8 Plan of enclosures, banks and walls in western Canna. The conjoining elements at the east belong predominantly to the later townships, but those partial elements on the left mostly represent relict prehistoric boundaries and field lines. HES GV006086

teeth') which can be partly traced in the peat and may represent land boundaries and field divisions. The greater majority occur on the western half of Canna where they can be viewed as part of a wider prehistoric landscape, although there are at least two examples in moorland on the eastern part. There are no definitive examples recorded from Sanday. Many of the hut-circles have later structures, usually huts, either in the immediate vicinity, or in the circles themselves, presumably utilising the existing redundant stonework

The two most accessible examples lie on the higher moorland immediately west of the cultivated areas of Tarbert, at Cnoc Rugail[23] and, further south, at Cnoc

Loisgte.[24] At the former the hut-circle, together with a series of huts, mounds and other structures, is situated along an orthostatic wall that extends across a boggy terrace to the north-east of Cnoc Rugail itself. The wall can be traced for a distance of over 350m before dropping down a further 120m to the gully of Allt na Criche Tuatha to the west which forms a natural boundary across the island. There is also a further shorter length of wall adjoining it forming a T-junction, and running to the south. The hut-circle itself is visible as a low mound in the surface of the peat, measuring 8.2m in diameter overall, in which there is a central depression some 5m across. It has been partly exposed by peat cutting, and a shallow dip on one side may indicate the position of an entrance.

At Cnoc Loisgte, the hut-circle is slightly smaller, lying on a terrace within a bank 2m in thickness and up to 0.5m in height. There is a possible entrance at the east. A later hut nearby appears to have been built using boulders taken from a stretch of orthostatic wall that extends north-east from the terrace for a distance of at least 70m. Its projected course would meet another wall, extending up on to Cnoc Loisgte from the gully to the west. This can be followed for a distance of at least 400m, and probably connected with another wall climbing out of the gully further south. The boundaries around both these hut-circles suggest that large areas of this higher section of the island were enclosed before the ground was blanketed in peat.

A greater degree of complexity of boundaries is visible around one of the two hut-circles on the western

Fig 2.9 The surviving remains of a prehistoric hut-circle at Sron Ruail, Canna. HES SC369324

side of the gully Allt na Criche Tuatha. The more northerly one[25] sits on a boggy terrace below Ceann Creag-Airighe; it measures 9.3m in diameter within a stony bank spread up to 2.3m in thickness and 0.4m in height. A few outer facing-stones are visible on the west, but there is no obvious entrance and the interior is filled with peat. Its most exciting feature, however, is its apparent association with a number of orthostatic walls protruding through the peat within a distance of around 200m. Most of these cut across terraces, combining with the crags and outcrops to form a series of fields or enclosures, some of them D-shaped, but others drop down the slope from the crags of Ceann Creag-Airighe into the gully to the east. One of these can be traced intermittently over a distance of about 300m across the lower ground to the north. The other hut-circle[26] lies further to the south at Sliabh Meadhonach, sitting on a terrace below a rock outcrop. Several large inner and outer facing-stones are still visible, but the diameter is relatively small at 7.3m; there is a probable entrance on the south-east. The main system of orthostatic walls in this area lies

Fig 2.10 Prehistoric stone boundaries weave across the landscape, such as here in western Canna, and are almost certainly associated with hut-circles. HES SC369322

well to the south, looping round the west side of the hollow containing shieling huts and up the gully of Glac na Criche Deise. Several walls drop down into the gully, and at least one extends along the contour.

The use of contours appears to have been a characteristic feature of setting out the more major boundaries and this is clear from the boundary layout on the south-facing contours of Leob an Fhionnaidh at the far west of the island. There the main boundary seems to hug the 120m contour, with more minor boundaries dropping off down slope to form smaller land units. It is tempting to think that the more major boundary features indicate land division, while the smaller divisions indicate domestic enclosures or fields. This divided landscape would appear to be associated with two hut-circles near a burn named Allt Bhre-Sgorr, one being particularly small with a diameter of 4.4m[27] and the other, larger at 7.4m, set within a grass-grown stony bank. Boulders forming the outer wall-face can be seen on the smaller example, but there is no obvious sign of an entrance in either.[28]

A hut-circle at Sron Ruail, located on the west side of the same headland, may belong to the same complex of boundaries.[29] It lies at the foot of a rock outcrop, measures 8.4m in diameter and is particularly well preserved. Several stretches of orthostatic walls are visible running from the base of the rock outcrop across a higher terrace to the north, in one case forming an irregular-shaped enclosure. The structure itself appears to have been rebuilt on at least one occasion, the earlier phase being the ring of large outer facing-stones, which seem to have been replaced at some stage by a more irregular line of boulders. The entrance is on the east, emphatically defined by three orthostats. Probably also related to the same land division complex is a hut-circle at Glac Bhre-Sgorr located at a slightly lower elevation and nearer the coast.[30] It measures about 8m in diameter with an intermittent ring of boulders marking the line of the outer face. A fragment of orthostatic wall is visible nearby and other stretches link up the crags over a distance of 200m to the north.

The remaining two examples lie on the eastern side of Canna, on the slopes of Beinn Tighe. Both are relatively large, each measuring around 11m in diameter. One is partly buried in peat and visible as a low mound with a dished interior and a possible entrance on the south-east side.[31] The other, overlain by lazy bed cultivation, has no obvious entrance, but a few internal and external facing-stones can be seen on the west.[32]

Much in the way of boundary walling has clearly become buried in the peat and is now invisible, but the surviving traces, in some cases running for hundreds of metres (Fig 2.10), demonstrate the complexity of the land division and of the organised and co-ordinated society that devised it. Moreover, given the number of boundary traces where there are no hut-circles, notably in the north-west around the Garrisdale area,[33] it is also likely that there are other hut-circles still to be found.

Burials

As with the other islands, without archaeological investigation it is difficult to distinguish burial cairns from those cairns resulting from field clearance or collapsed structures, and therefore even harder to determine whether any are contemporary with the settlement mounds. Curiously, and possibly as a reflection of land use, all but one of the probable examples lie on Sanday. Only one is on Canna, at Creag a-Chairn on the cliff edge overlooking Tarbert Bay where the wasted remains lie on the summit surmounted by a later hut or pen.[34] The cairn is roughly oval, measuring approximately 16m by 12m standing to a maximum of 1.4m in height on one side. The perimeter appears to be defined by a boulder

Fig 2.11 Plan of the partially denuded remains of the cairn at Creag a-Chairn with traces of a boulder kerb. Much of its substance may have been removed to build the later pen or enclosure at its northern edge. HES GV006087

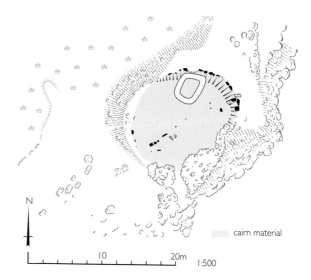

cairn material

N

10   20m   1:500

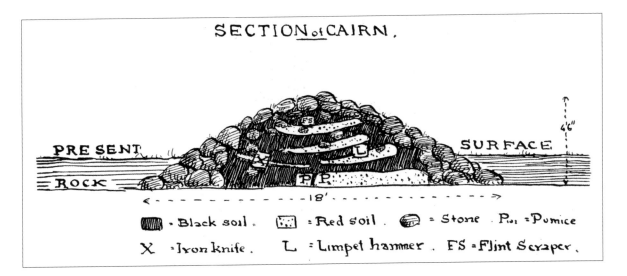

SECTION of CAIRN.

PRESENT ... SURFACE

ROCK

<----------------- 18' ----------------->

▨ = Black soil.   ▥ = Red soil.   ⬭ = Stone   P.u. = Pumice

X = Iron knife.   L = Limpet hammer.   FS = Flint Scraper.

Fig 2.12 T C Lethbridge's 1925 excavation section through the 'cairn' at An t'Oban. HES SC1524976

kerb which is now incomplete. The character of this setting is uncertain, for although it is evidently not the remains of a simple cist, the stones are too slight to be considered the slabs of a passage or chamber. However, the location is significant and the cairn would have provided an imposing landmark.

There appear to be a number of possible burial cairns at An Doirlinn on Sanday on the high ground above the bridge. The largest has a diameter of 9m and stands to a height of over 1m, with evidence of a possible kerb visible on its southern side.[35] A further example has a diameter of over 6m and there are three smaller grass-grown mounds to the north-east.[36] Cultivation patches lie nearby and it is conceivable that the smaller cairns may represent field clearance cairns. That said, however, their elevated position is significant and can be compared to a similar group of six mounds standing on the next headland to the east at Rubha nam Feannag overlooking the harbour.[37] Here the largest has a diameter of over 8m. As with the An Doirlinn group, the smaller examples may represent other forms of land use, although here there is no evidence for cultivation to argue the case. Given the position of the smaller cairns on the two headlands there is some argument to suggest that these are traditional prehistoric burial locations, the larger mounds perhaps belonging to the Neolithic chambered variety, and the smaller to Bronze Age cremation burials as typified elsewhere in Scotland. There are no other identifiable prehistoric gravefields on either Canna or Sanday.

According to records, one cairn has been excavated. The excavator, T C Lethbridge, who published a paper

regarding the site in 1925, refers to it as being 'on the south side of Sanday and almost due south of Canna pier'. The later Commission *Inventory* places the cairn at An t'Oban, in the eastern moorland of Sanday, where later Commission notes indicate that Lethbridge's excavations were clearly visible. The notes also maintain that the cairn to which Lethbridge alluded was in fact the remains of a collapsed stone bothy. Lethbridge describes the 'cairn' as measuring approximately 6m in diameter, and his findings, including a section of the layers encountered (Fig 2.12), are illustrated in his report. He wrote that it 'probably represents the remains of a funeral pyre scraped up and covered by a heap of stones'. He also noted the absence of an urn or cist.[38] The confusion epitomises the problems of landscape survey and interpretation, even when excavation is involved; it also highlights the difficulties in identifying authentic burial cairns from other types of cairn or stone collapse, of which there are numerous examples. There is, for example, a turf-covered stony mound some 6.5m in diameter on a knoll at the eastern side of a small island called Eilean a'Bhaird sitting within the harbour between Canna and Sanday.[39] The location has a commanding view of the harbour entrance and would be a prime and typical position for a burial cairn. But it would also be a prime and typical position for a navigation marker for boats entering the harbour.

Later Prehistory

Settlement sites of the Iron Age, which spans most of the 1st millennium BC and spills into the 1st millennium AD, are notoriously difficult to identify from field survey. There are several amorphous mounds where rabbits have helpfully scraped out pottery sherds to the surface, but the coarse fabrics of Iron Age pottery are little different from those of later centuries. As elsewhere in the Hebrides, traditions of potting seem to have survived largely unchanged between the Iron Age and the post-medieval period. Forms of pottery vessels are more useful for identifying the period, but this requires rim or base sherds to be recovered. Numerous sherds of coarse pottery have been recorded as 'stray' finds over the years on both Canna and Sanday, but it is usually only possible to say that they are neither Neolithic nor Bronze Age rather than that they belong to any specific period thereafter. Spearman's catalogued descriptions of recorded finds makes this point well.[40]

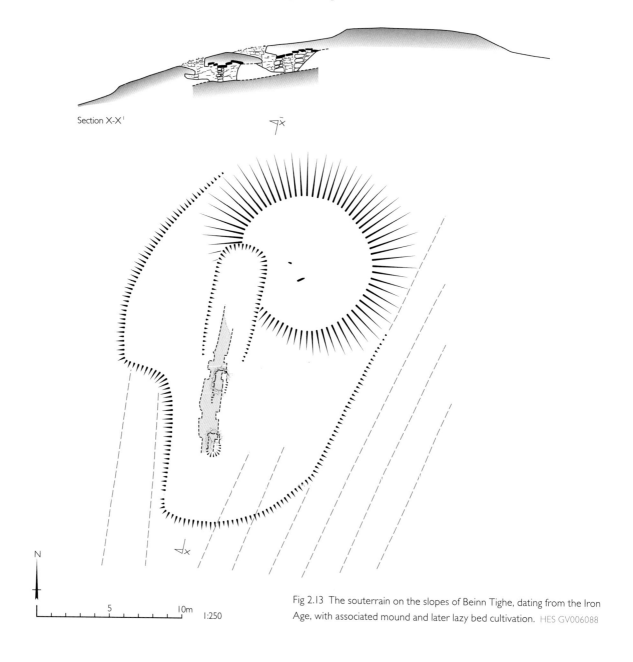

Section X-X'

Fig 2.13 The souterrain on the slopes of Beinn Tighe, dating from the Iron Age, with associated mound and later lazy bed cultivation. HES GV006088

However, there are several monument *types* that can be confidently ascribed to the Iron Age provided that their general shape and character can be determined. These include promontory forts and souterrains (earthhouses) both of which are evident on Canna, the single example of the latter being unique in the Small Isles. Souterrains seem to occur in the middle part of the Iron Age and typically consist of an underground chamber with stone walls and roofing accessed by a long, often curving, stone-built passageway. Opinion suggests that they were not used as dwellings as such, but that they were used for storage purposes, possibly for grain, but there are suggestions that they may also have held a ritual connotation.[41] Souterrains have an interesting distribution: in the west of Scotland they appear limited to the Western Isles (around 37 examples) and Skye (around 20 examples). The main distribution clusters lie on the eastern side of the mainland. The example on Canna is located on the south slope of Beinn Tighe just below a grassy summit.[42] It was originally considered to be two souterrains, but it now seems almost certain to be a single monument surviving in two sections with modern breaks providing access through the roof into the passageway. One section of passageway measures 6m in length, the other almost 4m, with an average width of around 1m (Fig 2.13). The sides are rock-cut, but in places stretches of stone walling survive, and

the stone lintels of the roof are partly supported on at least three pairs of drystone pillers set against the sides. The course of the passage appears to narrow as it rises northwards where it becomes lost, although a depression in the ground surface may indicate its continuing line. At this point a grass-covered mound some 15m wide may indicate the location of a structure associated with the passage. Rabbits have been active in the mound, but the coarse pottery sherds recovered are undiagnostic and therefore cannot be closely dated.

The main evidence for an Iron Age presence undoubtedly comes in the form of natural coastal promontory sites, suitably modified by walling and ramparts, and described on OS maps (probably inaccurately) as 'forts'. Canna has three (possibly four) of these monumental features, Sanday just one. While they doubtless offer some defensive capability, they are vulnerable as fighting platforms, and not particularly useful as places of refuge given their size and coastal locations. None of the examples here contain any internal features that can be argued to be contemporary. Moreover, there appear to be no known associated dwellings, although Iron Age remains

Fig 2.14 The walled entrance of the Dun Channa promontory 'fort', seen here from the landward side, is only accessible by braving a rocky outcrop. HES SC1470326

Fig 2.16 Dun Teadh fort from the south-west showing the single
wall enclosing the promontory. HES SC1500516

may lie beneath the post-medieval townships. Current
opinion sees these 'forts' as more likely to be ostentatious
symbols of wealth – visible testimony of power and
control to anyone approaching the island. But no matter
how they are interpreted, their construction signifies
the presence of a population which was both reasonably
large and co-ordinated from the early 1st millennium
BC through into the 1st millennium AD.

Perhaps the most impressive and spectacular example
is at Dun Channa on the western tip of Canna.[43] This
fort occupies a coastal stack and is only accessible by
way of a narrow spine of outcrop jutting out from the
foot of the cliffs. Even here, however, the stack presents
a vertical rock-face over 3m in height, and it is only
possible to reach the top by scaling the ledges above a
precipitous drop to the rocks on the shore below. The
summit of the stack measures approximately 35m by
30m and is defended by a single wall extending along
the cliff edge the length of the landward side. At the
entrance, immediately above the spine linking the stack

Fig 2.15 The fort of Dun Channa, located below the cliffs,
may have been a symbol of status rather than a military
stronghold. HES DP109399

to the shore, the wall draws back from the cliff edge,
leaving a steeply sloping forecourt in front of the
passageway. Here the wall is almost 2m thick and still
stands to a height of 2.4m in fourteen courses (layers
of stones and slabs). Immediately behind the wall, one
to each side of the entrance, there are traces of two
rectangular buildings in the grass, one some 11m by
6.5m, the other 6.5m by 5.5m. The relationship of
the buildings to the wall is not known, but in their
present condition they have obscured the line of the
inner face of the fort wall and are presumably from a
later date.

At Dun Teadh, approximately 600m north-east
of Dun Channa as the crow flies, is a neighbouring
fort situated on a broad promontory at the foot of
steep cliffs.[44] Its defences comprise a single wall
cutting across the landward side and elsewhere by the
cliff-edge. There are also traces of a possible external
ditch running out into the gullies on either side of the
promontory. The wall, which is over 40m long and
3m thick, is faced externally with massive boulders

still standing up to 0.8m in height in two courses, while the inner face is built of smaller boulders in rough courses. There is a probable entrance near the south-west end, and the interior contains two possible field clearance cairns and traces of what may have been a subrectangular building set against the inner face of the wall, enclosing an area of approximately 10m by 3m. There is a further possible structure set against the outer face near the entrance. Neither appears to be contemporary with the defences of the fort itself.

It seems odd that two monuments of this type should be located so close together, but the remaining five or six kilometres of coastline at that end of Canna mostly lack further suitable promontories capable of modification. It would seem that it was the natural feature itself as opposed to the precise location that was significant. The only other promontory of note in the west of Canna is at Rubha nic Eimoin[45] where the third fort (Fig 2.17) is located at the foot of the coastal escarpment due south of Tarbert and where a low bank crosses the headland. The fort is defended by a single rampart which encloses an area measuring approximately 30m by 20m on the highest part of the promontory. The rampart forms a stony bank up to 5m in thickness and 1m in height directly on the landward side but has been reduced or lost at the edges. The interior is featureless. The entrance is probably on the east, opening outwards onto the lowest part of the promontory, and the only approach from the neck on the landward side is overlooked by the rampart.

The eastern part of Canna also lacks much in the way of appropriate promontory locations, but there is a likely, but as yet unproven, site at Coroghon where a monumental stump of basalt columns provides a ready-made, if inaccessible, coastal fort location.[46] One side of the mass of columns, near the top, is the site of a 17th or 18th century 'castle' (see below) which may have destroyed any evidence of earlier walling or fortification on the landward side. However, modern construction work nearby has identified that this was an area of likely Iron Age occupation; it is surely implausible that a location as impregnable as this should have been overlooked in the Iron Age.

The single fort on Sanday (Fig 2.18) is at Sean Dun, located on an isolated stack of basalt, facing westwards, on the southern part of the island.[47] For the most part, the stack is defined by no more than a cliff, but on the north-east landward side, a drystone wall up to 2.2m thick has been built with the outer

wall-face still standing several courses high. The entrance is marked by a 2m wide break in the wall with a massive boulder on one side. The internal area measures approximately 60m by 25m and appears to have been divided diagonally by a stony bank. The date of this is unknown, but a small enclosure and hut, both apparently overlying the stone wall, are clearly later. Outside there are other small huts in a slight hollow below the fort, as well as traces of a further stone bank.

Fig 2.17 Plan of the fort at Rubha nic Eimoin where the headland is protected by a single rampart. HES GV006089

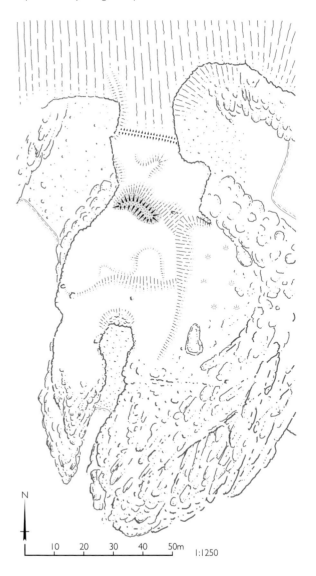

N

| 10 | 20 | 30 | 40 | 50m | 1:1250 |

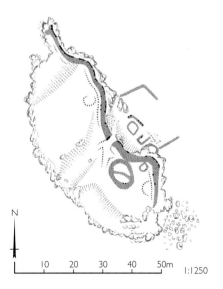

One final monument that might be related to the Iron Age consists of a large circular grass-grown mound, upon which traces of at least five superimposed structures and one subrectangular hut can be seen.[48] This sits on the line of a modern fence that extends along a terrace cultivated with lazy beds (Fig 2.19) overlooking Tarbert Bay. The mound appears to incorporate a massive circular structure some 14m in overall diameter and has an external kerb of large boulders. The superimposed structures are a mixture of shapes and sizes and are likely to have been built using stones robbed from the mound itself. In his notes, Lethbridge considered the underlying structure to be a wheelhouse – a circular building with internal walls radiating from a central point, and well attested in the later Iron Age in many parts of northern and western Scotland. The monument is also large enough to be a small broch or other circular structure falling within the generic term 'Atlantic roundhouse' from the middle and later Iron Age. There is a distribution of many of these in Skye and the Outer Isles, and no good reason why they should be absent from the Small Isles. Only exploratory excavation will be able to take the understanding of this monument further.

Fig 2.18 The Iron Age fort at Sean Dun, Sanday, showing walling along its north-eastern edge, and later structures. HES GV006090

Fig 2.19 This stony mound overlooking Tarbert Bay incorporates a massive circular structure. HES SC369339

Early Christian and Viking

Canna is probably the most remarkable of all the
Small Isles in terms of its visible testimony to early
Christianity. The island was placed under the
jurisdiction of the Benedictine abbey of Iona by the
Pope in 1203, with a church dedicated to St Columba.
This may not have been the original church, and
Campbell has put forward a convincing argument to
support the view that Canna is the mysterious island
of 'Hinba' alluded to in Adamnan's *Life of Columba*,
where a monastic foundation was established as part
of the Columban mission in the 6th century AD.[49]
Adamnan mentions Hinba on several occasions,
including references to miracles which occurred when
Columba visited;[50] he also mentions the erection of a
cross there.[51] The identification of Canna with 'Hinba'
is, as yet, unproven but at the suspected site of the
Columban foundation there is a standing cross in what
may be its original base (Fig 2.21). There are no visible
structural remains of a church or chapel in what is
now an empty field at A'Chill (or Keill; Gaelic *Cille*
'chapel') on the southern fertile flank on the eastern
part of the Island. However, the 1805 estate map shows
the site denoted as 'Keill', which was one of the main
townships on Canna.

In a lengthy missive to the Pope in 1428 the Abbot
of Iona drew attention to the effects of local feuding
on the Abbot and convent on Canna. This clearly
indicates the continued presence of an ecclesiastical
community there at that time.[52] However, in the
mid 16th century Monro mentions only a 'kirk',[53] and

Fig 2.20 A'Chill, one of the townships on Canna, was a focal point
for early Christianity. This later burial ground incorporates a railed
family mortuary enclosure and the foundations of a Mass House.
The buried remains of an earlier chapel and the standing cross
(Fig 2.21) are located in the adjacent field to the left. HES SC875172

an account in the mid 17th century describes a cross
'well carved with strange figures' in the cemetery of
St Columba.[54] This was presumably the cross which
stands there today decorated with human and animal
images (below). The late 17th century account of
Martin Martin records a chapel on the island,[55] and
a century later Thomas Pennant refers to 'ruins of a
chapel, and a small cross' – the first indication that
the chapel was no longer in use.[56] In 1788 a report of
the British Fisheries Society mentions a broken carved
cross and an old chapel that appeared 'quite ruinous',
but interestingly, the writer observed that 'the shape of
a window pleased me a good deal' which suggests that
part of the building was still upstanding.[57] The Report
also refers to a 'Mass House' nearby, presumably the
replacement for St Columba's chapel, where services
took place. It mentions too a 'new' burial ground that
was covered in weeds. This is likely to be the present
burial ground shown as an enclosure abutting a rock
outcrop on the Clanranald map, probably dating from
the 18th century. There is also a crevice in the rock just
south of the enclosure where poles for carrying coffins
used to be stored. Inside the enclosure, grass-grown
foundations on a broad but significant east–west

Fig 2.21 The early standing cross at A'Chill from the west (left) and the east (right) (drawing no. 12 in Fisher's list).
HES SC1523059, SC450730

alignment were recorded during the Commission's survey in 1995, and further clarified by an NTS Thistle Camp clearance in 2013. These may represent this Mass House. It stands just to the south of a railed mortuary enclosure dedicated to the MacNeill family and is visible as a low rectangular outline measuring some 8m by 5.4m.[58] On the pre-Clearance 1805 Clanranald map numerous buildings are depicted, but none are annotated as a church, although the position of the standing cross is clearly marked (Fig 2.35).

Also *not* appearing on the Clanranald map is the so-called 'punishment stone' first described by T S Muir in 1856 as a 'tall red-coloured pillar worn bare' located on a slight knoll nearby.[59] However, this appears on the 1881 OS map and stands some 2m high, now set in a concrete base.[60] The origin and function of the stone are unclear, but a small hole near the top of the southern face is said to have been where offenders had one of their thumbs wedged in a form of punishment similar to the stocks. There is no specific evidence for this and it seems possible that the pillar may have been a reused architectural component, originally being a door jamb built into the earlier Columban chapel, or its replacement Mass House, both of which were ruinous by the time of Muir's visit.

Research excavations around the standing cross in 1994 uncovered the foundations of a rectangular building, probably a successor to any original wooden structure but likely to be medieval. On the basis of geophysical survey the stone-built chapel measured some 20m by 6m, with evidence for a burial ground wall beyond.[61] Keyhole excavations showed that the chapel foundations included stones exotic to Canna indicating, perhaps, the special status of the building; moreover, the foundations overlay pre-existing (disturbed) burials, and probably a cairn which suggests that there was long tradition of burial in that place. A similar phenomenon is also evident at Kildonnan on Eigg (see Chapter 3). During the middle of the 19th century there are records to show that the enforced clearance of the township at Keill involved demolition of the dwellings in order to provide stone for building dykes. The requirements were for a sheep dyke over 5 feet high separating the arable ground and the hill grazing.[62] The chapel is not mentioned, but given its ruinous state it may also have been dismantled for the same reason. The well was infilled, and carved stones from the old graveyard broken up and used for building. Some of the inhabitants took the step of rescuing two of the most ornate crosses and buried them in the ground for safe keeping. Their locations are unknown.

The *New Statistical Account*, produced in 1845, makes it quite clear that there was no church on any of the Small Isles at that time, worship taking place in houses or even in the fields.[63] T S Muir visited Canna in 1856, five years after the Clearance. He wrote of the 'ancient' church that was dedicated to St Columba, noting that 'only slight traces remain'. He also referred to two 'places of sepulture', one old and the other new, but both 'open and in a shocking condition'.[64] The 1st edition of the OS 6-inch map (surveyed 1877, published 1881) uses an antiquities symbol to depict the general location of the former chapel; the later enclosed graveyard is also shown, but the Mass House is not marked.

Additional evidence for an early Christian foundation survives in the form of a number of carved crosses, several being discovered in the vicinity of the former chapel at Keill, together with the standing cross that survives today. Most of these are described and illustrated by Fisher in his comprehensive volume on early medieval sculpture published in 2001 and are ascribed to the 7th–9th centuries. His numbering system is followed here.[65] Fisher has recorded thirteen stones: five of these were recorded from the 'new' burial ground where they had probably been moved to before the Clearances, and where they still stand *in situ*.[66] Seven further examples, also from the burial ground, or discovered in nearby field walls or from ploughing, have now been collected and housed inside Canna House on the island. The final example is the standing cross

itself. The majority of the carved stones are formed from pillars or slabs of Torridonian sandstone; the standing cross is of yellow sandstone. An additional stone – the prayer stone – was later discovered in the burial ground in 2012.[67]

The five still in the burial ground are relatively large, between 0.75m and 1.15m in length, but their widths and thicknesses show a greater degree of variation and reflect the sizes of the natural slabs selected. The taller examples are likely to have been used as upright rather than recumbent grave markers, the lower undecorated half being buried; this would explain the presence of the awkwardly shaped slab (10). There is no evidence of any having been dressed and many of the surfaces are irregular. Three exhibit simple Latin crosses inscribed into the surface (1, 6 and 7),[68] one with forked terminals (6) and one with expanded terminals (7); a further example shows a simple cross but with a V-section groove and barred terminals (4).[69] The final, awkwardly shaped, example is the only one of the five decorated on both faces (10): one face bears a thin sunken cross, the other an outline cross where the top and the arms extend out to the slab edges.[70] Several of the stones appear to have eroded surfaces (Fig 2.22 drawings nos. 1, 4, 6, 7 and 10).

As part of the Canna House collection there are three small carved stones which are of similar simplicity (2, 3, and 5), each bearing a plain cross and each probably representing a grave marker. One of them (2) is decorated on both faces, but the foot is broken and the stone was originally much larger and intended to be set upright.[71] Another was discovered on the shore near Tarbert and is also broken, but it is not clear whether it is the top or the foot that is missing (3)[72] However, the third is complete (5), showing a Latin cross extending the full face of the pillar, which was intended to be recumbent.[73] There is also a fourth small carving which was found in a field wall (11), not of a cross, but of possible trial decoration on a stone that was too small to have been used as a marker.[74] It bears two thinly cut and irregular circles, each with a shaft through the centre, possibly representing some experimental template. Two others are more ornate. One small example broken at

Fig 2.22 Drawings of the Canna sculptured stones (scale 1:15), taken from Fisher 2001. (Drawing no. 12 see Fig 1.8) HES SC373303, SC373284, SC373287, SC373268, SC373289, SC373292, SC373296, SC373291, SC373306, SC373293, SC373282, SC373302, SC1360292

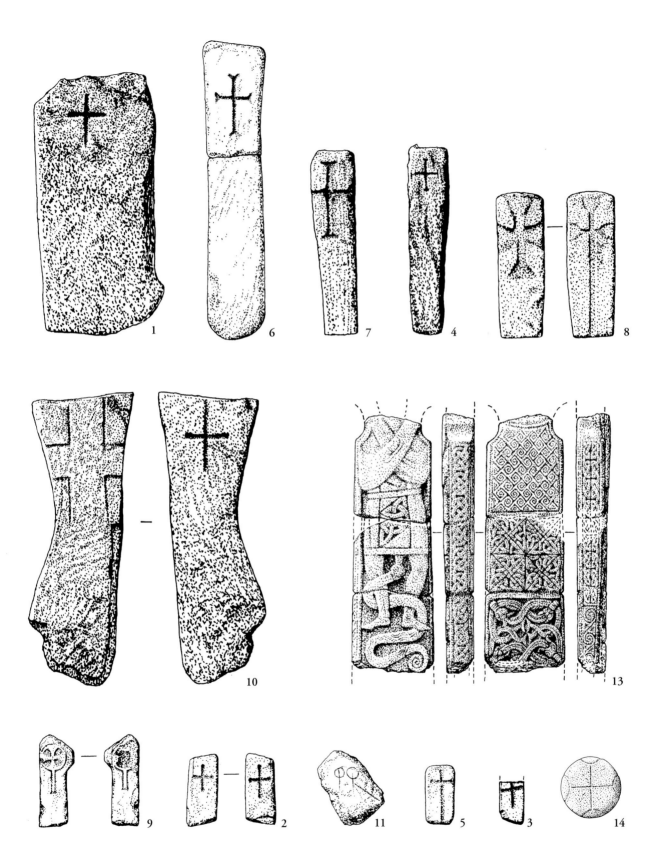

Fig 2.23 Sgorr nam Ban-Naomha from the north-east showing enclosures and structures. HES SC665405.

the foot was found during ploughing at A' Chill in 1947 (8); on one face there is a broad sunken cross, with its side-arms extending to the edges of the slab, but the other face is filled by a Latin cross.[75] The other (9) is more complex and was probably originally roughly disc-headed, but the foot and one edge are broken off disguising its original shape.[76] On one face there is a cross with pocked-out armpits inside a circle; on the other face there has been a similar cross whose head has been much damaged by flaking. In addition to these, and discovered inside the Mass House after Fisher's volume had been published, is the so-called 'prayer' or 'cursing' stone. This is a small rounded (diameter 25cm) beach stone incised with a simple equal-armed cross with arced terminals; several similar examples are known from Ireland. The stone was used by slotting it into the hollow of a larger stone and turning it manually when prayers (or curses) were being offered (Fig 2.22 drawing no. 14).

The final two crosses, one in the Canna House collection, and the free-standing cross in the A'Chill field are both highly decorated with animals, figures

Fig 2.24 The 'altar' from Sgorr nam Ban-Naomha. HES SC701074

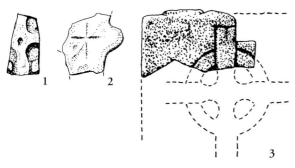

Fig 2.25 The three carved stones from Sgorr nam Ban-Naomha identified during the 1994 survey (scale 1:15). HES SC373298, SC373299, SC373301

and interlace patterning. Taken as an entity, they both reflect a traditional Christian symbolism but displayed through figures and animals which are depicted with strong western influence, reminiscent of animals on the illuminated pages of early Irish manuscripts as well as on Pictish symbol stones. They present a fascinating admix of original pagan imagery adapted to Christian purpose.

The remaining early carved stone in the Canna House collection comprises two fragments of a cross-shaft which were discovered in the wall of the burial-ground not long before 1895 (13).[77] A third fragment was discovered later, and a fourth fragment was found in a ruined house near the harbour. The cross is carved from a medium-grained reddish-brown sandstone and is decorated on both faces and both edges; the top is unfortunately lost. The front of the shaft shows a single scene, a large standing figure wearing a tunic, lacking the head, whose legs are entwined with a serpent and whose arms are crossed on the breast. There is ring-knot decoration on the tunic, and the upper part of its body is much worn. On the other face there are three surviving panels of complex line decoration: the uppermost contains diagonally set spirals; the middle four identical squares of knotwork, and the lowest four symmetrically interlaced snakes. Both edges are incised with tightly set interlace of spirals. Throughout, the carving is intricate and shows much attention to detail and symmetry (Fig 2.22, drawing no. 13).

The free-standing cross (Fig 1.8, Fig 2.21) has been the subject of much attention (drawing no. 12).[78] It measures over 2m in height from the ground surface, has a width of some 0.5m, a thickness of around 0.25m and stands in a socketed slab. It has been extensively decorated, but the top and one arm is missing and the whole piece is very weathered. It has also been extensively drawn and photographed over the years – this itself provides an interesting record of imaging and interpretation, not to mention a measure of the cross's gradual erosion. The illustrations reproduced here include the Commission's late 20th century flashlit photography (Fig 2.21) and drawings published in 2001 (Fig 1.8).

The east face shows a series of figure and animal scenes: there is a dog-like creature at the base, below an antlered stag; above them are two figures, one female carrying a child in what would appear to be an adoration scene; higher up is a horse-backed rider, and above that, towards the top of the shaft, two unidentifiable animals are engaged in snarling. The circular centre-piece is very weathered, but may contain two animals and a central figure. The surviving cross-arm is supported by a colossus-like figure standing on a thin band of interlace. The west face is divided into a series of panels: the lowest shows two creatures with gaping jaws attacking a human figure, with a serpent-like creature in the panel above; two intertwined beasts each fill the next two panels, and the uppermost panel is filled with diagonally set spirals. The circular centre-piece is very weathered but seems to show four roundels of interlace. Only the north edge survives, but this shows two human figures; each appears to be carrying an object.

There are three additional fragments of carved stone within the Canna House collection. These derive from Sgorr nam Ban-Naomha ('Cliff of the Holy Women') – a south-facing coastal site located at the west of Canna. This is a remarkable location at the base of a steep scree cliff rising some 90m and with no access from the sea. It was the type of spot that would have been favoured by hermits or anchorites and may have been associated with the more major monastic establishment at A'Chill; in fact the 1428 reference to a 'convent' (above) may allude to this very site. One mid 16th century source describes 'old Columban cells at the foot of a steep cliff'.[79] The site bears all the hallmarks of an early Christian establishment based on the Celtic model and is unique in the Hebrides. It consists of an oval enclosure measuring some 37m by 31m defined by a wide drystone wall standing up to 2m in height; there is a circular structure 5m in diameter in the centre and a number of small huts or platforms on the exterior. A natural water course

Fig 2.26 The dramatic location of Sgurr nam Ban-Naomha below the southern cliffs on Canna. HES DP109403

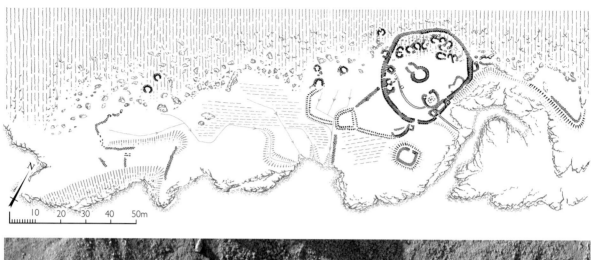

Fig 2.27–28 At Sgorr nam Ban-Naomha the archaeological survey reveals details not visible from the air.
HES GV006091, DP109401

appears to have been adapted to provide a running water system. Early monastic sites based on the Celtic model held the enclosure not as a defensive measure, but as a delineation between the religious and the secular worlds; it was symbolic rather than practical. In the south-east part is a small D-shaped enclosure containing kerbing and loose stones (Fig 2.24). This was known locally as the 'Altar' and it was here that the three carved stones (Fig 2.25) were discovered on a raised platform during Commission survey work. All are of Torridonian sandstone and are in fragmentary form only. The largest (3, using Fisher's numbering) consists of two adjoining pieces from a stone, with worked edges showing a small part of the end of a cross-arm and a quadrant of its ring. This was probably a recumbent grave slab.[80] A second may have been of similar design but here the background has been cut away to form a relief cross (1),[81] and the final piece

consists of a worn, equal-armed cross, probably with original arms on the stone (2).[82]

The demise of Early Christian communities and the emergence of the Vikings tend to go hand in hand, but there is no evidence, historical or otherwise, that the raids which inflicted Iona from AD 797 also made their presence felt on Canna. Common sense suggests that Canna was unlikely to have been spared, but it is mostly the numerous place-names, particularly of natural features, that indicate Scandinavian influence.[83] Commenting on the place-names, one visiting Scandinavian linguist described coming to Canna as 'like coming to the west coast of Norway'.[84]

Two stray finds may lend weight here: one, a glass bead with four bands of inlaid chevron pattern,[85] and a badly corroded Viking-type ring-headed bronze pin found on the site of the present Church of Scotland in 1938. Decorated beads are notoriously difficult to date but the ring-headed pin can be more specifically dated to this period.

Much confusion has arisen over the interpretation of 'Viking' graves, originally recorded in the Commission's 1928 *Inventory*, but these have been looked at in detail by Professor Alcock and largely dismissed. There are a number of sites, typically rectangular, stone-kerbed and unique to Canna and Sanday, which were originally interpreted as being Viking ship burials. A distinguished Scandinavian professor visiting the island in 1943 agreed with this suggestion of Viking burials and, walking down to the shore at Langanes, identified 'a whole cluster of Viking graves'.[86] However, there were so many that Alcock sarcastically mused that the islands must have been used to bury an entire fleet.[87] He pointed out that the oval, boat-shaped, triangular and circular setting graves known in Scandinavia are absent from Canna and Sanday, and that the regular parallel-sided, open ended settings on the two islands are absent from Scandinavian cemeteries. So what were they? He concluded that those on the coastal parts of the islands were likely to be kelp kilns (discussed below), and that those further inland were more likely to be some form of farming structure, possibly peat stands, although not of a type known from the other three islands. The best example illustrating the problem is at Rubha Langanes where the footings of a rectangular 'structure' some 10m long and around 2m wide lies with its long axis down a slope. It appears to conjoin a smaller, more amorphous stone-based feature at the hillward end which sits at a slight angle.[88] There are a number of irregular stones in the vicinity and more obvious hut bases nearby. The traditional view that it was the grave of the King of Norway has no historical justification, nor does it have any similarity with known Viking longhouse structures. It probably represents some form of crude bothy or peat stack, but is nonetheless unusual. A similar example lies in the moorland at Beul An Iola Sgoir, at the south-west end of Canna.[89]

Fig 2.29 Despite being known as the King of Norway's Grave, these boulders at Rubha Langanes are more likely to be the surviving foundations of a store or shelter. HES SC370002

Fig 2.30 Survey plan of the 'grave'. The stones in black are those which are firmly set into the ground. HES GV006092

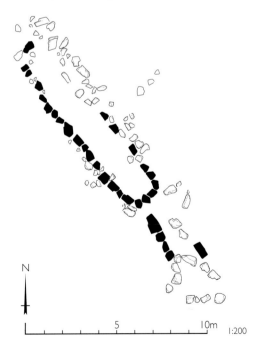

N

5   10m   1:200

Fig 2.31 Coroghon Castle perched on a stack of basalt pillars at the south-east of Canna. HES SC369334

Medieval and Post-Medieval Landscapes

Coroghon 'Castle'

One of the most pronounced features, albeit a higher status one associated with the later landscape, is Coroghon Castle, which stands on top of a stack of basaltic pillars rising some 20m to 25m sheer at the south-east end of Canna. The stack juts out into the sea and is accessible only by a perilous path that ascends a narrow neck of land connecting it to the mainland. It was described by Thomas Pennant in 1772 as a 'horrible path' leading to a 'little tower'.[90] The surviving portion of the castle gives the impression of being precariously tacked on to the north-west corner of the stack's summit, from where it overlooks the approach from the mainland; in fact the second *Statistical Account* refers to it as 'Corra Dhun' (unsteady fort) which may have led to the 'Coroghon' place-name.[91]

The structure of the building consists of random rubble which has incorporated natural rock-faces to form the walls of internal compartments. A narrow doorway with a dressed stone lintel in its north wall gives access to a small ante-chamber from which a series of four rock-cut steps provide entry to the upper floor, which comprises two main rooms. The first is directly above and is subdivided into two smaller chambers by a partition wall; at some stage, the northern of the two chambers appears to have been roofed independently, and traces of its pitched roof-line can still be seen. The second room on the upper floor, which is the larger, has five narrow openings through its north and west walls, all of which are at slightly different heights. A cellar of narrower dimensions lies below but it is not clear how it was reached.

This curious building is traditionally held to have been a prison, used in the late 17th century by a jealous husband to confine his wife. This tradition appears to refer to Donald MacDonald of Clanranald and his wife Marion MacLeod; Donald died on Canna in 1686. However, the earliest record of the building's existence belongs to the late 16th century, where it is referred to as a place of refuge, although no structure or building is mentioned in this description.[92] The castle itself probably belongs to the 17th or 18th centuries. Given the stack's position overlooking the best harbour in the Small Isles and the extent of its natural fortifications, it is highly probable that it would have been used defensively before the castle was built. Unfortunately, any earlier remains have been erased by the castle construction. There is local memory of Lethbridge excavating there, but there is no report of any findings.

Fig 2.32 The plan and elevation of the castle show its perilous position. HES GV006093

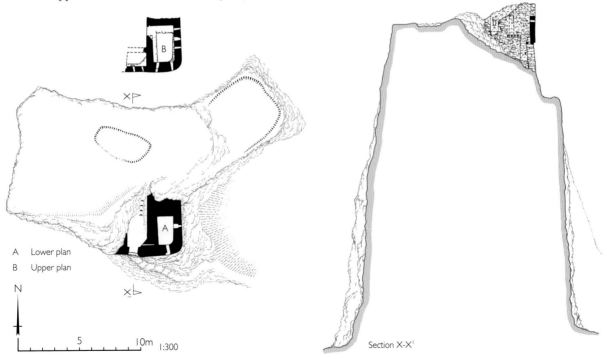

A   Lower plan
B   Upper plan

N

5   10m   1:300

Section X-X¹

Fig 2.33 The unusual character of the castle has attracted visitors since the 19th century, some more adventurous than others. HES SC1113661

Fig 2.34 *The Witch's Home No.2, 'She's Off'* by Richard Doyle. This watercolour was inspired by the rocky coastline of Canna, which Doyle visited in 1875. © Victoria and Albert Museum, London.

The stack is illustrated by Pennant at the end of the 18th century where the castle is shown to be roofless, but still standing to a height of several metres. Later, it appears to have become a popular strolling place for summer visitors, no doubt partly inspired by Doyle's 1875 sketch *The Witch's Home* which portrays the castle as a scene of Gothic horror.

Townships

The more mundane aspects of island life occurred in the fields and pastures where the community lived and worked. We achieve our earliest glimpse of Canna's evolving community through an amalgam of three main sources: a report from the British Fisheries Society (1788), the *Statistical Account* (1796), but predominantly through the Clanranald map (1805) (Fig 2.37). None of them take us back into the perceived gloom of the Middle Ages, but together they provide us with some evidence for how the landscape may have been used in earlier times. Medieval settlement on Canna and Sanday is an unknown quantity but we can assume, on the basis of later population figures (Fig 2.3), that the population probably numbered into three figures and had already identified the most appropriate habitation sites on the basis of shelter, convenience and available resources. The choice of sites is unlikely to have changed significantly over time. Some of the dwellings and clustered foundations of buildings identified in the sources at the turn of the 18th/19th centuries, and indeed seen on the ground today, are almost certainly the latest in the pattern of building and rebuilding through the centuries, robbed time and again of their structural elements.

By the time of the Clanranald map in 1805, the islands appear to have been divided into six separate farms whose boundaries probably equate with the land previously held by townships. Four of these are on Canna (Garrisdale, Tarbert, A'Chill and Coroghon), and two are on Sanday (Upper Sanday and Lower Sanday). These are depicted at the beginning of the 19th century, a time when the population was approaching its peak. The four Canna townships were also noted in the *British Fisheries Society Report* of 1788 in which the houses were 'scattered here and there' and described as being 'formed of loose stones and in every sense mean'.[93] However, there are other settlements that are not depicted: a settlement is recorded at Lagg a'Bhaile near the harbour, and a series of foundation remains and enclosures can be found lying at Conagearaidh on the north-west side of the island. Any, or all, of these may contain structural precursors.

It was the great Clearance during the summer of 1851 that brought about the most dramatic change, when all the tenants on Canna were removed to Sanday. The declining population in Canna was matched by an increased population in Sanday, as evidenced by the number of dwellings which appear there on the 1881 OS map but not on the 1805 map. We might have expected, although it is not evidenced on the ground, an increased level of cultivation on Sanday at that time. The township of A'Chill, which had been inhabited for hundreds of years, was cleared and the buildings and enclosures flattened.[94] There is now nothing at all to be seen on the ground. A'Chill was the largest of the settlements; it was the main township on the island, centred on the ruins of St

Fig 2.35 Detail of the Clanranald map showing the township of A'Chill (labelled 'Keill') and depicting individual houses. The enclosed burial ground and standing cross are also shown. HES SC378353

Fig 2.36 Sketch of Canna harbour by Lieutenant Pierce of the British Fisheries Society. Coroghon Castle is visible in the background, as is a series of dwellings nearby and Coroghon House at the head of the bay. HES DP233885

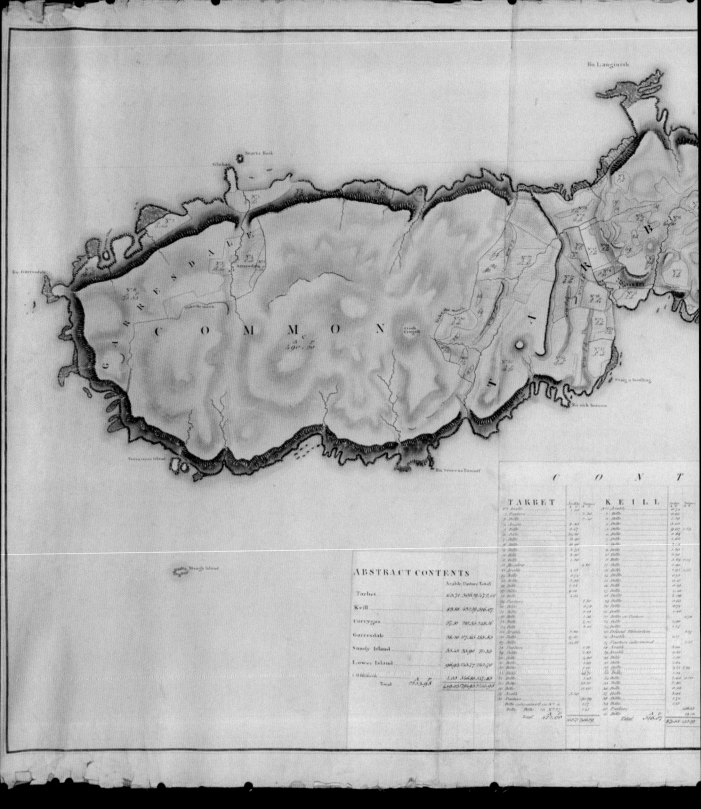

Fig 2.37 The Clanranald map of Canna, which shows individual population centres, is an

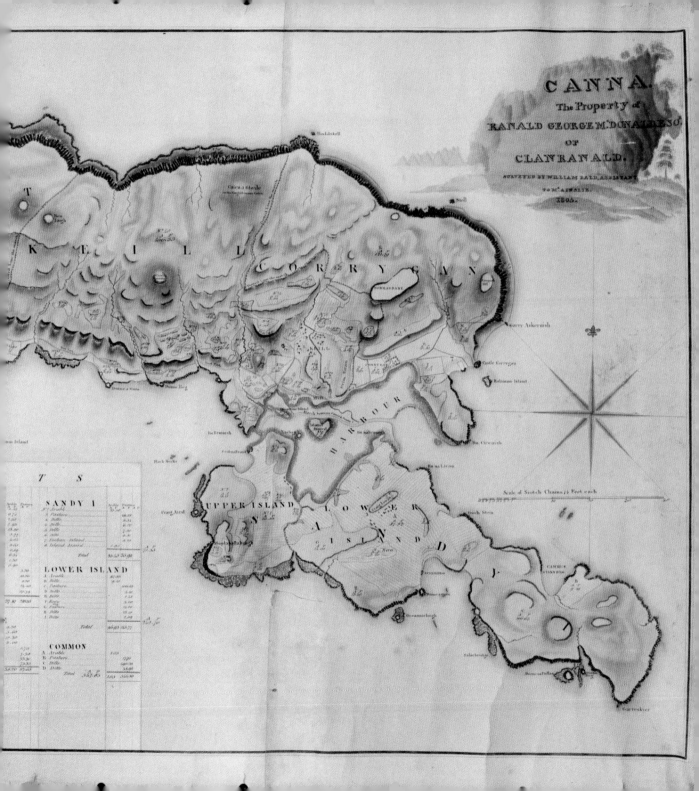

CANNA.
The Property of
RANALD GEORGE M.c DONALD ESQ.
OF
CLANRANALD.
SURVEYED BY WILLIAM BALD, ASSISTANT
TO M.c AINSLIE.
1805.

Scale of Scotch Chains 74 Feet each

Fig 2.38 Remains of the head dyke from the township of Coroghon to Compass Hill, so named because of its magnetic effects on compasses. HES SC665176

Columba's chapel and the free-standing sculptured cross. The 1805 map depicts some 30 structures and at least a dozen enclosures all lying concentrated to the east of a more complex farm configuration (Fig 2.35). A'Chill was separated from the neighbouring farm of Coroghon to the east and Tarbert to the west by now ruinous turf and stone walls (dotted lines on the map itself) which probably originate from the lands held by the earlier townships. The eastern march (boundary) with Coroghon runs roughly south from above the cliffs on the north coast but appears to follow a dog-leg eastwards before running south again down to the harbour. This dog-leg may result from redefining earlier boundaries. Little hint of any subdivision of the farm can be detected on the map, but a series of ruinous dykes cutting across the island may belong to an earlier pattern of land organisation.

To the east lay the township of Coroghon, but nothing is left of this either, although lengths of the head dyke (Fig 2.38) are still visible on the upper slopes.[95] The British Fisheries Society's map of Canna Harbour of 1788 shows nine houses above Coroghon Bay in the valley known as Lagg a' Bhaile (Gaelic 'Dell of the town').[96] These appear as about 20 buildings on a sketch of the harbour drawn by Lieutenant Pierce of the Society, probably from memory (and probably inaccurately) after the Society's visit in 1788. The sketch also appears in the first *Statistical Account*.[97] However, the depiction at least demonstrates the existence of settlement there at that time. It seems likely that their inhabitants were moved to Sanday for the purpose of making kelp or fishing by the time of the 1805 map, possibly to Creag Liath (below).

The farm and township to the west of A'Chill is at Tarbert where the 1805 map shows some 11 houses and an enclosure (Fig 2.39) on the fertile ground at the southern side of the isthmus, standing in a field unusually named Na h-Athannan (Gaelic 'The Kilns').[98] The remains of at least nine of these

Fig 2.39 Detail of the Clanranald map of 1805 showing the
township of Tarbert and associated cultivation. HES SC369356

rectangular buildings can still be seen, together with
three enclosures and a cluster of field clearance heaps.
Most of the buildings have been reduced to little more
than stone footings, but one appears to have been of
turf and survives only as a low grass-grown mound.
With the exception of a large building incorporated
into the modern field-wall, they range in overall
size from around 6.1m by 4.5m to 12.9m by 5.2m.
The largest, which comprises three compartments,

has been remodelled, and overlies an earlier building
belonging to the township. It is shown roofed on
the 1st edition of the OS 6-inch map by which
time the rest of the township had been abandoned.
An enclosure associated with this building appears
to be the only one depicted on the 1805 map. The
cluster of cairns to the south of the township have a
regular layout that has prompted suggestions of early
Christian pilgrimage cairns (Fig 2.41), though it seems
safer to view them as field clearance gathered in the
furrows between plough rigs. At least 24 are visible,
measuring between 2m and 4m in diameter, and there
are also three linear heaps forming low stony banks.

Tarbert was cleared in the mid 19th century, but lazy beds and field boundaries are still visible.

To the west lies an area denoted as the 'Common' on the 1805 map (Fig 2.42) which separates Tarbert from the settlement at Garrisdale, the most westerly farm and township.[99] The map shows not only the extent of the farm, bounded in part by a now ruinous wall, but also the area of ground which was then under cultivation. The stony banks which defined its fields and enclosures can still be seen, together with traces of

Fig 2.40 A current photograph of Tarbert and Na h-Athannan (compare Fig 2.39 and Fig 2.41) showing the fertile area between the moorlands to the east and west. The Tarbert township and the cairns lay towards the coast at the south. HES DP109419

lazy bed cultivation, other banks and numerous small huts and mounds, many of which are undoubtedly earlier. Three roofed buildings are depicted, but the 1st edition of the OS 6-inch map (1877 survey) shows

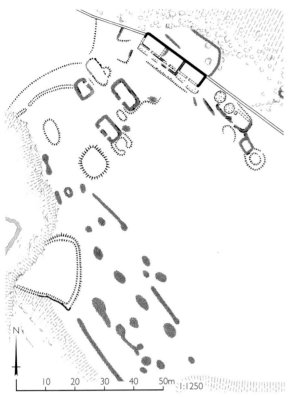

Fig 2.41 In the field known as Na h-Athannan, Tarbert, the survey plan shows evidence of buildings, enclosures and the regular layout of cairns. HES GV006094

Fig 2.42 Detail of the Clanranald map showing the township of Garrisdale. HES SC639018

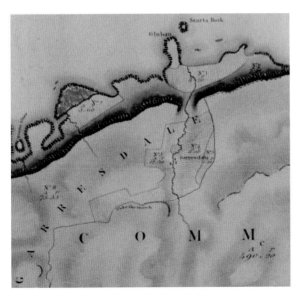

only a string of five unroofed buildings. The three buildings all probably belong to a farmstead, which replaced the township buildings, the largest being a byre measuring approximately 14m by 4m, later modified for use as a livestock pen.

Not far away on the lower slopes to the north at Conagearaidh (Fig 2.43), but not depicted on the 1805 map, is a cluster of two subrectangular buildings, at least six other structures and two enclosures.[100] The two buildings and enclosures are sited at the leading edge of the terrace, the larger building measuring 10.6m by 4.9m within a faced wall; its east side has been entirely robbed but one rounded internal corner is still visible. The end of the second building, which is in a better state of preservation, has been filled with field clearance. The associated enclosure lies immediately to the south-west. The terrace on which they sit has been cultivated and several plots of lazy beds can be seen, together with field clearance heaps and stretches of stony banks. One bank runs across the terrace from the foot of the cliffs to the foreshore and four of the structures lie along its line. These are all subrectangular and defined by grass-grown banks; they range in internal size from 1.9m by 1.3m up to 4.7m by 2.2m. The remaining two structures lie towards the rear of the terrace; the first is oval and crudely formed by tumbled boulders, while the other is set within a grass-grown bank.

It is far from clear how these two settlements relate, how they can be dated, or how far back in time their antecedents might stretch. Garrisdale and Conagearaidh are both depicted on the first edition OS 6-inch map surveyed in 1877 which shows five and three buildings respectively, all unroofed. Conagearaidh, however, does not appear on Langlands' rather schematic map of 1801. Conagearaidh contains a possible burial enclosure which may have provided a facility for the small township there and at Garrisdale before they were cleared.[101] The low grass-grown walling of the enclosure lies near a burn below steep cliffs and measures about 13m by 11m. A small number of burial plots are visible on the surface, some with upright stone slabs, but there is no memory of any burials ever taking place here, nor does it appear on any of the relevant maps.

On Sanday, the map shows the island divided into two by a boundary running from north to south in a reverse S-shape across the neck of ground between

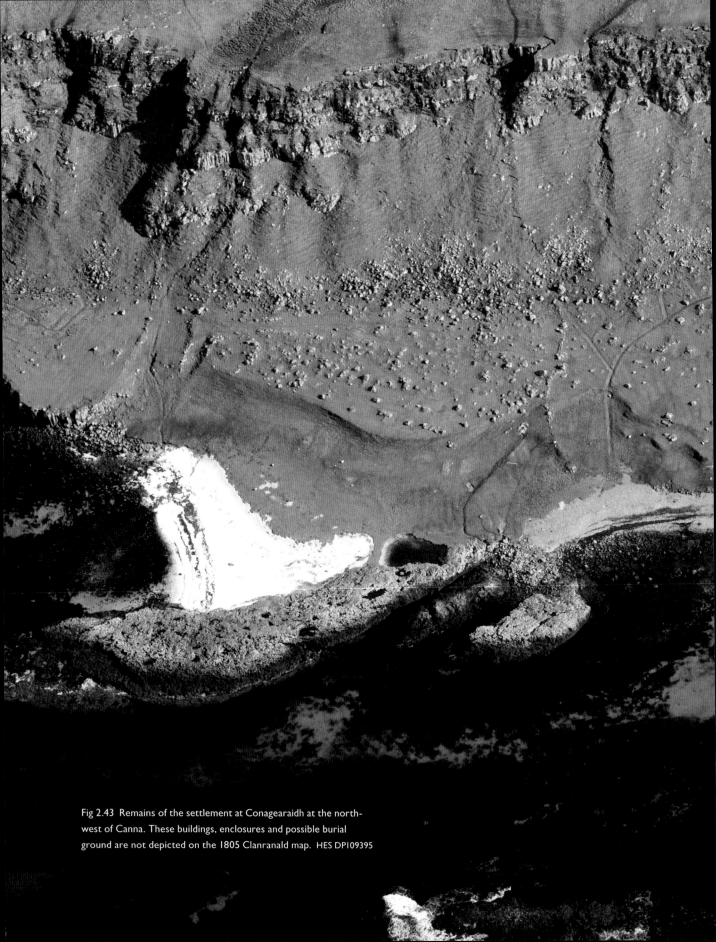

Fig 2.43 Remains of the settlement at Conagearaidh at the north-west of Canna. These buildings, enclosures and possible burial ground are not depicted on the 1805 Clanranald map. HES DP109395

Tallabric and Cnoc an Tionail. By 1805 both east and west units appear to be operating as separate farms, whose boundaries presumably equate with the land held by two earlier townships. The eastern unit is the larger of the two; it contains the moorland which provided pasture for the township there, and is annotated as the Lower Island. No buildings or structures are depicted at this far eastern part of the island on the estate map, nor on the first edition of the OS 6-inch map. Some areas of arable ground shown on the map take in the east side of the bay at Camas Stianabhaig defined partly by the coastline and by rocky crags. Several stretches of walls can still be followed linking up the rocky crags and apparently enclosing the area shown on the map. This end of Sanday has never been intensively cultivated, and the clusters of huts and stretches of ruinous field walls that survive suggest the ground was only ever used sporadically or on a seasonal basis. They are impossible to date; some of the walling lines may be prehistoric, part-buried in the moorland.

The township of Lower Sanday may be depicted on the 1805 map (Fig 2.44) by two scatters of buildings nestling below the rocky knoll of Creag Liath. These are depicted in an irregular scatter of seven structures, with a further series of five slightly to the south-west. Traces of the former can still be seen partly overlain by a row of later buildings, all of which are oriented in a linear manner along the foot of the knoll.[102] Although reduced to their grass-grown footings, these later buildings are all similar in size, measuring on average 10m by 4m within faced rubble and may represent the dwellings of people Cleared from Canna. The surviving rentals for Sanday show that the 'Lower Island' had ceased to exist as a separate farm by 1818; the township was abandoned by the late 19th century and nothing is

Fig 2.47 The remnants of buildings at Am Mialagan, Sanday. HES SC1499342

Fig 2.44 (opposite, top left) Detail of the Clanranald map showing dwellings in the Lower Sanday township which lie below the rocky knoll of Creag Liath. HES SC639018

Fig 2.45 (opposite, top right) Later remains at Creag Liath, probably the result of Clearances from Canna. HES SC575755

Fig 2.46 (opposite, below) The later buildings at Creag Liath were located to optimise on the shelter of the knoll outcrop. The Catholic church is on the right of the picture. HES SC871434

depicted here on the first edition of the OS 6-inch map published in 1881 although a number of later roofed buildings are shown along the shore.

There are a number of structural ruins situated round the northern coastal fringes of Upper Sanday, many showing rebuilding and replacement. The first edition of the OS 6-inch map depicts over 20 roofed buildings in 1881, but the 1805 map shows only five roofed buildings, all on the eastern side. These presumably represent the survivors of the Upper Sanday township located at Am Mialagan on the peninsular shore.[103] Only two remain in the form of grass-grown footings, rectangular in shape measuring approximately 8.4m by 4m and 6m by 5.3m respectively. There are possible remains of what may be a third robbed building nearby. The map also shows four unroofed buildings and a subcircular enclosure at An Doirlinn. The latter may have been incomplete; the buildings and enclosures that survive there today appear to be of more recent date.[104]

Shieling

The survey data recorded by the Commission on both Canna and Sanday show a multiplicity of structural foundations of small buildings, mounds, earthwork features and small cairns occupying all parts of the landscape, both within and outwith cultivated areas. The structures of most of these do not conform to known prehistoric monument types and can be associated with more recent activity. Many lie adjacent to clusters of township dwellings, but many others lie in open landscapes in locations more removed from daily activity. A number are likely to have been shieling huts – small stone or turf-built structures that provided temporary accommodation during the process of transhumance in the summer months. There are thought to be over 100 such structures on Canna and Sanday, surviving as small grass-grown foundations, or as mounds, but they are harder to interpret than, for example, those on Rum where the vegetation is less obscuring. They most obviously occur in the moorland zones in the far east of Canna, in the areas of 'Common' in the west of Canna, and across the eastern parts of Sanday. They can be seen in small clusters, often associated with small enclosures and lazy beds. The majority probably relate to the townships and reflect the summer movement of livestock into the higher pastures, but many will date before this era, and the size of the mounds on

Fig 2.48 In common with many shielings, the mounds and foundations at Fang Na Fola reflect building and rebuilding over the centuries. HES SC36931 I

which some of them sit suggests several generations of accumulated seasonal occupation.

A typical group lies at Bual Thial Sgorr on the slopes of Canna's Compass Hill where a large oval enclosure occupies an area of gently sloping ground embracing a group of seven huts and three mounds.[105] For most of its circuit, the enclosure is defined by a stony bank. Two small plots of lazy bed cultivation can be seen within the enclosure, and a stretch of grass-grown stony bank runs across the interior, forming a link between several of the huts. These huts are set on top of low mounds, which are undoubtedly the remains of earlier huts. The huts on top are subrectangular in plan, the largest measuring 6.5m by 4.6m sitting on a much broader mound. There are also other earthwork features in the vicinity.

There is a particular density of huts on the moorland slopes of Beinn Tighe, to the west of Compass Hill. There are several groups, particularly

Fig 2.49 The remains of scattered shieling huts lie in the shelter of the outcrops at Fang Na Fola. HES DP109400

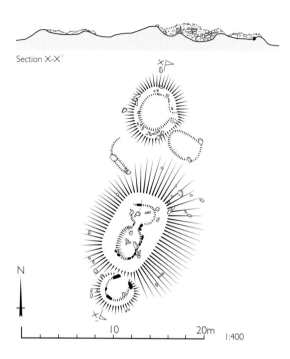

Section X-X¹

N

|_____|_____|
10   20m   1:400

Fig 2.50 Detail of three shieling huts sitting on mounds at Blar Na Carraigh. Two are circular, one figure-of-eight, with associated features in the immediate vicinity. HES GV006095

on the south-western slopes typically consisting of hut foundations and mounds, where the mounds almost certainly represent former collapsed huts. There are several clusters variously containing between three to six huts and four to ten mounds each.[106] The largest group, however, sits at a little distance away at Blar Na Carraigh where there are no fewer than twelve huts and eighteen mounds evident on the ground.[107] All these clusters occur within a few hundred metres of each other. To the south-east of Beinn Tighe is another cluster of two huts and three mounds,[108] and to the north of these there is a group of three huts and seven mounds.[109] Nearly all of them lie in association with other less decipherable earthwork features and are reasonably representative of clusters elsewhere on the island. Several appear to be deliberately located adjacent to running water, and two of them yielded pottery from rabbit scrapes suggesting that the sites may have been partly selected in view of an existing earlier building which could be robbed. Sizes are small, ranging typically from 2m by 2m to 4m by 2m with a maximum surviving height of over 1m; one was divided into two internal compartments.

In a further cluster of five huts at Allt Gheodrain nearby, one of the structures has two adjoining cells in the shape of a figure-of-eight,[110] the second chamber possibly having been used for storing dairy produce. Similarly configured huts are also found on the south coast of Sanday, at Easubric[111] and Suileabhaig.[112] There is no specific size, shape, or material used that marks out a shieling hut from any other type of hut; the only realistic criterion is that they must stand within the higher pastures. They are difficult to date without archaeological intervention, and even then there is no guarantee that datable evidence in the form of diagnostic pottery will be forthcoming. There is a group of four at Garrisdale[113] at the far west end of Canna which appear to have been overlain by cultivation shown on the 1805 map, and some groups are incorporated within earlier field systems, such as at Druim Na Tire[114] to the east of Garrisdale where the structures are defined by parallel rows of boulders and are associated with orthostatic walls. One of the Blar Na Carraigh huts was excavated by T C Lethbridge in 1925. This remains unpublished, but in a letter to the Commission he wrote:

On Canna, I dug a house in a shieling but it was late medieval, probably 15th-16th century. It was the largest of a complex of hut sites and there were several successive floors of peat ash but the few potsherds were all medieval[115]

Lethbridge's dating criteria for the pottery are unknown, but he was certainly aware of the successive levels of floor ash which presumably indicated several phases of occupation. Many huts sit on accumulated mounds which suggest that any seasonal occupation may have taken place for much longer than just a few years. Good examples of huts on mounds are evident at Beul Lama Sgorr,[116] north-west of Compass Hill, and at Glac Na Criche Deise where a total of sixteen mounds and two huts in a natural hollow suggest a lengthy period of use.[117] There is no definitive structural method: eight huts at Sgorr An Duine[118] are all outlined by rows of boulders, at Fang Na Fola[119] to the south-west of Tarbert there is a large cluster of which two appear to be mostly of turf, and nearby, at Buidhe Sgorr[120] by the cliffs on the north coast of Canna, natural rock elements and boulders have been used. All the evidence points to the structures being of a temporary nature, presumably recreated seasonally in locations appropriate to summer grazing, and where building materials were readily available.

Fig 2.51 Canna's harbour in the 1960s.

Alasdair Alpin MacGregor. © National Museums Scotland. Licensor Scran

Maritime Remains

Like the other islands in the group, Canna and Sanday made use of local fishing for domestic needs and enjoyed the benefits of kelp harvesting. Unlike the other islands, however, they had the benefit of a natural harbour that had greater potential prospects for a maritime economy based on fish and trade. The harbour sits enclosed against the prevailing westerly winds, sheltered to the north and the south by Canna and Sanday, with an entrance to the south-east. It appears in a sketch, albeit in slightly schematic manner, in the first *Statistical Account*, complete with sailing ship and two kilt-wearing islanders (Fig 2.36) in the foreground. It was also adjacent to good fishing grounds. In 1824 MacCulloch found the quantity of coal fish being hauled out of the sea by hand nets 'incredible'.[121] Thomas Pennant, writing in 1776, was one of the first to point out how this fishing potential had not been realised, noting that the investment and equipment necessary to promote fishing was completely 'past the ability of these poor people' on the island,[122] and how their current supply of fishhooks was almost exhausted.[123] The first

Statistical Account noted that it was safe for ships, but only of moderate size and that ships needed a favourable wind to enter or leave.[124] Clarke's visit of 1825 pronounced it to be 'small, but safe and commodious' and (remarkably) compared its scenic location as being second only to that of Naples.[125] It clearly had an international reputation as both *Statistical Accounts* allude to the earlier presence there of Baltic traders.

The British Fisheries Society visited Canna in 1787 and 1788 with the intention of identifying locations for fishing stations; the harbour was given serious consideration. The visits resulted in two reports.[126] The first (1787) commented on the fitness of the harbour, the proximity of fishing grounds, the fish that could be caught, and the support of the present tacksman (Hector MacNeill), but stressed the need for a pier and warehouses. The second (1788) was of very different tenor and contained more about the

Fig 2.52 The natural harbour between Canna and Sanday brought the islands into consideration for industrial fishing in the 18th century, although the plan never achieved fruition. HES DP109393

landscape and the islanders than the fishing potential. The Society identified a piece of land suitable for a fishing station but differences over payment between the Society and the owner, the Clanranalds, eventually achieved stalemate and nothing resulted. This all occurred in the wider context of kelping with its competing manpower requirements, and with the problems encountered in acquiring sufficient quantities of salt for the preservation of barrelled fish for export. The latter had much to do with the duties, the cumbersome conditions for obtaining it, and the distance to the nearest Custom House (Tobermory) from where it had to be collected and its use justified – issues already brought to the fore in the first *Statistical Account* of 1796.[127] Lack of enthusiasm appears to have continued until 1892 when a pier built of green-heart oak was finally constructed in the harbour to support the herring fishing. Canna's coastline is harsh, and there is no evidence to support domestic boat use in the form of minor jetties or slipways as evident, for

example, on Eigg. Nor did the survey identify any fish traps, although there is some recorded evidence of one on Canna.[128]

Kelping was a mainstay of the island's economy throughout the late 18th and early 19th centuries and Canna (with Sanday) exhibits more kelp kilns than any other island in the group. The process was a relatively simple one (see also 1797 description in Chapter 1). Seaweed (kelp) was collected from the shore, spread out to dry, then burned in a kiln until it turned into a red-hot liquid and was worked with irons until it was hard. Buchanan, writing in the late 18th century, commented that the whole kiln measured up to 3m by 1m in size and that other layers of seaweed could be burnt on top of

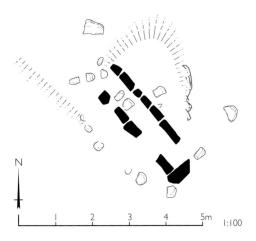

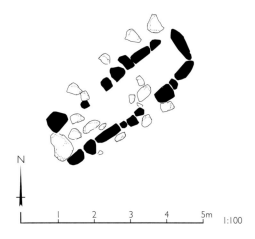

Fig 2.54–5 Kelp kilns tended to be formed by rectangular stone settings with one end open, such as here at Garrisdale (left) and Suilebhaig (right). HES GV006096, GV006098

Fig 2.56 The kelping industry had a major impact throughout the Small Isles, although few traces remain. This kelp kiln at Conagearaidh is one of the few reminders of the trade left today. HES SC378338

the previous one.[129] Many of these kilns appear on Sanday, which has a lower, more appropriate coastline on which the seaweed could be dried. These include sites hitherto interpreted as Viking graves. One small kiln at Suileabhaig takes the form of a narrow rectangular structure situated on a rocky ridge overlooking the foreshore. It measures 4.8m by 1.4m defined by two parallel rows of small boulders set on edge. One end was formed by a boulder. A part excavation of this kiln in 1994 showed that the edge stones were earth-fast, but that between them was a sporadic layer of beach cobbles containing patches of burnt soil.[130] No other deposits were observed, nor was there any evidence of a superstructure. The general shape of kelp kilns seems to have been long and narrow, defined by earth-fast stones, often with one end left open, possibly being used as a flue. Others on Sanday can also be found at Suileabhaig (5m by 0.9m),[131] Creag Nam Faoileann (two kilns measuring 7.6m by 1.7m and 6.6m by 1.7m respectively)[132] and at Rubha Camas Stianabhaig (12m by 1.3m).[133] None of them, however, appear to be sunken in the manner of some of the Irish examples recorded, and this may explain why they are often difficult to recognise.[134] The Sanday examples are of consistent width with their Irish counterparts, but are significantly longer (the maximum Irish length was 3.6m). Three putative examples at Ceann An Eilean, also on Sanday, measure between 17m and 25m in length, but these longer versions are more likely to be peat stands.[135] On Canna, the most visible kiln sits on a grassy terrace below the cliffs at Conagearaidh. It has an open end facing the sea and is relatively small measuring 3.4m by 0.5m.[136]

Later Buildings

Several of the buildings on the present landscape have their origins in the late 18th century and survive today in modified form. A small number of buildings are shown scattered along the north side of the harbour on both the British Fisheries Society's 1788 map and the 1805 Clanranald map. These include Coroghon Barn,[137] the Changehouse and barn,[138] and Coroghon House.[139] Coroghon Barn, the most easterly, is located near to the 'lost' township of Lagg a'Bhaile north of the harbour, and is a fine example of a bank-barn occupying a sloping site above Coroghon Bay. It was designed as a multipurpose agricultural building, with rooms for stabling horses, providing a byre for cattle, storage space for hay and working floors for winnowing. The building is rectangular and of random rubble construction with rubble dressings and a slated roof with two floors, each subdivided. The lower floor is cobbled and the upper storey is accessed by way of an external stair leading to a central door in the gable, as well as directly from the higher ground behind. The 1805 map shows two buildings at this location, while the first edition map

Fig 2.57 Early photograph of the barn in use showing upper storey access from rear. HES SC1249121

Fig 2.58 The Coroghon Barn was built into a bank. The lower storey is accessed from the front and the upper storey from the side and rear. HES SC794199

shows four roofed buildings, two adjoining enclosures and a well.

The Changehouse and associated steading was built in the late 18th century by Hector MacNeill the tacksman and is now the oldest inhabited building on Canna. It sits in 'the Square' on the shore below A'Chill. The house itself was a three-bay single-storey cottage constructed of whitewashed rubble with an attic beneath a slate roof, and is traditionally said to have been used as an inn. The steading lies immediately to the south-west and is of similar construction. The upper storey contained a barn to which access was gained from one end. Hector MacNeill also built a water-powered corn mill which features on a plan of Canna Harbour produced by the British Fisheries Society in 1788. It also appears on the 1805 map together with a dam, mill-pond and two outflows. The mill itself no longer survives, having

been replaced by a steam-driven mechanical grain mill, but the dam, built of coursed rubble, can still be seen. Other contemporary features that also survive include a culvert which carries the outflow of water from the dam and traces of a lade which runs under the adjacent road.

Hector MacNeill was also responsible for the earliest 'main' residence on Canna in the 1780s, Coroghon House, situated at the head of the harbour on the road frontage. Lieutenant Pierce's drawing of 1788 shows it to be a rather grand edifice, having a central element of three floors with a single-storey wing either side. The British Fisheries Society report records it as 'a neat house of four rooms on a floor, two stories high'.[140] The Society's second report, a year later, mentioned that it had a 'miserable interior'.[141] It was later replaced by the construction of Canna House[142] in 1860 and reduced to a single floor, before more recent renovation, and is now known as 'The Bothy'. The current Bothy, 6m wide and 11.5m long, was constructed out of its central shell using the front wall and shortened gable walls, with a new build for the rear. During redevelopment, excavation in 1998

Fig 2.59 The Bothy, a single-storey building, was built from the shell of the taller late 18th century Coroghon House.
HES SC369352

Fig 2.60 Canna House, built in 1860, was later home to the island's owners John Lorne Campbell and his wife, who passed Canna over to the National Trust for Scotland in the early 1980s. HES SC1078147

showed that the original Coroghon House had an upper floor and was of more than a single build; it originally had flagged floors with cobbled edges.

Canna House, which replaced Coroghon House as the principal residence, was built to its rear at a short distance from the road by Hector's son Donald in 1860. It was occupied by John Lorne Campbell and his wife when they purchased the island in 1938 and is now in the care of the National Trust for Scotland; it houses their library and their collections which include Gaelic music, early Christian sculpture and an archive of moths and butterflies. The building mostly survives in its original form today as a two-storey villa with an attic beneath a slate roof which is hipped, sloping to all four walls. The south-facing front elevation is symmetrical, with a shallow pediment, bay windows and a porch. The walls are of coursed dark squared rubble with ashlar dressings, the darkness of the stone creating a rather austere presence on the landscape. A lower two-storey wing was attached to the rear, and a

single-storey conservatory with a corrugated iron roof abuts the east end, originally used as a billiard room.

There are several interesting later items in the Canna House collection of sculpture, notably a piece probably belonging to the 16th or 17th centuries. Fisher describes it as being a 'crudely carved' grave slab;[143] it appears to be complete and decorated on one face only. It was found in the 'new' burial ground and photographed (Fig 2.64) sometime

Figs 2.61–2.63 The hallway, dining room and study at Canna House. The bay window of the dining room houses a collection of early Christian carved stones. HES SC1330137, SC1330151, SC1078156

Fig 2.64 Local workmen display a carved medieval slab found in the burial ground at A'Chill. Not knowing which way up it should be presented, both display options were given, although the slab was almost certainly intended to be recumbent. HES SC1470322, SC1470390

before 1925. Not knowing which way up it should be presented, the gentlemen in the images offered both options, although in actual fact the slab was probably intended to be recumbent. The images also show the MacNeill family mortuary enclosure in the background. The slab's carvings are in two zones, one at each end, separated by a blank panel that may have been intended for an inscription. Parts of the carvings are difficult to make out but one end depicts, according to the 1928 Commission *Inventory*, 'a heterogeneous assemblage of objects', together with a bird centred around a figure holding a sword.[144] The other end appears to show two trees as well as an interlace pattern based on a cross saltire. Problems of interpretation here are explored in a helpfully annotated illustration in the Thistle Camp report.[145]

There are two 'modern' churches that stand today, a Presbyterian building on Canna,[146] and a Roman

Fig 2.65–67 The Presbyterian church provides a local landmark with its pointed round tower, an ornamental wrought-iron gate and a simple unadorned interior. HES SC664042, SC369316, SC1499331

Fig 2.68–69 The now-disused Catholic church on Sanday differs in style to other buildings on the islands. The Presbyterian church can be seen in the background.
HES SC684140, SC369347

Catholic one on Sanday.[147] The Presbyterian church, designed by P MacGregor Chalmers and overlooking the harbour, was built as a memorial to Robert Thom by his son between 1912 and 1914. Small and rectangular, the construction is of random rubble; the roof is of stone, rendered externally, but visible internally as a pointed tunnel-vault. The building has an Irish feel to it with a pointed round tower lying central to the west gable, vented by similar openings which match the pointed leaded windows in the nave. Unusually, the pews are arranged length-wise in the nave. The church lies within a stone-walled burial ground, which has a fine ornamental wrought-iron gate decorated with birds and fishes.

The 'new' Catholic church is a different beast altogether. It was designed by William Frame and built by the Marchioness of Bute as a memorial to her father, Lord Howard of Glossop, between 1886 and 1890. The dedication is to St Edward the Confessor. The church is an imposing landmark and consists of a rectangular nave, a semi-circular chancel with neo-Romanesque arch, a three-storey rectangular tower with belfry and louvered vents, and a gabled porch. The construction is of coursed dark rubble with sandstone dressings and the roof is of slate with decorative red ridge tiles. The windows in the nave and chancel are round-headed, the exception being in the west gable where there is also a rose window. Internally, there is a corbel course around the nave, carved by Thomas Nicholls, with five evenly spaced stone heads of knights and priests on each side. The communion rail by Robert Thompson still survives in front of the chancel arch, and the altar, square font and organ are still *in situ*. The building was closed in 1963, and is no longer used, attempts to convert it into a hostel being unsuccessful. It sits somewhat incongruously on the landscape, but the tower makes a convenient marker for shipping.

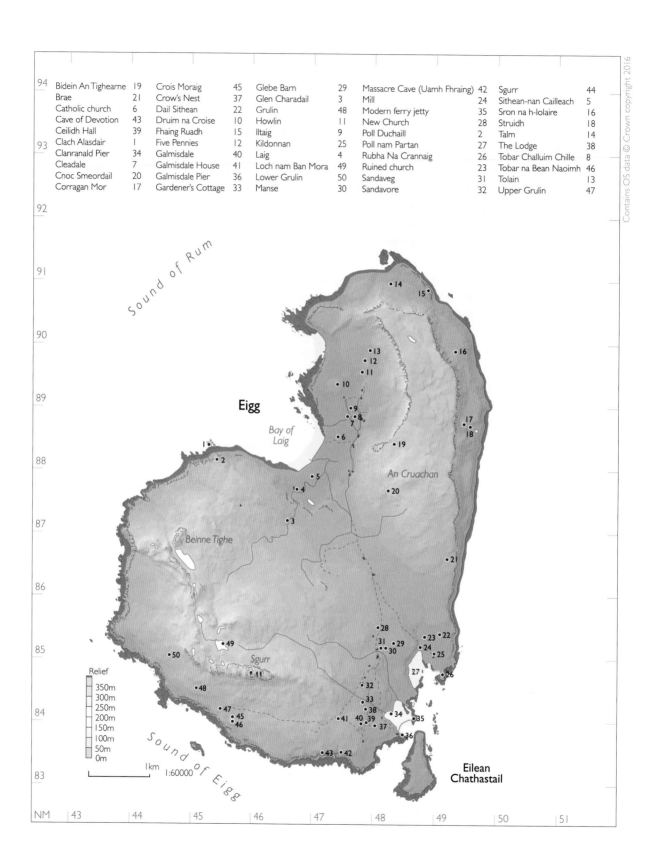

Bidein An Tighearne	19	Crois Moraig	45	Glebe Barn	29	Massacre Cave (Uamh Fhraing) 42	Sgurr	44

Sound of Rum

Eigg

Bay of Laig

An Cruachan

Beinne Tighe

Sgurr

Relief

350m
300m
250m
200m
150m
100m
50m
0m

1km   1:60000

Sound of Eigg

Eilean Chathastail

NM 43 44 45 46 47 48 49 50 51

Chapter Three
Eigg

History has tended to view Eigg as the parent island within the Small Isles parish. The landscape was the most suitable for farming settlement, and even although it was not the largest of the four islands (around 3,000ha), it housed the highest recorded population of all four with over 500 souls at the turn of the 19th century. The Small Isles parish was formed in 1740, and by the late 18th century Eigg was home to both parish clergymen (from the Church of Scotland and the Catholic Church) and the parish school, which served all four islands at that time. Both ecclesiastical livings required their incumbents to preach regularly on all four islands and, given the distances involved and the often dangerous sailing conditions, they were argued by one visitor to be the most arduous ecclesiastical duties in the Christian world.[1] The schoolmaster and the parish surgeon both lived on Eigg,[2] and it was the only island in the group with a proper manse, built in 1790.[3] Eigg also features prominently in the accounts of 18th and 19th century travellers and visitors, no doubt reflecting its dramatic historical background and legacy of wild superstition, including the 7th century bloody martyrdom of St Donnan and his monks, and the supposed massacre of the entire island population suffocated in a cave in the 16th century. There are also tales of magic wells and

giant women – legends and superstition that underlie the alternative island name of Eillan nan Banmore ('Isle of the Great Women'), a name only used to describe the island from the sea, first recorded by Martin Martin in the late 17th century.[4]

Eigg's history of ownership is equally absorbing. It lay under the tenuous powers of the MacDonalds of Clanranald for several centuries before being sold off in the early part of the 19th century. Since then it lists among its proprietors: Professor of Greek at King's College Aberdeen; his son, Professor of Scots Law (and interested antiquarian) at Glasgow University; a journalist and arms dealer; two Edwardian shipping magnates (one of whom, Sir Walter Runciman, was also a government minister), and a mysterious German artist who eventually transpired to have part-financed the purchase by a loan from a Hong Kong clothing exporter. Eigg was also the focus of an acrimonious divorce settlement and eventually, in 1997, became the possession of the islanders themselves as the result of a community buy out. The chief island residence, 'The Lodge', only came into being as a new build from less stately origins in the early part of the 20th century.[5]

Like its neighbours Canna and Muck, the shape of Eigg's landscape is the product of basalt lava flows emanating from Rum. These manifest themselves as a series of step-like escarpments, with the softer flows weathering down, augmented by blown sand, to produce the best soils. They occur on the lower plateaus below the more exposed upper terraces which are found

Fig 3.1 Eigg, showing locations mentioned in this chapter.
GV006099

Fig 3.2 The rocky Sgurr, seen here from the south, is Eigg's most prominent geological feature. HES DP109442

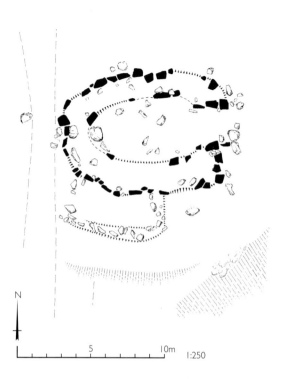

Figs 3.3–4 The Small Isles have been populated for several millennia, and these foundations at Galmisdale on Eigg may be part of a Neolithic house. HES SC771464, GV006100

at the north and south ends of the island. A long geological slit or groove running from north-west to south-east separates the two areas of higher ground and may have been the reason for the island's name, Gaelic *Eagg* meaning 'hollow' or 'groove' according to the *Statistical Account*.[6] In the southern part of the island the landform is broken by a massive column of pitchstone, the Sgurr, almost 400m high formed in a series of hexagonal columns not dissimilar to those found on the island of Staffa off Iona, but of a magnitude and character that made embodiment with the supernatural inevitable. Robert Jameson, Regius Professor of Natural History at Edinburgh, climbed to the summit in the late 18th century and described the Sgurr as being 'characteristic of the wildest and most inimitable work of nature'.[7] James MacDonald, writing on behalf of the Department of Agriculture in the early 19th century likened it to a 'threatening tyrant',[8] while Hugh Miller, a geologist, devoted several pages of his book *Cruise of the Betsey* to it, effusing over its formation and beauty. He was the first to identify the casts of ancient tree roots fossilised in the Oolite (limestone) beneath it.[9] The Sgurr gives the island its unmistakable profile and its mystical aura, and makes Eigg instantly recognisable on the skyline.

The *Statistical Account* of 1796 recorded that the island was 'pretty equally divided as to crop and pasture grounds',[10] presumably reflecting the lower and upper landscapes respectively. It recorded eight ploughs at that time, more than any of the other three islands.[11] It was also relatively rich in peat and heath – a valuable source of fuel – and was sufficiently well endowed to supply the fuel needs of Muck in addition.[12] The fertile soil attracted settlers from Neolithic times, and generations of dwellers have subsequently left their mark there, from Bronze Age hut-circles and Iron Age forts to a cemetery of Pictish square cairns, a series of early Christian crosses and, finally, the nucleated townships which were cleared during the 19th century to be replaced by the regimented layout of croft walls to be seen in Cleadale today.

Throughout the centuries, the prime areas of settlement seem to have been in the lower-lying areas, principally around Galmisdale and Kildonnan in the south-east, and around Cleadale, Howlin and Laig in the north-west. These areas, which are still inhabited today, contain several prehistoric monuments, including burial cairns and hut-circles. Kildonnan was the focus of a multi-period burial tradition, while the other four show extensive landscapes of the 18th and 19th century fields and lazy bed cultivation around the old townships. There are also dense concentrations of archaeological remains on the narrow strips of rough pasture below the cliffs on the north and north-east coast where scores of shieling huts, stock pens, enclosures and rock shelters, many of unknown date, lie among the boulders and scree. But within this wild landscape there are two relatively fertile oases, at Talm and Struidh, both of which were later occupied by groups of summer shielings in the early 19th century. In a similar topographical position, on the south coast below the Sgurr, forts and hut-circles stand within an extensive system of later fields surrounding the old townships of Upper Grulin and Lower Grulin. Elsewhere on the island, the north-east and western uplands are much less hospitable, though even here small groups of shielings of medieval or later date can still be identified, some of which have been built over the remains of prehistoric hut-circles. All these monuments have been recorded by the Commission through a programme of field survey and aerial reconnaissance and published in broadsheet form, as well as being available on the Canmore website.[13]

Early Prehistory

Structures

Given the presence of Mesolithic activity on neighbouring Rum, it would be surprising if Eigg, with its more subsistence-friendly landscape, was not also a base for groups of hunter-fishers during the Mesolithic period (7500–4000 BC), perhaps using some of the rock shelters in the scree slopes on the east coast. Moreover, Eigg would have been directly visible on the shortest sailing routes from the Mainland to Rum, as well as visible from Rum itself. In the subsequent Neolithic period (4000–2500 BC), which saw the introduction of agriculture and new types of stone tools, there is a modicum of artefactual evidence for activity on Eigg (below). Additionally, in Galmisdale there are the footings of a building that may be the foundations of a Neolithic house, situated on a terrace at the edge of later field cultivation, and one of the few known examples in the region.[14] The foundations are oval in plan, measuring approximately 8m by 4.3m, with double-faced stone walls some 2m thick but with many of the inner facing stones missing. The entrance is at the east end and is unusually wide, possibly reflecting the original use of timber posts, flanked by the remains of a flat façade. An upright stone stands on each side of the entrance at its outer edge, immediately in front of the façade, but it is not clear whether these are original features. A subrectangular cell built against the outer face is probably a much later structure. The closest parallels for this building are to be found among the oval prehistoric houses on Shetland. Many of these (eg Stanydale Temple or Benie Hoose) have stone facades, and one site (Loch of Collaster) features a pair of boulders outside the entrance similar to the stones at Galmisdale.[15] Most of the Shetland houses have small cells or alcoves set into their walls; no such features can be identified at Galmisdale, but this has not been tested by excavation.

The earliest dates from the oval houses of Shetland are from House 1 at Scord of Brouster, constructed in the late Neolithic, around 3000 BC, but the form continues in use into the Bronze Age, and with variations, into late prehistory.[16] The only other comparator in the west is at Northton, Harris, where occupation of the house was associated with Beaker pottery, and a single uncalibrated radiocarbon date of approximately 3080 ± 150 bc was obtained for a sample of animal bone.[17]

Hut-circles

Eigg contains most of the hut-circles in the Small Isles, all representing the stone wall-footings of round buildings probably dating from the Bronze Age (c2500–800 BC). Around 30 individual sites have been located, although not all of these have been verified and only one has been partly excavated. The distribution of these sites tends to show that most (two thirds) occur on higher ground, between the 100m to 200m contours on the southern lower terraces of An Cruachan in the east, and on the northern and north-eastern slopes of Beinn Tighe to the far west. But there are several examples on the lower slopes (below 100m) which suggest that the original overall distribution was probably quite dense before becoming obliterated by the field clearances and ploughing of later agriculture regimes. Many of the hut-circles have been disfigured by robbing, those on the higher slopes for the construction of shieling huts which have been superimposed or sit nearby; many have collapsed and spread, their surviving walling standing to heights typically between 0.3m and 0.8m. Any associated field boundaries and enclosures to which the hut-circles

Fig 3.5 Cleadale, Howlin and Laig in the north-west. HES DP109456

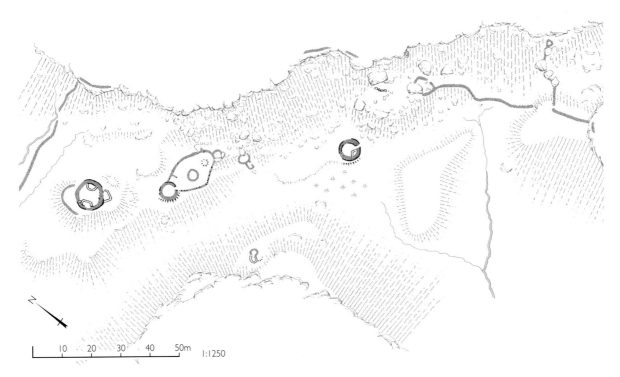

10   20   30   40   50m   1:1250

were integral have usually become degraded, or lost to the undergrowth. As a result survey measurements can often act only as a guide.

Some of the best surviving examples can be seen at Cnoc Smeordail[18] on the south-west slopes of An Cruachan where there is a group of at least three, possibly more, of different sizes, together with enclosures and traces of an associated field system. The group sits in a shallow valley located on the natural ledges of the slope between rock outcrops. Their diameters range between 7.5m and 10m with walling up to 1m thick. The remains probably represent a small farming unit, active in the first millennium BC when ambient temperatures were more amenable to working the higher slopes; their survival reflects a gradual but widespread abandonment of farming to lower levels as the climate deteriorated, or as soils became exhausted. Some robbing has taken place: two of the hut-circles contain vestiges of later structures, probably shielings, utilising the original walling stones.

Fig 3.6 Now degenerated into moorland, the high slopes of Cnoc Smeordail were once home to Bronze Age communities, traces of whose huts and field systems are still partly evident. HES DP109450

Fig 3.7 Plan of a group of hut-circles at Cnoc Smeordail. HES GV006101

Another small group, also with later shieling huts, lies on the north side of Beinn Tighe.[19] Two hut-circles, one with a diameter of 5m, the other more oval in plan and slightly smaller, stand about 25m apart. A later shieling hut has been built into the former, and at least two other huts stand adjacent, suggesting that the shieling location was probably enjoyed for its easy robbing of hut-circle stone. There are at least five other hut-circles in the general area of Laig;[20] these mostly stand in isolation from associated features but one appears to connect with a sinuous wall visible for around 150m and two others have stone-built structures of unknown date standing nearby. Their diameters vary from 4m to 11.5m – a range that is evident across the island and which may reflect the availability of building materials or the individual functions of the structures.

The only formal excavation to assess this took place at a hut-circle at Galmisdale on the higher edge of the 100m contour and set into rising ground.[21] The hut itself measures about 10m in diameter and shows some mutilation, presumably from robbing. There is a levelled platform slightly further to the south, possibly the remains of a second hut-circle. Two trial trenches were excavated through the former to assess its condition and likely date in view of a possible association with a Late Bronze Age metalworking site located nearby.[22] No direct correlation was made, but the discovery of the metalworking site itself is of major significance – it was found by a local resident in 2001, followed by formal excavation which produced fragments of crucibles, clay moulds for casting several types of object including bronze socketed axes and knives, and stone tools for grinding and sharpening. The finds were recovered from inside a rough setting of small boulders created around a larger boulder to form a later pen or shelter.[23] The large boulder itself was an immoveable landscape feature and the discovery of a cache of some 40 flint flakes and tools buried against it, within an earlier ground surface, suggests that this was already a significant marker before any metalworking ever took place. The metalworking is estimated to have been undertaken in the period 1000–800 BC and was relatively short-lived, perhaps lasting only a few days. It introduces the concept of nomadic craftspersons and raises

questions regarding patronage and ownership of resources. In Britain and Ireland as a whole, sites producing evidence of Bronze Age metalworking activity are rare and in Scotland only a handful of sites are recorded, most recently at Cladh Hallan in South Uist.[24]

Of the hut-circles on the lower slopes, a pair at Howlin are worthy of note, one superimposed on the other, standing on a slight rise within enclosed fields to the north of Five Pennies township.[25] The later of the two, which makes use of the north-east arc of the wall of the earlier, measures 8m in diameter within a rubble wall. The earlier hut-circle was slightly larger, and a later subrectangular hut has been built against its outer face on the north-west. Possible examples also survive at Struidh on the remote east side of the island, but these too have been extensively robbed; their outlines are now blurred by later huts and collapse, and concealed under vegetation.[26] A final large example, some 10m in diameter, survives in apparent isolation in Manse Wood, Sandavore.[27] Although heavily overgrown, there is some evidence of associated banking, possibly representing a field system.

Burials

In 1878 the owner of the island, Norman MacPherson, Professor of Scots Law at Glasgow University and an enthusiastic antiquarian, made the first published record of antiquities discovered in Eigg.[28] Several of the objects he identified were not from specific locations, such as a leaf-shaped flint arrowhead found in ploughsoil near Kildonnan.[29] However, a small polished stone axe and fragments of bone were found when a (now lost) cairn containing two cists at Sithean-nan Cailleach, above the Bay of Laig, was quarried for building work in 1853.[30] The axe is now held in the National Museums Scotland and has been ascribed to porcellanite rock from Northern Ireland.[31] A later Viking grave at Kildonnan may have utilised a Neolithic chambered cairn (below) but this is not clear from MacPherson's description. A further donation made by MacPherson to the Museum, but without reference to the source from within the island and almost certainly from a burial, was a bronze socketed axehead of the Late Bronze Age, later denoted as being of Yorkshire type.[32] Interestingly, modern excavations within the ecclesiastical area at Kildonnan (below) have since

Fig 3.8 Plan of the hut-circles at Howlin, with the smaller, later hut-circle superimposed on the earlier one. HES GV006102

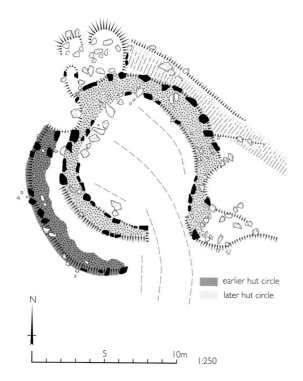

earlier hut circle
later hut circle

N

5   10m
                1:250

Fig 3.9 A bronze socketed axehead and a leaf-shaped flint arrowhead found on Eigg by the then-owner, Norman MacPherson. © National Museums Scotland

identified the remains of a robbed Neolithic cairn containing sherds of a Beacharra bowl – a type of pottery usually dated to around 4100–3350 BC.[33] This gives further credence to the putative chambered cairn nearby, reused by Vikings, and suggests that Neolithic burial was more widespread on the island than the current landscape indicates. Eigg is something of an outlier in the distribution of Beacharra bowls but the presence of this pottery on the island, together with that of the porcellanite axe and the socketed axehead, indicates that even in early prehistory Eigg had wide-ranging contacts.

There are a number of circular burial cairns on the island; most of these probably belong to the Early Bronze Age (c2500–1400 BC) and most seem to have been damaged by stone robbing. MacPherson records one that was dismantled at Kildonnan in 1861 by workmen building a road; he describes a stone cist as being covered by 'a fine earthy matter, containing some small pieces of charred bones', but there is no diagnostic evidence of date.[34] Several cairns are still visible: the most accessible lies in woodland adjacent to the Eigg Lodge driveway and shows traces of a kerb of large stones on one side of its 8m diameter.

An earthen ramp that runs up its side may reflect an attempt to incorporate the mound into a landscape design within the Lodge grounds. Its centre has been hollowed out, probably for the same reason, or through excavation.[35]

At the north end of Eilean Chathastail (Castle Island) two grass-grown cairns stand some 40m apart occupying prominent positions on a headland overlooking Galmisdale Bay.[36] One, measuring 8.4m in diameter, has occasional kerb stones surviving but has been disturbed, exposing a core of rounded stones. The other, slightly smaller, stands on the edge of a low cliff and has partially collapsed into the sea; a depression on the top suggests that it too had been dug into. On Eigg itself there are two further cairns standing together on the edge of an escarpment overlooking Galmisdale Pier from the west.[37] One measures some 7.5m in diameter, the other slightly less. Both have a number of kerb stones still *in situ* but both have been disturbed and have a hollow top indicative of robbing. A particularly large cairn, 12m in diameter, stands in a prominent position on the summit of Druim na Croise, just to the north of the Cleadale settlement, and it probably survives because it was situated in the common grazing outside the arable land.[38] This cairn has been mutilated too, but in this case the location suggests it may have been robbed for its antiquarian content rather than for building stone. The unfortunate story continues: the final cairn stands on a rise along the road from Galmisdale Pier to the Lodge. It probably had an original diameter of around 6m but its centre has been disturbed as a result of its use as a base for a flag staff. In 1878 MacPherson noted that there were still 'many artificial circular mounds unexplored,'[39] but sadly this appears no longer the case.

Later Prehistory
The principal monuments of the earlier and middle parts of the Iron Age (c800 BC–AD 100) are forts or duns. At least six are now known on Eigg, all but one occupying rocky stacks or promontories around the coast, and defended by a stone wall. 'Fort' is probably a slightly incorrect term for these monuments, for although they present defensive capabilities around the island periphery, they also offer a number of logistical difficulties in supporting a community that might seek refuge there. Moreover, in many instances their 'defences' do not appear to be ideally

fit for purpose. Opinion differs as to their consistent function through time; one plausible alternative sees them as symbols of authority vested in a visual display of wealth evident to all those who approach the island. Either way, they represent the result of controlled communal activity and are indicative of local power.

On Eigg the largest of these commands the island from the summit of the Sgurr, a pitchstone ridge whose striking profile forms a landmark visible for many miles around. The ridge rises towards the east from a plateau of high moorland and becomes increasingly precipitous towards the summit, culminating in sheer cliffs on three sides. The only approach to the summit is barred by a single drystone wall, in places up to 1.8m in height and some 2.5m thick, which can be traced for a distance of about 80m. This wall, together with the top of the natural cliffs, encloses an area of some 5ha, but with no internal structures evident. Although described by Martin Martin in the 17th century as a 'natural fort'[40] and as offering 'very good strength against enemies' by Macfarlane, it was a place that hardly lends itself to any form of permanent occupation.[41] Miller's opinion of it as being 'one of the most inaccessible [hillforts] in the kingdom'[42] is probably more correct in terms of its

Fig 3.10 Image of Loch nam Ban Mora taken from the Sgurr c1860. HES DP233888

geography than its function; this fort in particular may hold more significance for its spectacular location than for any real defensive purpose.

Nearby, on high ground to the north-west of the Sgurr, Loch nam Ban Mora contains what was originally considered to be a crannog, an ancient dwelling in the loch, some 50m from the shore.[43] The loch was so named ('Loch of the Great Women') as being the place where, according to legend, the female warriors who martyred St Donnan and his monks lived and eventually met their demise. However, this 'crannog' transpires to be a small dun or fort, typical of many of the poorly built island fortifications in western Scotland. It occupies a D-shaped natural rocky islet which has probably been artificially enlarged with walling around the perimeter and measuring overall 14m by 8.5m transversely – small but adequate to hold, according to one early 17th century account, 'a certain number of men and women with their bairns'.[44] The drystone walling is best preserved on the straight landward side on the north-east, and is built of similar pitchstone blocks and in the same style as the fort wall on the Sgurr. Elsewhere the walling has mainly collapsed and the position of the entrance is not visible; the interior in uneven and heavily turfed, and there are no obvious structures.

Fig 3.11 Under the spine of the Sgurr, a dun sits in Loch nam Ban Mora. HES SC729720

Fig 3.12 The Poll Duchaill fort looks out from the cliffs of
Eigg to the mountains of Rum. HES SC686860

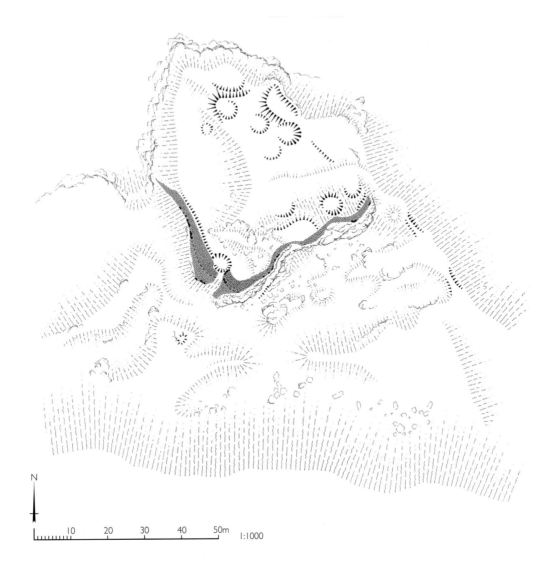

N

|___10___20___30___40___50m___| 1:1000

Fig 3.13 Plan of the Poll Duchaill fort, showing internal features that may date back to the fort's construction. HES GV006103

On the north-west coast of the island the fort at Poll Duchaill is set on a steep-sided, rocky promontory; it commands extensive views and can be seen by any vessel sailing from the north or west.[45] Defended by an outer stony wall, it defines an area which is roughly triangular, measuring internally 55m by 45m. There is some revetment visible, but the walling is much reduced and survives, turf-covered, as banking up to 3m thick. Steep-sided natural gullies afford protection on the south-west and north-west sides, but it appears to have been necessary to increase the depth of natural ditching on the south-east; this was quite a considerable achievement and has resulted in a ditch some 50m long, 4m broad and up to 1.5m in depth. The interior of the fort is grass-grown and contains three slight terraces – on two of which there appear to be house platforms or small enclosures. There are six, possibly eight, such platforms ranging in size from 3m to 7m in diameter, but their surface relief is not very pronounced. As far as can be seen, these platforms would appear to be an integral part of the original construction; if so, this would be the only fort in the Small Isles to exhibit contemporary internal features.

Fig 3.14 Galmisdale House on Eigg with the Sgurr in the background.
Erskine Beveridge took this early photograph in 1883. HES SC743160

Fig 3.15 The triangular-shaped fort at Rubha Na Crannaig below Kildonnan on the south-east coast. A later pier can be seen leading out from the adjacent beach. HES SC1500513

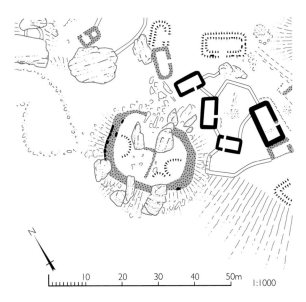

Fig 3.16 Seen from the air, the fort at Grulin is barely visible under later buildings. The survey plan, shown at approximately the same scale, is able to pick out greater detail. HES DP109440, GV006104

Three forts overlook the south and south-west approaches to Eigg, one at Grulin and two in the area of Galmisdale, one of these lying west of Grulin and the other overlooking the sound at Eilean Chathastail. At Grulin the fort occupies a rocky knoll at the edge of the old township.[46] It sits on the same level terrace as the township, but the two are separated by the remains of a poorly defined collapsed rubble wall. Within the Grulin fort, which measures about 20m in diameter, there appear to be at least three platforms and some later structures, built from the robbed wall of the fort, all possibly associated with the adjacent township. The fort west of Galmisdale House lies on a flat-topped rocky knoll and is at least in part defined by a stone wall some 2m thick.[47] The interior measures approximately 40m by 37m and contains two circular foundations, probably later huts or small houses, the walls of which appear to merge with the fort wall.

Perhaps the most strategically positioned fort is at Galmisdale Point[48] opposite Eilean Chathastail, overlooking the sheltered area of harbour immediately above the mid 20th century pier. The fort's proximity to modern development has reduced

it to little more than an outline with the road from the pier running through its centre – earlier uses have included a tearoom and a car park. Kidney-shaped in plan, it measures about 28m by 25m with its outer walling best preserved on the south and south-west, where stretches of inner and outer face can be seen, though nowhere standing more than one course high.

Eigg's eastern approaches are guarded at Rubha Na Crannaig[49] below the farm at Kildonnan and, further north, at Corragan Mor[50] against the steep cliffs at Struidh. The former occupies a slight rise on a rocky promontory to the south of the farmhouse and is probably more complex to interpret than others. Roughly triangular in plan, it measures about 36m from north to south by up to 24m within a low wall now largely reduced to a grass-grown stony bank up to 5m thick. The outer face can be traced intermittently around the circuit of the wall; the entrance is now represented by a simple gap on the western side. Within the interior are the confusing remains of several structures and stretches of stony bank, including subrectangular depressions that may mark the sites of buildings. Where a relationship with the fort can be shown, these features are clearly all later. There is nothing in the character of the structures within the fort to support the suggestion by the Ordnance Survey that they represent the remains of St Donnan's monastery. In the absence of further evidence, it is more prudent to assume that the monastery was centred on the area occupied by the medieval church to the north (see below). Also within the defences, on the east side, there are the remains of a concrete plinth which once supported a cast statue of St Donnan made by local artist Wesley Fyffe in the late 1970s.[51] On the shell beach beneath there is a small drystone pier, constructed in the late 19th century by the tenant of Kildonnan, who maintained a profitable business exporting potatoes to the Mainland during a period of potato blight.

The final fort, at Corragan Mor, lies on a craggy knoll on the hillside below Eigg's eastern cliffs. The monument is in the most remote part of the island and difficult to access by land, but would be readily visible from the sea, and commands extensive seaward views to the east. The fort has been created by the construction of a drystone wall to supplement

Fig 3.17 The distinctive outline of the fort at Corragan Mor looking north. HES SC771507

Fig 3.18 Survey plan of the Corragan Mor fort showing how walling was built to supplement the natural rock face. HES GV006105

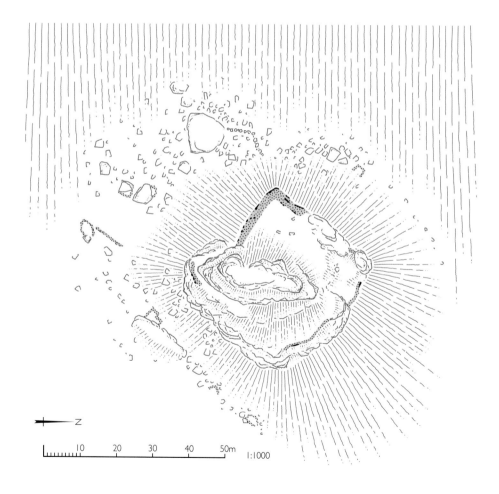

10   20   30   40   50m   1:1000

the natural rock scarps which defend much of the perimeter of the knoll, although the walling seems barely necessary on the steep eastern side. Where it survives best on the southern side, the walling is some 2.5m thick and faced with large stones externally. There are no signs of internal features.

At Sron na h-Iolaire, towards the north end of the Struidh area, there is a puzzling structure, built partly underground, which would appear to be prehistoric in character but the function of which is unknown.[52] Among a jumble of boulders beneath the cliffs a substantial platform has been constructed, on top of which there are the remains of a circular enclosure, possibly a roundhouse, of the later Iron Age, measuring about 6m in internal diameter. The wall is about 2m thick around most of the circuit, but at the entrance it thickens to 4m on either side of a narrow passage. Opening from the interior is the entrance to a large boulder cave that runs westward beneath the enclosure wall. The main chamber of this cave measures about 7m in length and there are other, smaller chambers opening off to either side and at the west end. The cave entrance and the sides of the chamber have been modified by the insertion

Fig 3.19 The dramatic position of the Corragan Mor fort on the eastern cliffs. Later enclosures lie below to the north. HES SC875724

of rough walling, and the thick deposit of midden material that covers the floor includes animal bones, shells and broken hammerstones, some of which have a concretion of crushed shell on their points.

Thus far, the site is unusual, but not unique: at Usinish on the east coast of South Uist there is another circular structure built around the entrance to a boulder cave. What makes the Eigg site stand out is its position within the landscape. The cliffs on this side of the island are characterised by horizontal banding of different lavas, but immediately above the site here these bands are broken by a dramatic eruption of vertical basalt columns, soaring to the top of the cliff, and easily visible from the sea. Standing in front of the structure the eye is immediately drawn upwards, and the view is framed by two enormous boulders, one to each side. Moreover, it is difficult to argue the

case for a defensive or domestic function for the site. It is hidden away in the scree, over 400m of difficult terrain separating it from the shore and, while there are shieling-huts and fragments of enclosure walls on grassy terraces close by, any access is hindered by the extent of boulder scree. The resources involved in constructing the platform and the structure suggest something of more importance than a mere farmhouse or herdsman's hut. Like the forts, it suggests co-ordinated, organised effort in its construction. The sense that this has been a 'special place', possibly in keeping with Iron Age religious practices, is inescapable.

Fig 3.20 The unusual site at Sron na h-Iolaire with the vertical basalt columns behind. HES SC729717

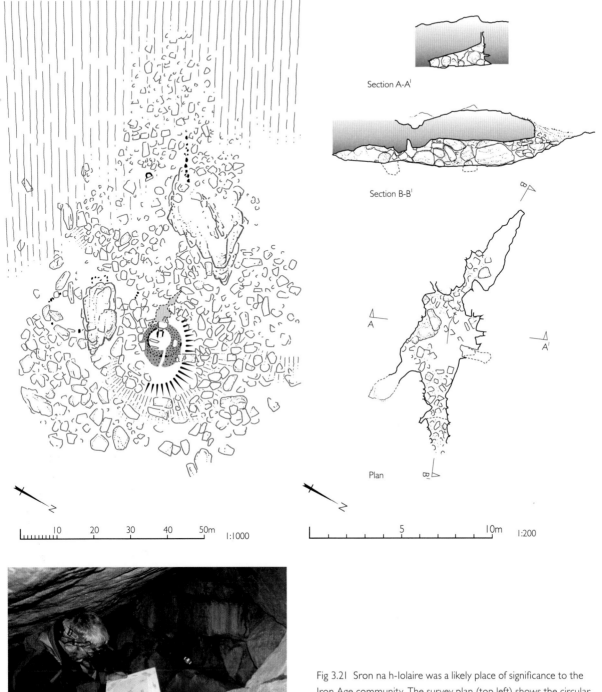

Section A-A¹

Section B-B¹

Plan

10   20   30   40   50m   1:1000

5   10m   1:200

Fig 3.21 Sron na h-Iolaire was a likely place of significance to the Iron Age community. The survey plan (top left) shows the circular enclosure among the rocks, and the plan and sections of the underlying cave (top right) illustrate its internal shape and height. The photograph taken during survey (bottom left) gives a realistic perspective as to the cave's nature and internal walling.
HES GV006106, SC1523859

Early Christian and Viking

The Early Church

The principal evidence for Early Christian activity on Eigg focuses on the monastery founded by the monk Donnan, and on his martyrdom there together with a community of monks around AD 617. There are no visible traces of this early monastery, but it is likely that it was in the same area as the ruined church at Kildonnan, which is probably of early 16th century date and the likely parish church referred to by Monro in 1549.[53] Tradition holds that Donnan's monastery lay nearby, and the place-name itself, Kildonnan ('Donnan's chapel'), is a reflection of this tradition. The vicinity has been used for burial from both prehistoric and Viking times. According to the Reverend Donald Maclean writing the *Statistical Account* at the end of the 18th century there was only one barrow or tumulus within the whole four islands and that was on Eigg 'near the old Popish chapel', and said to be the burial place of Donnan.[54] The location of this mound has not been identified.

The ruined church itself lies at the north-west of a defined ecclesiastical area, some 130m by 60m, stepping in a series of terraces down to Kildonnan Farm. This area is defined by a stone field-wall to the south-west, but on the north-east there is no boundary

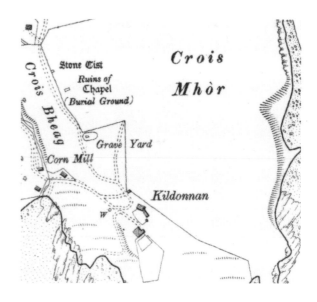

Fig 3.22 Christianity has had a presence of Eigg since the 7th century. The 1st edition OS 6-inch map extract of the Kildonnan area depicts church ruins, an elliptical 'Grave Yard' and stone cist.

Fig 3.23 The ecclesiastical area at Kildonnan contains the ruined church and enclosed burial ground. HES SC1500512

Fig 3.24 The botanist Michael Pakenham Edgeworth sketched on Eigg, including the ruined church. As is often the case on the island, the Sgurr provides an unmistakable backdrop.

Eigg Archive

other than a modern fence as the land levels out. At the south-east end there is a curiously formed subrectangular walled enclosure containing post-medieval burials. It is depicted as an elliptical 'Grave Yard' on the 1st edition OS map surveyed between 1875 and 1877 but its boundary wall has evidently been rebuilt in more recent times. Catholic burials are located immediately to the south of the ruined church, with non-Catholic burials immediately north of the 'Grave Yard', leaving an open area between the two. The most prominent feature here is a cross-shaft made of schist and decorated with plant scrolls and animals. It was re-erected, presumably out of its original position, on a modern base on the highest point of the upper terrace. This has been ascribed to the Iona school of sculpture, grouping it with the late 14th century Campbeltown Cross and other 14th and 15th century carvings on Islay, on Oronsay and at Inveraray.[55]

MacDonald tradition credits John of Moidart, Captain of Clanranald from c1529 until his death in 1584, with the building of the church, which consists now of a simple roofless rectangle, measuring about 15m by 5m. There is a single surviving doorway towards the west end of the south wall but the east gable end (shown in a ruinous state in one of the later 19th century sketches in the Edgeworth diaries) has been removed. Both the sketch and an early photograph show the church in an open landscape, quite different from today, the photograph showing it surrounded by sheaves of corn. The principal feature of the interior is an arched tomb-recess in the north wall, at the back of which there are two panels, the upper bearing the date 1641, the lower featuring a version of the Clanranald coat of arms. Also mounted in the interior is a curious small piece of crude sculpture showing the upper part of a human figure. The figure (Fig 3.26) either has very distinctive ears, or is resting its head on a pillow, according to interpretation. Although impossible to date precisely, the piece has an 'early' feel to it and Dressler suggests it may be a representation of the Celtic mother goddess.[56] Sadly, its findspot is unknown.

The floor of the church is significantly higher than the surrounding ground level and is covered with grave slabs. Five fragments of cross-shafts dating to between the 7th and 9th centuries have since been removed from the chapel. Previously on display at the Lodge, they can now be viewed in the Catholic church: a sixth fragment has been re-erected inside the church. Four of the fragments are very small, the largest measuring only some 0.55m by 0.33m. More detailed descriptions can be found in Fisher's magnificent volume *Early Medieval Sculpture in the West Highlands and Islands*.[57]

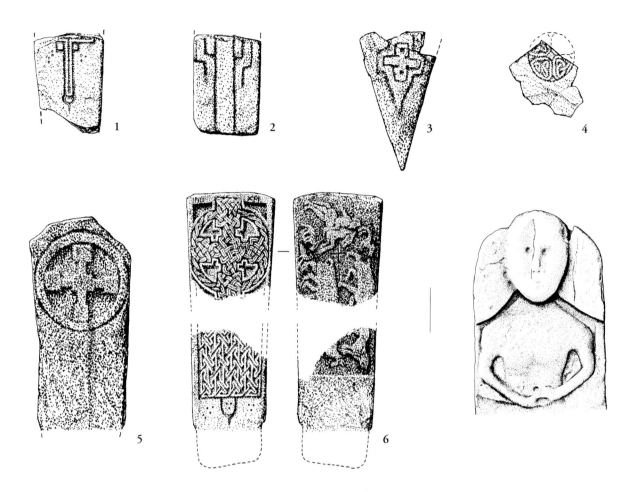

Fig 3.25 Drawings of the cross fragments discovered in the church (1:15 scale; from Fisher 2001). HES SC406074, SC406075, SC406077. SC406078, SC406079, SC406080

Fig 3.26 Susan Walker-White's sketch of the Kildonnan 'goddess' – very little is known about this intriguing early sculpture. (Approximate scale of 1:5) © Susan Walker-White.

His numbering system is adopted here for ease of cross-reference (Fig 3.25).

Two of the rock fragments are of mica-granulite, both being broken at the head and foot. One bears the lower part of an outline Latin cross with a grooved cross superimposed on it (1); the other has the grooved outline of a cross-shaft with stepped bands at the sides (2). Fisher suggests that one of the edges may have been trimmed or dressed for reuse on this example.[58] More ornate is a fragment of Torridonian sandstone which bears part of an equal-armed cross inside a circle produced by shallow pecking; the quadrants between the arms contain a simple knot decoration (4). The final small example is a curious triangular slab of

flagstone surviving in five separate pieces (3). It shows a rather crude outline of an equal-armed cross defined by pecking. The cross sits within a roughly pecked triangular outline which appears, in part, to respect the shape of the stone. It is not clear what this fragment represents. A further small cross-slab (Fig 3.28) was discovered in the enclosed graveyard to the south during clearance work in 2012. It was lying flat on the surface and the cross outline was noticed on the reverse side when it was turned over. It shows a simple incised cross and might be dated with the others.

The other two examples are more substantial; both are of Torridonian flagstone. One is set upright in concrete in the church, with a visible height of 0.86m

(5). The face shows an equal-armed cross within a broad circular margin. The cross has square terminals and a square centre, and its edges are neatly bevelled down. There appears to be no decoration on the opposite face. Pride of place, however, goes to the final piece (6) which consists of two fragments (upper and lower) of a cross-slab of reddish Torridonian flagstone, lacking the central portion, which has been made good with concrete. On one face there is a ringed cross-head filled with interlace, below which, on the other fragment, is a panel of diagonal key-patterning. Most interesting, however, across the head of the cross, are the Latin abbreviations: IHU XPI ('O Jesu. Of Christ' according to Fisher; or '(the cross) of Jesus Christ' according to Clancy).[59] This is the only example of an inscription among the carved stones in the Small Isles. The back of the slab is carved in low relief with a hunting-scene running down its vertical axis. The upper fragment depicts a bearded rider on a rearing horse following two dogs. One dog appears to be pursuing a bull and also possibly a wild boar, while the other looks at a bird. The lower fragment shows parts of two other animals. In the space between the horse and the two large animals on the upper fragment, there is an incised cross with expanded terminals. The cross resembles that at Bagh na h-Uamha, Rum, but it has presumably been added to the hunting-scene, which has strong Pictish connotations. Interestingly, the animal scene runs along, as opposed to across the slab, which has given rise to the possibility that

Fig 3.28 A small incised cross-slab recently discovered in the enclosed graveyard. Camille Dressler

the slab may have been used horizontally as one component of a stone shrine in which saintly relics may have been contained.[60]

At the time of Donnan's arrival, Eigg lay outwith the comparatively safe kingdom of Dalriada to the south and west, where the missions established by his contemporary, Columba, were mostly sited. What is not clear, however, is whether the island was situated in Pictish territory or in a no-man's land between the two. Whatever the case, it found itself within a very challenging political arena. Some of the confusion that surrounds Donnan's demise may be based on the perceived matriarchal nature of Pictish society, namely that he and his followers encroached upon land used by a Pictish queen who grazed her sheep there. She sent men with orders to kill them, the monks being allowed to finish celebrating mass before being beheaded. There are various credible Irish sources, including the *Annals of Innisfallen* and the *Book of Leinster*, that provide variations on this theme.[61] The most factual account,

Fig 3.27 The interior of the ruined church contains a number of early grave slabs. John Hunter

Fig 3.29 (above) Early undated photograph showing the isolated ruins of the church at Kildonnan. An earth-fast stone can be seen on the bottom right. Eigg Archive

Fig 3.30 (below) The ruined church and schist cross-shaft at Kildonnan, photographed in 1972. HES SC969817

however, which contains little scope for interpretation, belongs to the Irish *Martyrology of Donegal*:

> *Donnan of Eigg, abbot. Eigg is the name of an island in which he was after he left Ireland. And sea-robbers came one time to the island, while he was celebrating mass; he begged them not to kill him till he had concluded the mass; and they gave him this favour. And afterwards he was beheaded, and 52 of his monks along with him. And all their names are in a certain old book of the books of Ireland.*[62]

'Sea robbers' is a phrase usually applied to Vikings, but this is far too early for Viking assaults. There is no mention of a female leader and the precise number of 52 followers appears to be the general consensus of other sources suggesting the presence of a fairly substantial religious community. However, the few bare historical facts have since become embroidered: legend has it that the queen sent not men, but her warrior women to undertake the task, but after the beheadings, the women saw bright lights above the bodies and heard strange voices. They became enchanted, following the lights away from Kildonnan and up towards the Sgurr where they were led into Loch nam Ban Mora ('Loch of the Great Women') and drowned.

Fig 3.31 Below Left: The walled burial ground at the south end of the ecclesiastical area. The black line shows the position of the earlier enclosure and ditch. Below Right: Excavation against the angled junction of the burial ground and field wall showing the infilled ditch and post hole. HES SC1500512, John Hunter

Donnan's remains are said to have been buried separately from his followers in a revered place north of the present roofless chapel. The location was shown to Martin Martin during his visit in the late 17th century: he observed a 'sepulchural urn' about four feet deep and the same in diameter 'covered with a flat slab'. He described it as being 'full of human bones, but no head among them'.[63] He also observed a narrow stone passage underground nearby. Martin's description was largely dismissed by MacPherson who describes a stone basin rather than an urn, probably a font or piscina, 'full to the brim of ordinary earth' and containing ten or twelve fragments of human bone. He describes Martin's measurements as being 'quite inaccurate'.[64] The first *Statistical Account* of 1796 records that a sepulchral urn had been ploughed up in this general location and that bones but no skulls had been found.[65] The 1st edition OS 6-inch map records a 'stone cist' just north of the ruined church (Fig 3.22) but this is no longer evident on the ground. Nor is there any evidence of Martin's underground passageway. Interestingly, however, the early photograph of the ruined church (Fig 3.29) shows an earth-fast stone north of the building which may have been a marker stone for this cist. The stone is no longer there.

In 2012 archaeological excavations were undertaken around the ruined church and graveyard in order to clarify issues concerning the site of Donnan's foundation as well as the history of the site in general.[66] The results were astonishing in demonstrating that the site was of long-standing burial tradition starting in Neolithic times, thus by the time of Donnan's arrival at the end of the 6th

century the area had already been a 'special place'
for some four millennia. This is almost certainly the
reason why it was chosen for monastic activity. The
presence of stake holes, burnt daub (clay) and Late Iron
Age pottery south of the church indicate activity there
around the time of Donnan, and traces of a ditched
and fenced enclosure underlying the eliptical 'grave
yard' at the south of the site is indicative of the type of
monastic *vallum* (a wall or ditch defining a boundary)
characteristic of the brand of Celtic monasticism
to which Donnan belonged. Moreover, excavations
against the walls of the ruined church indicated earlier
stone structures below, attesting to a more complex set
of structures predating the 16th century building.

Donnan's martyrdom provided only a temporary
halt to religious activity. Irish sources, including
the *Annals of Ulster*, record that Eogan, '*princeps*'
of Eigg, died there around AD 725.[67] *Princeps* is a
significant term and might be viewed as reflecting
headship of an important and wealthy foundation,
indicative perhaps of royal patronage in the power
struggles between Picts and Dalriadans.[68] The death of
Cummine 'the religious of Eigg' is recorded for 752.[69]
The description 'the religious' is in the singular – he
was probably an eremitic rather than part of a wider
religious community, and his documented death
may indicate some level of monastic decline. Indeed,
there is a credible argument to suppose that monks
may have sought this more eremitic style of devotion,
living in crude cells, perhaps at Glen Charadail in the
north-west where a group of small remote beehive-
like structures differ from those usually interpreted as
being shielings (below). A tenable argument has been
put forward that they might represent the structures of
a small monastic community there.[70] Any demise of a
monastic presence in this way would be commensurate
with the growing threat of Scandinavian seafarers at
that time, leading to the sacking of Iona later that
century.

Further possible evidence of Eigg's religious
significance occurs with the name Tobar na Bean
Naoimh ('Well of the Saints')[71] below the remote
south side of the Sgurr, and with the cross place-
name Crois Moraig[72] at Upper Grulin further south
and depicted on the 1st edition 6-inch OS map.
Donnan is also said to have raised crosses in some
parts of the island: appropriate place-names survive
on the headland at Crois Mhor ('big cross') not far
from Kildonnan and at Druim na Croise ('ridge of

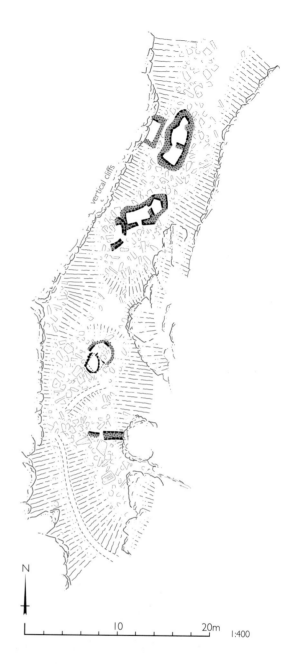

Fig 3.32 Plan of some 'beehive' huts at Glen Charadail, possibly once occupied by monks, alongside other ruined features. HES GV006107

Fig 3.33 Young girls collect water from St Columba's Well, around 1910. © National Museums Scotland. Licensor Scran

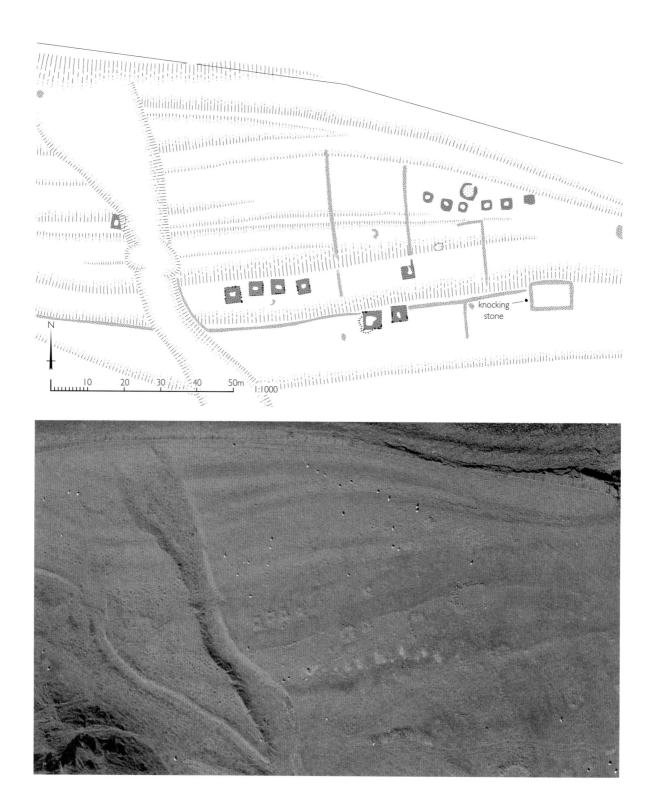

Fig 3.34 The square burials cairns at the Bay of Laig are almost certainly of Pictish origin. Their depressed centres indicate earlier robbing. HES GV006108, SC875769

knocking stone

N

10   20   30   40   50m
                           1:1000

the cross')[73] at the north end of Cleadale; there is also a further cross (site of) identified just north of the present school on the 1st edition map, a fragment of which stands beside the road.[74] A well dedicated to St Columba (Tobar Challuim Chille)[75] lies in the area of Cleadale (Fig 3.33), but its origins are also unknown. Unfortunately, Martin Martin's record of St Donnan's Well located somewhere in the south-west of the island and held 'in great esteem by the natives' is unreferenced elsewhere.[76] It is unclear in what form or for how long any monastic community survived on Eigg, nor is there any record of the later Viking incursions which affected both Skye and Iona in the late 8th and early 9th centuries, and which may have curtailed its existence.

Roughly contemporary with Donnan, but at the opposite end of the island, there are at least fifteen square cairns on the grass-grown storm beaches that rise in a series of terraces from the shore at the south end of the Bay of Laig amid some later field boundaries (Fig 3.34).[77] Many of the cairns have suffered extensive disturbance, and a hollow in the centre of almost every one suggests a thorough robbing of their contents. Apart from two outliers, the cairns are grouped into orderly arrangements in two main clusters, with the better preserved examples lying in the south-west cluster. Here there are at least seven cairns laid out in regular alignments on two terraces; the mounds are square or nearly square, measuring up to 5m by 5m and standing up to 0.4m high. Most of them have traces of a low kerb of edge-set stones; there are also some with distinctive upright cornerstones. The six cairns of the north-eastern group are less well preserved, while two isolated cairns lie to the east and to the west respectively, the latter cut by an old burn gully. The nature of the site – above the shoreline, near the best farmland on the island and with splendid open views towards the mountains of Rum – may have been significant in the choice of burial location.

In eastern Scotland there can be little doubt of the association of groups of square cairns such as these with the Picts. A number of excavations have produced a clutch of radiocarbon dates clustering around the middle of the 1st millennium AD, while at least two cairns have produced fragments of Pictish symbol stones. Their distribution is concentrated in eastern Scotland, between the Moray Firth and the River Tay. Although there are a few examples as far afield as Shetland and Galloway, they are rarely encountered on

the west coast, the only other example being a single square cairn excavated in 1998 at Kilphedir, South Uist. The presence of a cemetery on Eigg brings into focus questions about the extent of Pictish influence on the Inner Hebrides, and the Picts' relationship with the monastery at Kildonnan, which itself has produced a Pictish-style cross-slab (Fig 3.25 no. 6).

The Norse

By the 9th century Eigg had fallen under Norse control, and Norse place-names are as relatively common as they are elsewhere in the Small Isles. Less common, however, are the tangible remains of a Norse presence: there are no visible foundations of the longhouses typical of the period (although robbing for later buildings and dykes may be responsible for this), and there are no burial monuments which can be clearly placed in this time period. Those graves which have been identified appear to have reused existing burial mounds. They were found in the 19th century, but the accounts are confusing and several of the objects have been lost. There seem to have been at least three burial sites identified, all lying in the general area of Kildonnan. MacPherson records a fine Viking

Fig 3.35 A Viking sword hilt which probably came from a reused earlier burial mound at Kildonnan.
© National Museums Scotland. Licensor Scran

Fig 3.36 Oak boat stem posts from Lairg, each about 2m in length.

sword hilt of silvered bronze together with some other artefacts recovered around 1830 during the levelling of a 'hillock' (presumably a burial mound) in a field recorded as Dail Sithean ('the field of the fairy hillock') to the north-east of Kildonnan farm.[78] The information was not first hand, but provided by 'a blind old man of very retentive memory' which may cast some doubt on the credibility of the record. MacPherson also describes two cairns which he personally excavated south of Kildonnan and which produced grave goods.[79] Both cairns bear the scars of excavations conducted in 1875, which were clearly not backfilled at the time. The larger of the two cairns, approximately 12m in diameter, contained fragments of a sword, a silvered bronze penannular brooch used for fastening clothes, a whetstone, part of a leather belt with buckle and clasp, an iron axehead, fragments of woollen and linen cloth, an amber whorl, beads and fragments of bone. The cairn itself contained a cist and was almost certainly reused for this burial. Its primary form, its size and character, and especially the cist which is still partly visible, suggest it may have been of the chambered tomb type (see above, also Chapter 1, Fig 1.30). The other cairn, described as 'a tomb of much smaller size', produced another sword, a bronze brooch, a whetstone and amber and jet beads.

However, the most exciting finds of the Viking period on Eigg arguably derive not from a grave but from a 19th century chance find during moss draining in Laig.[80] Two waterlogged oak stems for the prow or stern post of a boat (Fig 3.36) were uncovered at the head of a former lake said to have been used by the Norse as a winter harbour. Each was about 2m in length and recognised by MacPherson as belonging 'not to a canoe but to a boat built of planks'[81] – a clinker-built vessel typical of Norse boats and with structural parallels in Scandinavia. One stem is bevelled, hollowed and stepped, with grooves to receive the ends of six pairs of overlapping planks. The other is bevelled and stepped with a flat face. The storage of partly worked stems under water is a practice that is well-attested in Scandinavia and would have served to keep the timber moist for ease of subsequent working. The discovery of the Eigg stems not only indicates the likelihood of some form of earlier water coursing to enable the boats to be launched but, more remarkably, also to the presence of boat-building on the island in Viking times.

Medieval and Post-Medieval Landscapes

Our understanding of the medieval period in the Small Isles is vague. We can only assume, in the absence of documentation and known landscape change, that the communities on Eigg, in common with those on the other islands, followed a lifestyle of mixed farming and lived in small settlements that grew into the townships recorded at the end of the 18th century. We assume too from the carved stones at Kildonnan and the discovery of likely medieval church foundations below the ruined chapel there, that there was an active worshipping community. But whatever dwellings existed probably lie beneath those of later centuries (below), and whatever systems of land use were employed have been subsumed under centuries of persistent agriculture. On Eigg we know that by the mid 16th century the island probably had a population of around 400, but we only know this because of a catastrophe of such magnitude that it receives mention in later sources.

The 16th Century Massacre

At a date likely to have been in the second half of the 16th century, the Eigg population of almost 400 was virtually annihilated in a gruesome event which occurred in a cave later to become known as the 'Massacre Cave' (Uamh Fhraing) at the south end of the island.[82] This occurred within the two centuries of disorder that followed the collapse of the Lordship of the Isles in the 1490s, and during a violent feud between the Clanranald MacDonalds, who owned Eigg, and the MacLeods of Harris. Tradition relates that a band of MacLeods, while sailing past Eigg, 'maltreated' a group of women who were working with cattle on Eilean Chathastail. They were pursued by a force of MacDonalds from Eigg and killed. In consequence, a large force of MacLeods was dispatched from Skye to seek revenge. This prompted almost the entire population of Eigg to retreat to a cave with a narrow entrance on the south side of the island. After three days of fruitless searching the MacLeods retired, but returned after spotting a scout, sent out from the cave. Following his footsteps (apparently in the snow) they reached the cave entrance, where they lit a huge fire, suffocating all those inside.

The cave is entered by a low narrow passage which requires crawling on hands and knees (the entrance was once concealed behind a waterfall) before broadening out into a cavern about 70m long. The traditional date for the massacre is 1577;[83] almost 400 islanders are said to have choked to death, men, women and children, and it seems that the bodies were not retrieved for many years. Even by the time of the *Statistical Account* some 200 years after the event, the bones were described as 'still fresh and some of the skulls entire, and teeth in their sockets'.[84] In the *New Statistical Account* of 1845, the Reverend Donald Maclean wrote of the eerie manner in which his torchlight reflected from the bones and skulls of the victims.[85] Miller's lengthy description, written after a visit in 1882, is probably the most memorable: he describes the cave as resembling a charnel house, how 'at almost every step we came upon heaps of human bones grouped together'.[86] By then the cave had become something of a tourist attraction with many visitors, including Sir Walter Scott, carrying off skulls as souvenirs. No doubt irritated and embarrassed by this increasing macabre interest, the parishoners and minister eventually removed the remains and buried them in the graveyard. Some of the remains clearly managed to escape their attentions and in 1979 a schoolboy on holiday discovered a small human skull which he took home to Birmingham before handing it over to the local coroner. The coroner verified that the skull was of some antiquity and belonged to a child of 5–6 years of age.[87] However, the extent of the massacre may have become partly confused with a less well recorded mention of an attack on the island which occurred slightly later. Campbell has suggested that reports of the cave episode may have been deliberately over-egged in order to cover up a wider raid on the Small Isles by the MacLeans for which Sir Lachlan MacLean was subsequently imprisoned.[88] It is debatable as to whether the entire island was depopulated as a result of the event, but a massacre certainly occurred in the cave in question.

Population and Change

From the later Middle Ages Eigg was held by the MacDonalds of Clanranald during which time the island was divided into eight townships, with leases held by tacksmen. As in most parts of the Highlands, evidence for early dwellings is hard to come by: successive generations of occupation have succeeded in concealing or reusing the stone from these original houses, and the ruins visible today are unlikely to be much earlier than c1700. Some are much later, although they all appear to have antecedents, and

Year	Population	Source
1764	459	McNeill (1764/5)
1768	501	Stat Acct (1796)
1796	399	Stat Acct (1796)
1801	500	Census
1811	442	Census
1821	469	Census
1831	452	Census
1841	546	Census
1881	291	Census
1891	233	Census

Fig 3.37 Recorded population figures for Eigg.

their overall evolution is a complex one. In the late 18th and 19th centuries the pattern of townships and the shieling system associated with them (below) was broken up when huge areas of land were leased to sheep farmers. Most farmers reared a few sheep for domestic needs but the first *Statistical Account* noted how one farm began to be flocked with black-faced sheep in the 1770s, and how they seemed 'to multiply and thrive well'.[89] Sheep provided greater profit than the rents from peasant farmers and displaced populations were put to task in kelp working which involved drawing in seaweed from the shore and burning it in kilns to provide the alkali for glass, bleaching agents, soaps and even gunpowder in a short vibrant period centred around 1790–1815. Many chose to emigrate instead.

The earliest detailed census was conducted by McNeill in 1764/5; it shows an island population of 459 and gives individual names and ages, and their religious affiliations.[90] Oddly, the male/female ratio is vastly different from the other three islands where the ratio is broadly balanced, but on Eigg McNeill recorded 183 males and 276 females (half as many again). It is difficult to explain this, other than perhaps by voluntary conscription to the military which was recruiting heavily at the time. The census also lists townships where the families resided, citing Galmisdale (*Gallmisdel*),[91] Grulin (*Gruline*),[92] Laig,[93] Cleadale (*Claidill*),[94] Tolain (*Toland*),[95] Five Pennies (*Five Penies*),[96] Sandavore (*Sandmor*),[97] Sandaveg (*Sand Beg*)[98] and Kildonnan (*Killdonan*).[99] Further evidence of island life is provided by a map of townships by

Fig 3.38 An early image by Victorian photographer Erskine Beveridge taken at Cleadale which shows the straight walling of the new crofting layout. HES SC743161

Fig 3.39 Cleadale croft is now open as a crofting museum. HES SC1499330

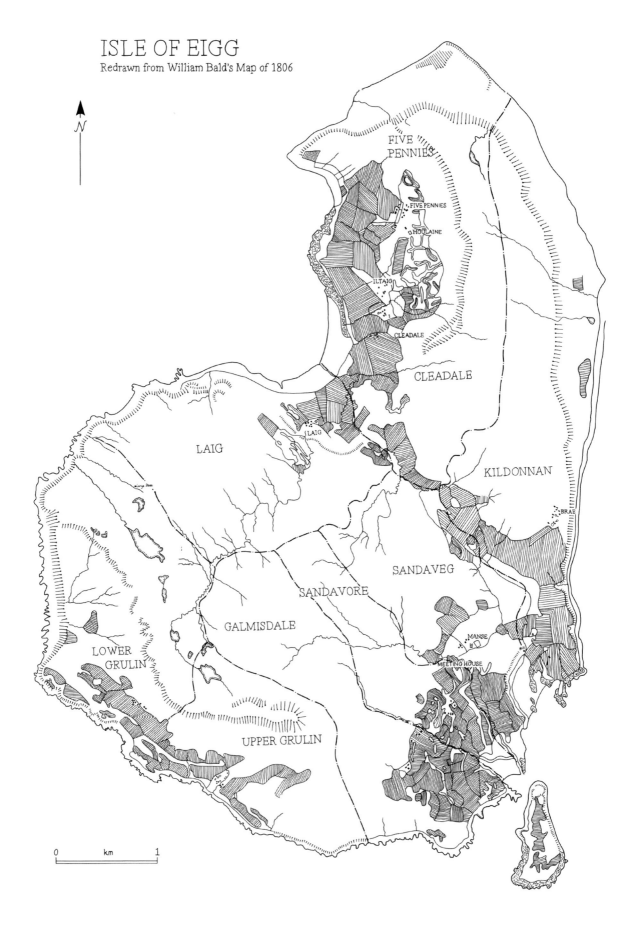

ISLE OF EIGG

Redrawn from William Bald's Map of 1806

N

FIVE
PENNIES

FIVE PENNIES

HOULAINE

ILTAIG

CLEADALE

CLEADALE

LAIG

LAIG

KILDONNAN

BRAE

SANDAVEG

SANDAVORE

GALMISDALE

MANSE

MEETING HOUSE

LOWER
GRULIN

UPPER GRULIN

0   km   1

William Bald in 1806. This was commissioned by the Clanranalds in order to aid the reorganisation of communal townships into individual crofts with the aim of creating part-time smallholdings to supplement seasonal income from kelping. Cleadale is probably the best example of how this occurred: it was divided into narrow strips in 1809 and is still a crofting township today with its straight boundary walls traceable from the cliffs to the sea overlying the earlier township enclosures (Fig 3.38). The Cleadale croft itself has survived unmodernised with much of its traditional homemade furniture and tools intact; it is now open as a crofting museum (Fig 3.39).

Bald's map (Fig 3.40) shows the division of township boundaries, indicating nine main units of land with parent farms: Five Pennies with Iltaig;[100] Cleadale; Kildonnan with Brae; [101] Sandaveg; Sandavore; Galmisdale; Laig; and Upper Grulin and Lower Grulin. The associated field systems are also shown and indicate the extent of cultivated land which even extended to Eilean Chathastail offshore.[102] Clusters of dwellings are depicted in all the townships, although within the Kildonnan land the main settlement appears to be at Brae. Kildonnan itself is shown as having only two buildings, one of which is likely to have been the farm, although it is not clear as to whether this is the present farmstead built in the early 19th century or its predecessor which stood to the north-east and which was incorporated into the current steading. This earlier version is likely to have been parent to the earlier township before removal of its stone buildings for sheep dykes. It sits adjacent to a rare surviving Lochaber-type bank barn and a horse gin which are both still visible (Fig 3.42).[103] A similar horse gin and bank survives at Laig. The map also depicts a mill at Kildonnan to the north-west of the later farmstead (Fig 3.41). This was rubble-built, the principal feature being the large suspended breast-shot wheel at the east gable, which had a rim drive.[104] James MacDonald, working for the Board of Agriculture in the early 19th century, noted the need for a windmill on the island, given that he considered there was insufficient strength in the streams to turn machinery.[105] However, a water mill was constructed shortly after his visit, probably in order to increase revenue by controlling the island's milling.[106] To power the wheel, water was diverted from the stream which ran past the manse to the west, from where a lade can be still be traced for about 600m across the hillside. Although converted into a holiday home in 1980, the building still retains its waterwheel and some of its internal machinery.

There are several maps which show the general township patterns, but none of them exhibit the detail, the boundaries, or nature of land use shown by Bald. The earliest is George Langlands' map of Argyllshire printed in 1801 around the time when Eigg's population was over 500. Less than a century later the population had fallen to under half this number. The orientation and spatial aspects of Langlands' map are rather confusing, but it appears to indicate seven settlements at that time, interpreted as being at Grulin, Galmisdale, Laig, Howlin,[107] Kildonnan, Cleadale and probably Sandaveg (Fig 3.44). Thomson's slightly more accurate map of 1824, which depicts a curving track or road running through the island, may confuse Sandaveg with Sandavore, but also includes the settlement at Brae on the east coast. Thomas Leslie's contemporary map (Fig 3.43) is not dissimilar, but divides Grulin into two townships (Lower and Upper) and introduces the name 'Five Pennies' at Howlin. At this time, and on the basis of the symbols used, the main townships would appear to have been at both the Grulins in the south-west, at Sandavore, at Kildonnan and at Brae at the east, and Cleadale, Five Pennies and Howlin to the north.

The collapse of the kelp market in the 1820s brought with it over-population and food shortage – every conceivable piece of cultivatable land was utilised for potatoes. Sheep had been brought in as a more profitable venture and emigration to the New World, initially voluntary, increased. Emigration had been underway for some time: MacDougall records the arrival across the Atlantic of John MacKinnon from Eigg in 1791, his son later becoming a bishop.[108] He also records the slightly later arrival of Hugh MacLean, 'a native of Eigg' who was married to a woman from Rum with four sons and four daughters. The family, he noted, was 'peculiarly gifted mentally', two of the sons becoming recognised poets.[109] According to the first *Statistical Account,* 176 people had already left Eigg between 1788 and 1790.[110] Others followed, notably those forcibly evicted from the two Grulin townships in the 1850s, and by the end of the 19th century five

Fig 3.40 Drawn copy of William Bald's 1806 map showing settlement concentrations and areas of cultivation. By kind permission of Susanna Wade Martins.

Fig 3.41 The mill at Kildonnan showing the breast-shot wheel at the east gable (top), the mill wheel (bottom left) and the surviving machinery (bottom right). HES SC1499334, SC1499332, SC1499343

Fig 3.42 The bank barn at Kildonnan with access to upper floor and platform for the horse gin. HES SC1499328

of the townships had become virtually deserted or abandoned altogether as depopulation took hold. The 1st edition of the OS 6-inch map shows both settlements there to be roofless by 1877. By then the settlement dynamic had shifted fundamentally, the population had dropped below 300, with the Five Pennies area in Cleadale and Galmisdale becoming the dominant settlements. Even with a reduced population the island remained reasonably vibrant, the 1881 census recording the presence of a mason, a seaman and even a cab-driver. As an example of self-sufficiency, in 1845 Hugh Miller purchased a pair of shoes created entirely from local materials –

> *from the skin out of which they had been cut, with the lime that had prepared it for the tan, and the root by which the tan had been furnished, down to the last on which they had been moulded, and the artisan that had cast them off, a pair of finished shoes.*[111]

Some of the best surviving remains of the former townships can be seen at Five Pennies which lies to the north of the later Howlin farmhouse. The name 'Five Pennies' presumably originates from the medieval assessment of Howlin, the earliest record of which is found in a charter of 1498, by which James IV granted '5 den. Terrarum de Houland' (five pennies on the land of Howlin) to Ranald Macallan, Captain of Clanranald. The Howlin farmhouse itself was built by Lachlan Mackinnon and his son Hector after they acquired the tack in 1770, and this is said to have been the first house with lime mortar and glass windows on the island. It was probably thatched until the late 19th century when the gables were raised and the roof slated. At some stage one of the front rooms was converted to a byre by opening up a window as a doorway, but this has now been re-incorporated into the house.

The concept of the 'pennyland' is of Norse origin and represents a portion of land the precise area of which (roughly 4 acres) was determined by the quality

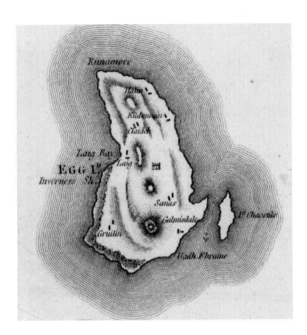

Fig 3.44 George Langlands' pre-Clearance map of Eigg, 1801.
© National Library of Scotland. Licensor Scran

notably at Brae, and contrasts with the rubble-cored walls which tend to characterise the later period buildings, such as those at Grulin. In one instance, close to the centre of the township, two buildings are joined along adjacent long sides, an arrangement commonly found amongst blackhouses in the Western Isles, where byres and other ancillary buildings would often be added to one side of the main house, rather than at its end.

Construction utilised local materials, and stone robbing was commonplace as one building replaced or became superimposed over the foundations of another. Turf was employed, as was any timber that might find its way to a predominantly treeless environment. Hugh Miller, an observant geologist visiting Eigg in the mid 19th century, also noted the presence of driftwood employed in the interior of the 'cottage' he visited:

> I observed, for the first time, in the interior of this cottage, what I had frequent occasion to remark afterwards, that much of the wood used in building in the smaller and outer islands of the Hebrides must have drifted across the Atlantic, borne eastwards and northwards by the great Gulf-stream. Many of the beams and boards, sorely drilled by the Teredo navalis [shipworm], are of American timber, that, from time to time, has been cast upon the shore, — a portion of it, apparently, from timber-laden vessels unfortunate in their voyage, but a portion of it, also, with root and branch still attached, bearing mark of having been swept to the sea by transatlantic rivers.[114]

Around Five Pennies there are well preserved fields of irregular plan, enclosed by substantial turf and stone dykes, within which fragments of rig cultivation can be traced. Their wide variation in size and their irregular form strongly suggest a gradual, piecemeal process of expansion and enclosure of arable land. Field systems such as these are common on the west coast of Scotland and the example here has probably survived because it lay outwith the Cleadale crofting settlement established immediately to the south in 1809, within which only fragments of any earlier system can be seen today. In fact none of the houses in Cleadale shown on Bald's map survived the change.

By the time of the 1st edition OS map the Five Pennies township had been reduced to two roofed buildings and one that was partly-roofed, six unroofed

of the soil. Its survival in place-name form gives some support to the strength of previous Scandinavian influence on the island; it was also a name used by Martin Martin who recorded the presence of a healing well at Five Pennies in 1695.[112] The visible remains at Five Pennies comprise the footings of about two dozen buildings, a corn-drying kiln and several small yards and enclosures at the edge of an extensive system of irregular fields. The buildings are all roughly rectangular, most of the walls having rounded external corners, constructed using a turf core faced inside and out with large stones and boulders, many of them set on edge. Bishop Nicolson who visited Eigg in 1700 observed that the houses were 'not constructed of wood like those of the Mainland', and that 'the two faces of the wall are of stone and the space between is filled in with earth in the manner of an embankment or rampart against the cold winds'.[113] This building style is found throughout the surviving remains of other pre-crofting townships on the island,

Fig 3.43 Thomas Leslie's detailed map of Eigg, 1824.
© National Library of Scotland. Licensor Scran

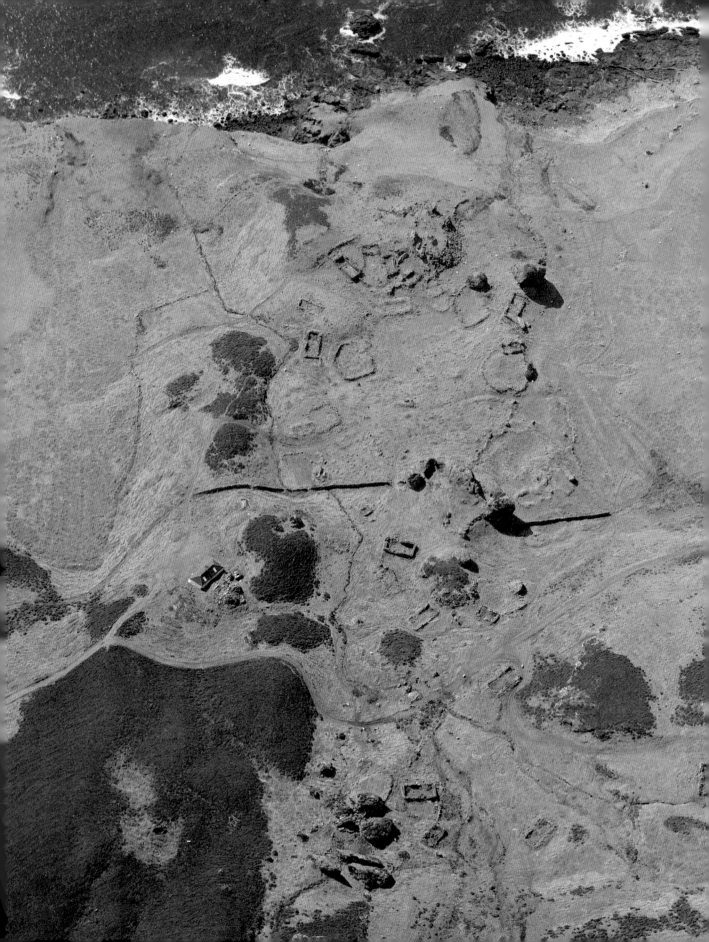

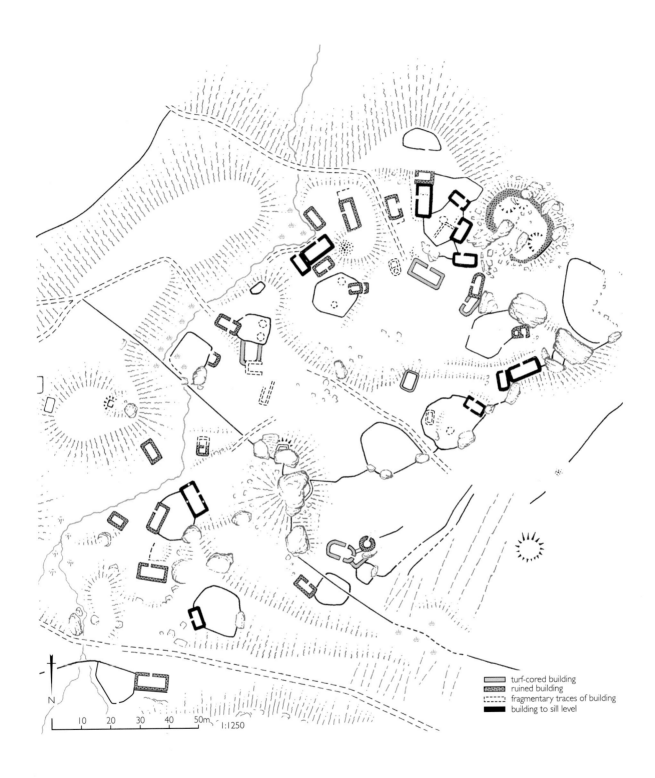

Fig 3.45 Aerial photo and plan of the Upper Grulin township which
was cleared for sheep in the 1850s. HES SC797070, GV006109

legend:
- turf-cored building
- ruined building
- fragmentary traces of building
- building to sill level

10 20 30 40 50m 1:1250

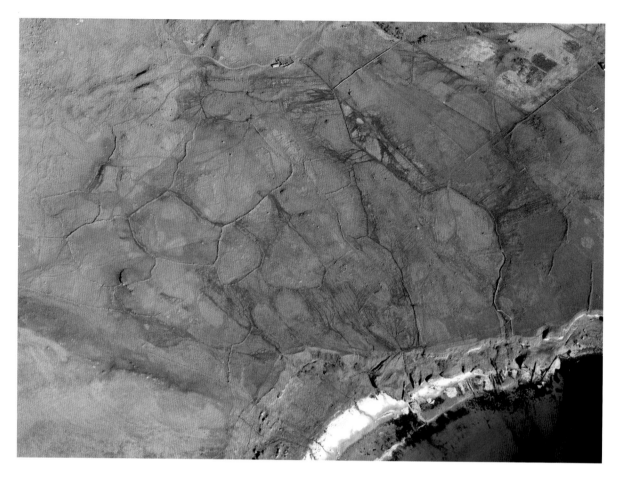

structures, two enclosures and a field system. We can
only surmise the nature of the other townships by
analogy, although the remains of Sandaveg can be
partly made out surviving as turf banks and robbed
hollows. At this time Upper Grulin is depicted as
having twenty structures, of which only one was fully
roofed, together with extensive enclosures, field systems
and lazy beds. Lower Grulin was slightly smaller, with
fourteen unroofed buildings together with field systems
and lazy beds. The structures in both are mainly
stone-built, as opposed to part-turf, and are probably
somewhat later than those at Five Pennies, most likely
of early 19th century date. The irregular field-systems
are especially well preserved at both Five Pennies and
Grulin. The township at Galmisdale appears to have
lasted a little longer: the first edition OS map depicts
fifteen roofed buildings at that time, although these
were demolished towards the end of the century to
make way for the new Lodge, and their inhabitants
relocated.

Fig 3.46 Enclosures of the Five Pennies township survived
the division into crofting units. HES DP109452

Fig 3.47 Turf-covered remains of dwellings at Five Pennies.
HES SC771504

Shieling

The women who were allegedly maltreated on Eilean Chathastail by the MacLeods were almost certainly working at the shielings there, a role often taken by women and girls. Until the breakup of the townships in the late 18th and early 19th centuries, transhumance was an important part of the farming year and involved herding and shepherding duties and the preparation of dairy produce. This took place on the hill pasture away from the townships and involved temporary accommodation during the few summer months of the year. There are probably well over 100 examples of shieling huts built for this purpose on Eigg, usually occurring in small groups or clusters. Most of them are simple rectangular turf bothies, now often reduced to little more than low grassy mounds, but some comprise two or more cells or chambers linked by narrow lintelled passages. The rear chamber is invariably constructed of stone within a turf embankment, and was probably intended to keep the interior cool for the storage of butter and cheese, the traditional products of the shieling. Their dates of origin on Eigg are unknown, but the tradition is one which reverts to Norse times, and many of the shielings show evidence of rebuilding within the same location. Some may well have been still active during Miller's visit in the mid 19th century – his exploration took him to the remote area of Struidh on the eastern cliffs where his description of a shieling hut is vivid (see Chapter 1 for details).[115] The building in question may have been one of two roofless structures shown on the 1st edition OS 6-inch map, and possibly part of an outlying farm rather than a shieling *per se*. His description, however, although no doubt romanticised, holds true for farming life at the time.

On Eilean Chathastail the grassy terraces of the central and southern parts bear extensive traces of lazy bed cultivation in numerous small patches. Within this area, and mainly clustered close to the centre of the island, there are at least twelve small shieling huts, two enclosures and two small pens. There are also numerous clearance cairns around and amongst the lazy beds. In the main, the huts appear to have been of turf and stone construction, their walls now reduced to grass-grown banks. Internal measurements are only possible for about half of them, the largest measuring 3.2m by 2.2m. This is likely to have been the setting where the women were abused by the MacLeods leading to the eventual massacre. Clusters of shielings like these can be found in several parts of Eigg's uplands, particularly in the north-east and north-west. There is a group of about twenty clustered in the Talm area to the north-east, below the cliffs, including a kiln which has a diameter of 2.2m set within a turf bank; this seems to have been carefully constructed, with its opening shielded by a short baffle wall, and a likely loading platform. It suggests a more sophisticated level of occupation than one of simple herding.[116]

Near Upper Grulin, and presumably associated with the township there, is a series of some thirteen huts and associated enclosures sited among the scree and the heather in the shelter of the Sgurr.[117] All lie within an area approximately 350m by 150m and are constructed of pitchstone rubble, some incorporating large blocks in their construction. Their floor plans seem to be contained within measurements of 1.9m to 6.3m in length and 1.4m to 3.2m in breadth, with walls generally surviving up to about 0.5m in height. Most are roughly rectangular on plan, but four huts are bi-cellular, with a smaller annex opening off the main compartment via a compact lintelled creep, thus giving the hut a figure-of-eight plan. One has a possible recess in the interior stone wall. The enclosures range from small pens formed among pitchstone blocks, to more formal structures measuring up to 8.3m square. At least some of them are associated with the huts, though others may be later, and at least one has a hut built over it. There is a cluster at Bidein An Tighearne, on the high ground south-east of Cleadale, where some ten shieling huts are set around a natural

Fig 3.48 Lower Grulin, smaller in size than Upper Grulin, has also left behind marked traces of habitation. HES SC875655

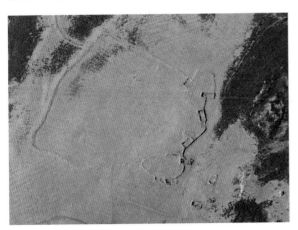

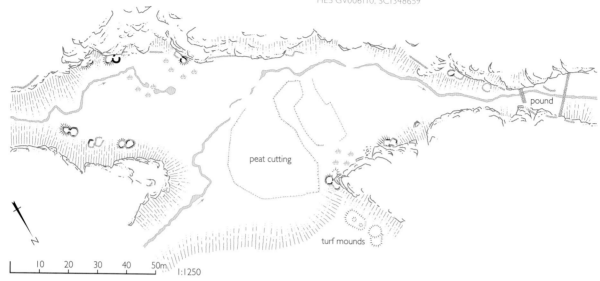

Fig 3.49 Plan and aerial photograph of shieling huts under Bidein An Tighearne showing a number of figure-of-eight structures.
HES GV006110, SC1348659

pound

peat cutting

turf mounds

10 20 30 40 50m
1:1250

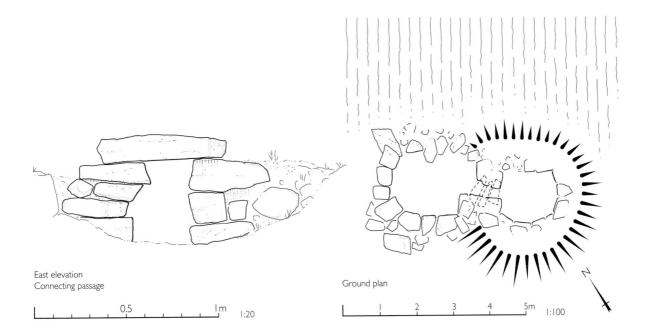

East elevation
Connecting passage

0.5   1m   1:20

Ground plan

1   2   3   4   5m   1:100

N

Fig 3.50 Detailed plan and section of a typical shieling hut at Bidein An Tighearn, inluding the passageway between the main hut and the annex. HES GV006111

contour with associated enclosures or pens, including a possible sheep wash in the stream (Fig 3.49).[118] Each of the remains has a figure-of-eight plan, and comprises an oval hut attached to a small annex or store, the two being linked by a low, lintelled crawl-way (Fig 3.50). In all but one case these lintels have been displaced, and the structures' walls, which presumably had upper portions made of turf, have collapsed into a tumbled mass of stone.

An interesting group lies at the head of Glen Charadail, but here there is some debate as to whether these are shielings or in fact a small group of six 'beehive' type huts, several of them double-compartmented, for a small eremitic community (above).[119] They sit clustered around a small basin of good grazing land along a scree-filled gully through which a stream drains. The largest examples are both 5m long internally by 2.5m wide and have an internal dividing wall. Although it has been suggested that the structures in the gully were places of refuge or even locations for ritual, it is more likely that they were cold stores for dairy produce, utilising the natural refrigeration properties of the water running under the boulders. In plan they are not unlike shielings, but the cold, damp location makes it seem highly unlikely that they were ever sleeping places either for monastic or transhumance purposes. There are other, more practical, small groups of huts at Struidh,[120] on Beinn Tighe,[121] and elsewhere in Glen Charadail, where they lie in clusters of two or three in both circular and rectangular shapes.[122]

The primary location of shieling huts may have depended as much on the availability of building materials as on the proximity of suitable grazing. Several clusters of huts which are located on or adjacent to prehistoric hut-circles were clearly sited to utilise existing building stone – at Cnoc Smeordail on the north-east coast,[123] at Struidh on the eastern cliffs, and on Beinn Tighe. The single hut at Howlin overlooking the Five Pennies township seems to have been built into the walling of a hut-circle, although it may not necessarily be a shieling.[124] Others would suggest, judging from the nearby grassy mounds, that the location was of long tradition and that the visible collapsed remains were the latest (and last) in a long line of shieling huts in that place. A good example is at Fhaing Ruadh along a shelf on the north-east cliffs where the number of collapsed huts and grassy mounds suggests use over a long period of time.[125]

Maritime Remains

The record of only one 'seaman' in the 1881 census is an interesting reminder of Eigg's maritime status – it was an island of subsistence farmers who also utilised the resources of the sea for domestic purposes, rather than an island of seafarers engaged in a predominantly maritime economy. One reason for this was the overt lack of appropriate harbourage for large-scale fishing, although commercial fishing began to take off in the 1860s following a relaxation in the herring laws. That said, given Eigg's heavy reliance on the export of kelp in the earlier part of that century, the existing harbour provision must have been reasonably adequate. By the end of the 18th century several tons of kelp per year were being exported.[126] In relation to this, the grass-grown remains of a few kelp kilns have been located on the coastal fringes, at Kildonnan in the south,[127] at Fhaing Ruadh to the north-east beyond the Struidh,[128] and at Clach Alasdair to the west of Laig.[129] Rectangular on plan and open at one end, all these kilns are approximately 3m in length and from 1m to 2m wide, with the sides and one end defined by edge-set stones. The largest kilns, however, lie on Eilean Chathastail which appears to have been a major focus of kelp activity and where two kilns have been located, the larger being about 5m in length.[130]

The *Statistical Account* notes 'a tolerable harbour for a few vessels' opposite Eilean Chathastail at Galmisdale where a pier had been built by the inhabitants, but only for small vessels 'for security of fishing boats' as the water was too shallow. The writer suggested that a 'properly planned' pier would facilitate herring busses.[131] The existing pier was unsatisfactory, built of roughly piled boulders, and was only accessible to vessels at high water.

The abundance of fish around Eigg had been noted as early as 1630, the possible date of an anonymous account (later included in MacFarlane's *Geographical Collections*) in which the reporter regretted to note that the inhabitants 'had no skill to slay the said fish'.[132] In the 1780s the British Fishery Society had plans to site a fishing village at Galmisdale, but the initiative was never realised. The Reverend John Buchanan, writing his advisory work, *A General View of the Fishery of Great Britain*, was sufficiently disgusted with the Society for considering the Outer Hebrides as a suitable proposition for locating government-sponsored fishing stations that he entitled (if clumsily) one of his chapters 'That the Inspectors

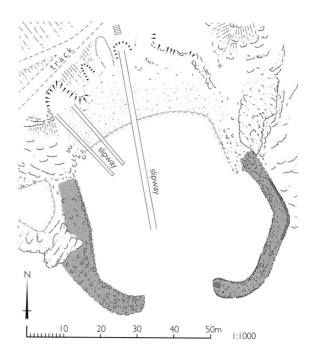

Fig 3.51 The arc of the original Clanranald pier on the right and the shorter curve of the 1877 addition on the left. There are possible boat nausts at the harbour's head. HES GV006112

of the proper Fishing Stations have been misled in their choice, is already too apparent to be doubted'.[133] In 1790, and as if in answer to the writer of the *Statistical Account*'s wishes, a well-built stone pier, known as the Clanranald pier, was constructed at the head of the bay.[134] It measures about 45m in length by 4.4m in breadth and stands up to 3m in height at the south end where a flight of steps leads down towards the water. But even this was still not seen to be satisfactory and by the time of the *New Statistical Account* of 1845 a safe harbour for large shipping was still seen to be a requirement.[135] In 1877 it was supplemented by the construction of a further pier, this time of rubble, on its western side. According to the Napier Commission report of 1883 it was still deficient. The two piers, each partly founded on a low reef, curve towards each other to create an enclosed harbour measuring roughly 50m by 50m with its mouth about 17m wide facing south. Both are shown initially on the 1st edition OS map. The harbour continues to dry out at low tide

Fig 3.52 The harbour with the Clanranald pier and fish traps on the left and the line of the modern jetty across the centre. The original pier built by islanders lies at the bottom. HES SC883568

Fig 3.53 Boats mooring in the calmer waters between Eilean Chathastail and Galmisdale c1880 near the original pier. HES DP233886

Fig 3.54 Fish traps, once an essential local fishing tool, are visible in the bay at low tide. HES SC771510

and is still only suitable for small vessels. There are two slipways within the harbour and possible boat nausts. One slipway, at least 50m long, carries a pair of iron rails; the other is more modern and made of concrete. Figure 3.52 shows the harbour during the construction of the modern ferry jetty;[136] the Clanranald pier can be seen to the north, as can the surviving submerged walling of fish traps on the west side of the bay which appear to have eluded documentary record.[137] Natural pools which are left isolated at low tide, such as that at Poll nam Partan, Kildonnan, may also have been baited, with the stranded fish collected when the tide receded.[138] Further to the east there is another pier (Fig 3.15) below Kildonnan farm.[139] Rather than being the result of maritime development, this was the result of an entrepreneurial Kildonnan farmer who, taking advantage of the absence of potato blight on Eigg in the late 19th century, built a pier below the house specifically to export island potatoes to those places where the blight had taken hold.

Later Buildings

The Catholic community on Eigg was quite considerable, numbering around 450 in the latter part of the 18th century according to Blundell.[140] Mass is said to have taken place in a cave (the Cave of Devotion) on the south side of the island,[141] then later at the house at Kildonnan until around 1810 when Cleadale House was made available. The Kildonnan arrangements had also been unsatisfactory: the house was too small to hold the worshippers, and the earth floor was so hard that members of the congregation had to bring peats to

kneel on.[142] Cleadale House served as both presbytery and church but, like the manse (below), left something to be desired in terms of durability and maintenance owing to the weather. Poor weather has always been a feature of life in the Small Isles, one incumbent of the presbytery complaining of storms that prevented him from travelling across to Arisaig to collect his Catholic newspaper (*The Tablet*) for a full 12 weeks.[143] The building of a new Catholic church dedicated to St Donnan was begun in 1910 on a new site a little way to the west of Cleadale, and completed by the outbreak of the Great War.[144] The old house was then demolished and a new presbytery (also now demolished) was built adjacent to the new church.[145] This was built of harled rubble, most probably using stones robbed from its predecessor. No architect has been identified yet for either of the buildings.

The reformation began in Scotland in 1560 and in the 1720s the Church of Scotland parish of the Small Isles was detached from Strathswordale on Skye, to which the medieval parishes of Eigg and Canna had hitherto been joined. The minister resided on Rum before moving to Brae, to the north of Kildonnan, in the 1750s, moving again 30 years later when the farm of Sandaveg was granted to the church, forming what was reputed to be the most extensive glebe in Scotland. A fine, prominent manse, with walled garden, was completed in 1790.[146] It must have been a striking landmark at the time, a symbol of the authority of the established religion over a predominantly Catholic island. But it was not until 1862 that a purpose-built Protestant church was constructed on the island, replacing the schoolhouse

Fig 3.55–6 The Presbytery, since demolished, stood adjacent to the early 20th century Catholic church (exterior above, Catholic church interior right). HES SC1504645, SC1499327

Fig 3.57 The new Established church (Church of Scotland) was not built until 1862, well after the Manse had been constructed. HES SC729676

Fig 3.58 The exposed position of the Manse, built around 1790, has made continued occupation of the building uncomfortable. HES SC1499321

which had formerly been used as the place of worship. The new church[147] was of simple rectangular design, built of local freestone under a slate roof, buttressed at the corners and lit with unadorned lancet windows (Fig 3.57). The interior is still lined with pine and adorned with quotations from the scriptures in Gaelic and English. The Manse was enlarged in 1889 when the flanking wings and dormers were added, but it lay in a location very exposed to gales and became both uncomfortable to live in and expensive to maintain,[148] eventually becoming uninhabitable (Fig 3.58). A programme of restoration was begun in the late 1980s during which the ground floors were removed, but the exercise proved to be abortive, although some work on the house has now been resumed. The associated Glebe Barn standing nearby, constructed in 1830, had a happier fate, being renovated and converted to a field study centre and hostel in 1999.[149]

The final building to receive mention is the main house on the island, the Lodge.[150] It sits facing the south-east coast of the island, enveloped in exotic wooded gardens, and standing as a slightly incongruous architectural feature in an island otherwise peppered with small stone buildings in open landscapes. It has a short but interesting history and is the latest in the sequence of laird's residences there

since the earlier part of the 19th century. The primary structure was originally an adaptation of a pair of cottages by the island's owner, Hugh MacPherson, lying to the south of the present Lodge. A two-storey rear extension was added followed by two side wings in 1880. The site later became tennis courts and is still a level area surrounded by a high hedge. Its Gaelic name Nead-na-feannaige ('The Crow's Nest') is recorded. Having inherited the island, his son Norman spent little time there, but Norman's sister Isabella made it her home and from 1854 was responsible for planting a large area of trees in the vicinity, partly to promote pheasant breeding. Norman created, albeit in a minor way, a small sporting estate in the gentlemanly genre of the time and set in train the footprint for the lavish gardens which survive today. An early photograph (Fig 3.59) epitomises the island's late 19th century gentrification, showing visitors fishing on the loch. Robert Thomson, who purchased the island in 1896, expanded MacPherson's lodge (Fig 3.60), retaining its Gaelic name. Thomson's son decided to sell Eigg in 1916 to the wealthy tenant who had leased the island

Fig 3.59 Photograph from c1880 album of visitors fishing on Loch Beinn Taighe – labelled 'Loch where we caught a fish'.
HES DP097507

Fig 3.60 The first Lodge during the ownership of Robert Thomson, who purchased the island in 1896. HES DP233887

Fig 3.61 The second Lodge (or White Lodge), complete with tower, was built by Sir William Petersen but burnt down in 1925. Eigg Archive

since his father's death in 1913 – the shipping magnate Sir William Petersen. Thomson himself is buried in a prominent iron-fenced tomb on the highest point of Eilean Chathastail.[151]

Sir William employed James B Dunn of Edinburgh to design a spacious new lodge on a more prominent site to the north of the previous house, although still within the Victorian plantation. The drawings, dated December 1920, survive in the archive of Newcastle architects Mauchlen and Weightman. The new house, known as the White Lodge, was timber-framed, with a prominent tower, and was by far the biggest residence ever constructed on Eigg. Terraced gardens were laid out below the house overlooking Galmisdale Bay, and these can still be seen in the woodland. A factor's house was also built (now known as Gardener's Cottage).[152] The Lodge, however, did not last long.

In 1925 the tower began to buckle and bend and in the same year it was destroyed in a catastrophic fire. Insurance was claimed and Sir William died a few months later.

The island was subsequently sold to the Rt Hon Walter Runciman MP in 1925. He was another shipping magnate and an acquaintance of Sir William's who had received lavish hospitality at the White Lodge. The Runcimans, who came from the north-east of England, also employed Mauchlen and Weightman to design their new Lodge – the third generation of a principal residence on the island. The architects had worked extensively for the Runcimans on their English properties, adopting a late arts and crafts style in the Lutyens tradition. Their adoption of a more striking modern style combining flat roofs and white walls for this new building is said to be due to the influence of Walter's son Steven (Figs 3.62, 3.63). The design appears to have been finalised by February 1926, 11 years before that of its closest Scottish parallel, Gribloch, Kippen, Stirlingshire, by Basil Spence. The location chosen was the levelled site of the previous

Fig 3.62 The third Lodge – a new design by Mauchlen and Weightman, originally with a flat roof – was built in the later 1920s under the ownership of the Runciman family. HES SC857939

Fig 3.63 The annotated architectural plan of the Lodge from the 1920s, with the original flat roof which which transpired to be insufficiently watertight. HES SC731165

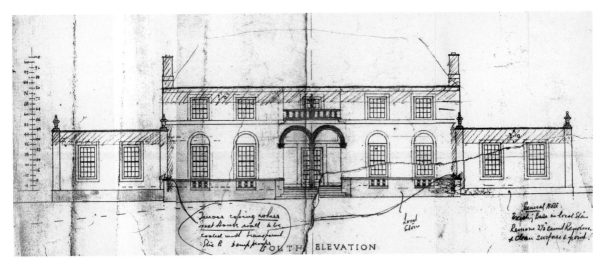

SOUTH ELEVATION

Lodge, making use of the existing platform and mature landscape, allowing the creation of spectacular gardens (Fig 3.64). Sir Steven Runciman recalled that he had been greatly influenced by Osgood MacKenzie's gardens at Inverewe. Within the grounds, on the east side of the drive and a little way south of the Lodge, there is a prehistoric burial cairn, modified as a garden feature. The Runcimans also had built the prefabricated Ceilidh Hall which still stands nearby for dances and social gatherings.[153]

A substantial house to the south of the Lodge known as the Crow's Nest (not to be confused with the original Lodge) was built in 1929 for the use of the island doctor; the large porch provided a waiting room, and the narrow central room was fitted out as a dispensary.[154] It became the factor's house in the 1950s when the doctor moved, first to the Gardener's Cottage, then in 1958 to a new surgery in the centre of the island.

The original design for the Lodge proposed a very modern open-plan living room and dining room, but was later altered to provide the more traditional separation between these rooms. The house was built of cavity walled brick and the roof was covered in bitumastic felt. The central loggia led both to the front door and the gunroom, with a central north–south corridor providing access to most of the rooms. The six principal bedrooms, including the master suite with its dressing room and bathroom, lay to the north and extended into the west wing. To the south, beyond the gunroom, was the study and then the large living room, which opened into the dining room. These latter rooms enjoy a southerly aspect and direct access to the rose garden. To the west of the corridor lay the service accommodation with the four servants' bedrooms on the first floor.

The flat roof presented problems from the start, with major applications of bitumastic felt in 1929 and 1932. One of the principal problems seems to have been waterproofing the junction between the chimneystacks and the flat roof of the central block. In 1935 Mauchlen and Weightman were called back to design a new pitched roof over the central raised block. The new hipped roof was covered in Norwegian blue/green slates giving the building a completely different aspect, drawing parallels with other 1930s villas such as Leslie Graham MacDougall's Sron Garbh in West Linton, Peeblesshire. The lodge has been little altered since and the drawings for all the original fixtures and fittings, including wardrobes, dressers, gunroom cabinets etc., survive in the Mauchlen and Weightman archive. In 1998, architects Simpson and Brown were commissioned to carry out a conditions report and options appraisal; their drawings and observations are housed in the Commission's collections.[155]

Fig 3.64 The Lodge and exotic gardens in the 1990s. HES SC729682

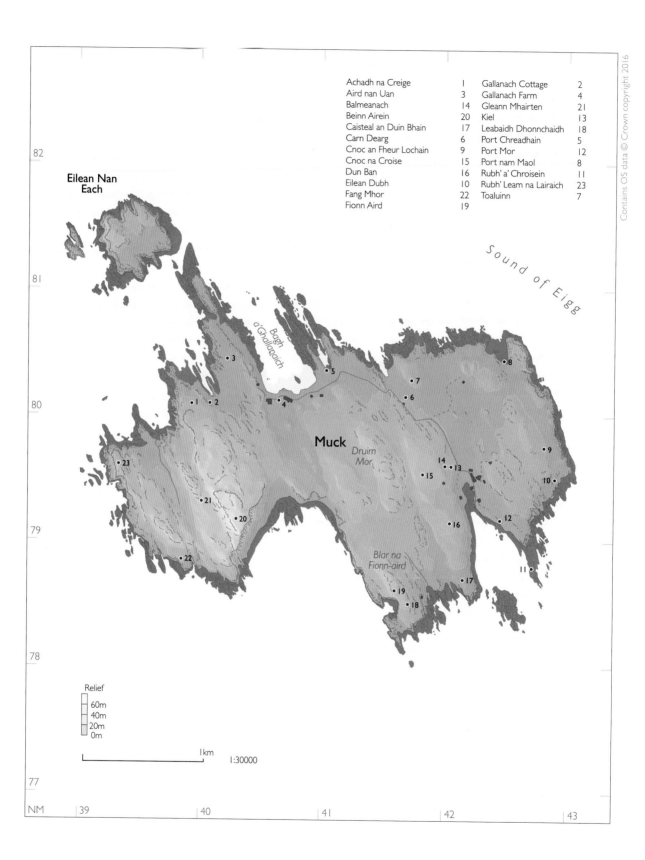

Eilean Nan Each

Sound of Eigg

Achadh na Creige	1	Gallanach Cottage	2
Aird nan Uan	3	Gallanach Farm	4
Balmeanach	14	Gleann Mhairten	21
Beinn Airein	20	Kiel	13
Caisteal an Duin Bhain	17	Leabaidh Dhonnchaidh	18
Carn Dearg	6	Port Chreadhain	5
Cnoc an Fheur Lochain	9	Port Mor	12
Cnoc na Croise	15	Port nam Maol	8
Dun Ban	16	Rubh' a' Chroisein	11
Eilean Dubh	10	Rubh' Leam na Lairaich	23
Fang Mhor	22	Toaluinn	7
Fionn Aird	19		

Contains OS data © Crown copyright 2016

Muck

Druim Mor

Blar na Fionn-aird

Bagh a'Ghallanaich

Relief
60m
40m
20m
0m

1km
1:30000

NM

Chapter Four
Muck

In many respects Muck is seen as the poor relation within the Small Isles, being the smallest in surface area with a land mass of around 560ha, and the lowest-lying with its tallest summit, Beinn Airein, peaking at around just 137m. Visually less exciting than Rum and perceived as being less interesting than the larger islands of Canna and Eigg, it was the least commented upon by 18th and 19th century travellers and visitors. Ironically, with its surprisingly varied and interesting landscape in its small compass, Muck is probably the most complex of the four islands to unravel in terms of settlement evolution over the centuries.

The name 'Muck' has an ambiguous origin, possibly from the Gaelic Eiltran nan Muchd (literally 'Island of Swine' as the *Statistical Account* asserts)[1] or, alternatively from the Gaelic *muc* [*mhara*] meaning 'sea pig' or whale, with a strong maritime connotation. The latter may be more appropriate, given the sightings of whales around local waters. It might also help explain an alternative version, the Gaelic Tirr Chrainne ('the Sow's Island'), which was used only from out at sea for superstitious reasons. Muck's late 18th century laird was embarrassed by the name, as Dr Johnson discovered while dining with his nephew on Skye. The nephew pointed out that it was customary to call gentlemen in Scotland by the name of their possessions. His uncle, it seems, was therefore known simply as 'Muck' which, understandably, he found socially embarrassing.[2] To rectify this he attempted to rename the island 'Monk' on the basis

of recorded earlier church ownership and a historical connection with the monks from Iona (noted in the *New Statistical Account*).[3] He had a modicum of success in that Muck appears as 'Monk Island' on Langlands' map (Fig 1.23) of 1801. Eventually he had to compromise by having himself addressed as 'Isle of Muck'. The problem was little different to that later encountered by his island neighbour Sir George Bullough who was embarrassed to find himself referred to as 'Rum'.

Muck's former ecclesiastical ownership and its Ionan connection were also known to Monro writing in the mid 16th century. He provides the earliest documented record of the island, referring to it as pertaining to the Bishop of the Isles. He describes it as the 'Swynes ile', but noting its value in crops and grass,[4] an observation fully backed up elsewhere, and in both later *Statistical Accounts*. This value can be explained by the basalt lava flows emanating from Rum which occur as small terraces, many with gentle slopes that combine with blown sand to produce a fertile soil well suited to agriculture. Such was the quality of the soil and grazing that in the late 18th century surpluses of corn were provided to neighbouring Rum,[5] and the cattle were seen as growing to 'a considerable size'.[6] But what was gained on the swings of fertility was lost on the roundabouts of natural fuel of which Muck possessed little. James MacDonald, writing for the Board of Agriculture in the early 19th century, wrote that the islanders burned cow and horse dung, sea tangle and dried weeds.[7] They were obliged to import peats from other islands when the weather permitted,[8] but in times of desperation had sometimes been forced to burn

Fig 4.1 Muck and Eilean Nan Each (Horse Island), showing locations mentioned in this chapter. HES GV006113

Fig 4.2 Muck from the west with Eilean nan Each (Horse Island) lying to the left – described in 1549 as 'guid for horse and uther store'. HES DP109154

furniture instead.[9] 'Muck', as one modern writer neatly phrased it, 'declines to flaunt her basaltic geology, boasts no volcanic peaks or slanting cliffs. Instead, green, peatless pastures slope gently down to the shore'.[10] Even the *New Statistical Account*, detailing the geologies of the four islands, found Muck insufficiently interesting and ignored it altogether,[11] although now the Jurassic and tertiary exposure on Camas Mor has been designated as a Site of Special Scientific Interest (SSSI).

Those 'green, peatless pastures' were the factors that almost certainly made the island so attractive for settlement, and we can distinguish three major changes in land use within the last few centuries which have had an impact on the landscape. All three have implications for the survival of sites and monuments, and how we might interpret them. The first (earliest) impact is clear from the vast areas of lazy beds, particularly in the central and eastern parts of the island, where extensive cultivation had spread in the later 18th and earlier 19th centuries. This spread of cultivation represents the most expansive

use of the land and marginal areas, presumably reflecting the peak in the island's population at that time, focused around three main townships and covering all but the far western moorland. Some of these lazy beds are contained within field banks of turf and stone, and others make use of natural topographical features with the terrace edges and outcrops doubling up as ready-made field boundaries. In these places any earlier traces of settlement or land use are likely to have been eroded by successive years of ploughing and planting. The best survivors of earlier monuments lie on the patches of moorland landscape which predominate on the higher contours, chiefly at the far west end of the island, or on marginal land at the coastal edges.

The second major impact occurred with the drawing up and part-implementation of a scheme

Fig 4.3 The western moorland of Muck with the 'green, peatless pastures' in the foreground that have been advantageous to agriculture on the island. HES DP109115

devised in 1809 to carve the landscape into a series of individual units, ostensibly in order to provide crofts to allow a greater degree of security to those working the kelp. A map (Fig 4.4) known as the Chapman map (after its cartographer), shows the island divided into 47 lots and served by a network of roads. The plan appears schematic and was prepared in advance of the subdivision in the same way as William Bald's map of Eigg around the same time. Only part of

the plan was implemented, but its impact on the earlier lazy-bed landscape and the survival of relict township features was significant. Several of the field boundaries and house sites are still evident. By the late 19th century the third and latest impact was being introduced and had an even greater effect on the erosion of lazy beds and their field boundaries. It involved a more formal arrangement of rectilinear enclosed fields as part of a model farm established for the existing site at Gallanach on the north coast of Muck. The improved field system was superimposed on the most fertile areas of the central and eastern parts of the island, effectively obliterating any earlier remains in those places.

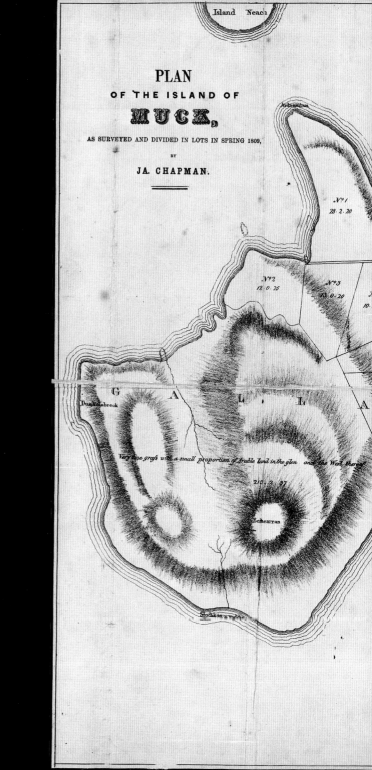

Island Neach

Ardnamhan

Nº 1
28 · 2 · 20

Nº 2
12 · 0 · 25

Nº 3
15 · 0 · 20

Nº
10 ·

G   A   L   L   A

Dunfidobreck

Very fine grass with a small proportion of Arable land in the glen and the West thereof

210 · 2 · 37

Behearran

Stockain a middle

Fig 4.4 The 1809 Chapman estate map of Muck showing
former township boundaries and a provisional division into
crofts. HES SC1386602

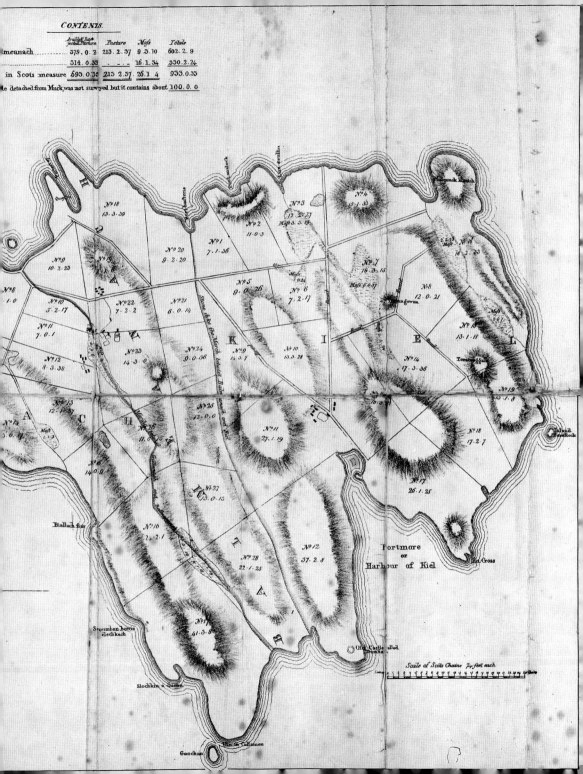

CONTENTS.

	Arable Improved Pasture	Pasture	Moss	Totals
...meanach	379. 0. 2	213. 2. 37	9. 3. 10	602. 2. 9
	314. 0.35	- - -	16. 1. 34	330. 2. 24
in Scots measure	693. 0.35	213. 2. 37	26. 1. 4	933. 0. 33

...le detached from Muck was not surveyed but it contains about 100. 0. 0

Portmore
or
Harbour of Kiel

Scale of Scots Chains 74 feet each.

Early Prehistory

Being a grassy, fertile and relatively low-lying island, the survival of any prehistoric or medieval remains has been severely curtailed by these three successive changes to the landscape. A number of chance finds have been recovered which hint at the presence of earlier peoples, notably flint waste (debitage) from the production of tools[12] at Port Mor from a small patch of disturbed ground, and further debitage from Gallanach lying on the surface of a pathway.[13] In addition the National Museums Scotland holds the upper half of a sword, identified as dating to the Bronze Age, probably between 950 and 750 BC, which was recovered from an inland boggy hollow at Carn Dearg in the east of the island during drainage work in 1920.[14] It shows some evidence of lengthy use in that the hilt was cast on later as a repair. Unlike the other three islands where scrapings from rabbit burrows often turn up sherds of pottery or other artefacts, Muck possesses no rabbits, and chance finds are commensurately limited. There are a small number of possible prehistoric features visible on the landscape; these tend to lie beyond post-medieval agricultural activity and include two likely hut-circles and at least six putative low burial cairns. All are truncated, eroded or robbed. There are also a few natural rock shelters, such as that on Eilean nan Each (Horse Island)[15] off the north-west coast which, in keeping with the hut-circles and cairns, are all difficult to verify or date without archaeological intervention.

Structures

Of the two hut-circles recorded, one survives on Beinn Airen as a circular grass-grown stony bank some 5m in diameter with several inner and outer facing-stones protruding.[16] Facing-stones are also partially

Fig 4.5 The upper half of a Bronze Age sword discovered in a bog at Carn Dearg in 1920. © National Museums Scotland. Licensor Scran

Fig 4.6 The complex earthworks on the summit of Beinn Airein illustrate the difficulties in identifying specific landscape features. HES GV00615

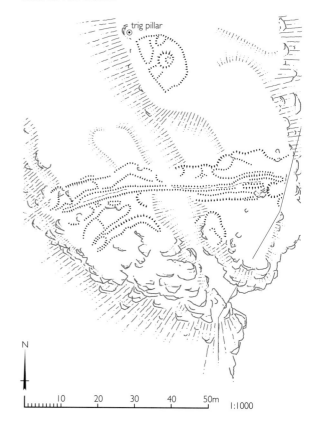

trig pillar

N

10   20   30   40   50m   1:1000

evident in the hut-circle at Gleann Mhairten which is slightly larger.[17] Both have been extensively robbed and adapted for later reuse. In the case of the latter, a field bank has been constructed directly across the original circle from north to south. Canna and Eigg are both much better endowed with some 40 examples of hut-circles between them, and the dimensions of those on Muck are also rather small by comparison. The paucity of hut-circles on Muck is more likely to be a reflection of land use and monument survival than of the original distribution.

Burials

There are several small prehistoric burial cairns on the island, all probably of Bronze Age date. One example, around 7m in diameter, at Port Mor,[18] would appear to have been originally constructed with a stone kerb; another slightly larger example, also at Port Mor, is surmounted by a recumbent stone slab and also by a modern memorial set in a concrete plinth.[19] Both lie in an area of early Christian burial and perhaps reflect a location of longer burial tradition. The other four are located away from known settlement or burial plots on the moorland Aird nan Uan peninsular at the north-west of the island: two lie at the tip of the peninsula,[20] and two lie on its crest.[21] The northerly one on the tip,

with a diameter of about 8m, is the best defined: it has kerb stones visible intermittently around its edge, but in one place the kerb has been moved to form part of the burial enclosure of the MacEwans of Muck dating from 1920. When this relatively modern burial was undertaken, burnt ashes were encountered, although there was no record of a cist. The other three cairns are less well preserved, but the general location of all four on marginal land has undoubtedly aided their survival. The existence of a group such as this in prominent positions might indicate an area traditionally designated for burial purpose.

The difficulties of interpreting landscape features such as these are well illustrated by earthwork features on the summit of Beinn Airein. Here, situated next to a cylindrical Ordnance Survey triangulation pillar, there is another possible burial mound, this time in turf.[22] It measures about 6m in diameter and the digging of turfs used to build the mound has left a shallow, now grass-grown, depression around it. Nearby is a thick turf bank which appears to isolate the cliff headland immediately to the south. It is not clear whether the two are related, what date they are or, indeed, what their respective functions were. They have in common the use of turf as a constructional material, and the places from where the turf was stripped are visible on the ground surface. A short stretch of trackway zig-zags from the banking down the steep rocky slope that forms the southern flank of the headland.

Fig 4.7 The peninsula at Aird nan Uan may have been traditionally used for burial purposes, and has since been used in modern times HES SC1383805

Later Prehistory

Muck boasts at least one Iron Age fort, which surmounts a basalt stack on a coastal promontory known as at Caisteal an Duin Bhain at the south-west of the island.[23] Although rendered broken by the presence of intrusive volcanic (dolerite) dykes, the Muck coastline lacks the stunning sea-girt locations used for fort building on the adjacent islands. But this fort's position, overlooking the western entrance to the main harbour and the traditional location of settlement, is impressive. The fort dominates approaches to the harbour and is depicted as a circular monument on the 1809 estate map (Fig 4.4), annotated as an 'Old Castle' – a warring reference reminiscent of Pont's late 16th century description of it being a 'rock or craig built by the Master and Superior of the island in times of wars which was betwixt him and certain enemies'.[24] The monument is also named on the 1st edition of the OS 6-inch map, surveyed in 1877 and published in 1880, with its perimeter outlined (Fig 4.10).

There are no outer ramparts or man-made defences other than the natural landfall of the promontory itself. Instead, the basalt stack rises to a height of some

Fig 4.8 The fort at Caisteal an Duin Bhain overlooking the western entrance of the main harbour. HES SC761113

Fig 4.9 Later structures outside the Iron Age fort at Caisteal an Duin Bhain. HES SC1383792

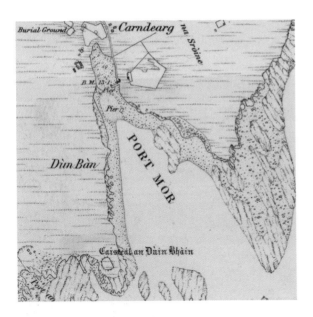

Fig 4.10 First edition 6-inch OS map showing the fort at the mouth of the harbour and the burial ground at the head of the harbour.

Fig 4.11 Plan of the fort at Caisteal an Duin Bhain showing structures and cultivation lines on the interior and further structures enclosed on the outside. HES GV006116

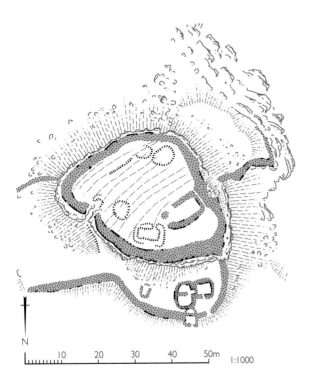

6m above the ground surface and the fort occupies the whole of the level summit, defined by a single stone wall which follows the lip of the stack enclosing an area with a diameter of some 30m. The wall is best preserved on the north where the outer face survives to a height of 1.4m in seven courses, but the inner face is less visible. For most of the circuit the wall core rises no more than 0.5m above the interior, being more impressive from the outside than from within; it appears to be thicker on the landward side than the seaward side, with a narrow entrance on the north-east.

Within the fort are the remains of at least two heavily robbed buildings and traces of lazy bed cultivation, the latter indicating the extent to which every available parcel of fertile land was eventually utilised. The lazy beds overlie four shallow scoops, three of which lie immediately inside the walling and which are likely to have been quarries for the wall itself. The largest building, which has rounded internal angles surviving at one end, measures approximately 8m by 4m and has a stone face and turf core. The second building is slightly smaller and lies within a low stony bank; there is a possible third structure, turf-built, and U-shaped on plan lying immediately within the fort entrance.

Below the fort on the landward side, a wall has been built isolating the stack from the landward approach. This cuts across the head of the promontory and effectively encloses a terrace on which two buildings and at least one hut can be identified. The wall is now ruinous and grass-grown, but survives up to 2.5m thick in places. Neither the wall nor the buildings appear to form part of the defences but they clearly relate to activities with which the promontory and possibly the stack itself were associated. The two buildings and the one remaining hut lie between the base of the stack and the wall. The larger building has two compartments and measures approximately 5m by 3m, with a faced rubble wall; a pen has been inserted into its north end. The second building is slightly smaller, and the surviving hut lies to their east. All appear to belong to a single unit, presumably for stock purposes for which the promontory, when effectively enclosed by the walling, provided a well-defined enclosure.

There are two other possible forts. One, at Fang Mhor, is defined by a short length of walling visible on a coastal promontory.[25] Perhaps less likely, on

Fig 4.12 The possible fort site at Fang Mhor on the remote south-west coast on the promontory at the centre. HES DP109119

Fig 4.13 A natural gully in the hillside divides the possible fort at Aird nan Uan from the main promontory. John Hunter

the east of Aird nan Uan not far from Gallanach there may be a fort on a small natural outcrop which projects from the side of the headland.[26] In the former, rather than cutting across the neck of the promontory, the wall extends along the spine of the promontory for about 20m, possibly originally enclosing two small cliff terraces on the eastern side. The walling is probably not part of the original fort and is more likely to be a feature built out of its abandoned ruins – the re-use of stone from earlier structures being a phenomenon that is commonly seen among the remains of early townships (below). The site lies in a most inhospitable environment and is difficult to access even from the landward side. Its interpretation as a place of refuge seem impractical, and there are no visible settlement remains nearby to which it might relate. As far as the Aird nan Uan site is concerned, the stack is some 20m in diameter, steeper on the seaward side, and separated from the main promontory by a natural gully. There is no evidence of internal features, but the ground round about contains remains of possible later walling lines and huts.[27]

Fig 4.14 Early chapel foundations and part of the burial ground at Kiel. The tall memorial relates to a boating accident. HES SCI383781

Early Christian and Viking

In common with the other three islands, Muck has a credible association with early Christianity, but mostly through the survival of two carved crosses rather than any documentary sources. Boswell's assertion that the island was formerly 'churchland belonging to Icolmkill [Iona]' has a documentary basis, but his view that it was also inhabited by a hermit is unsupported elsewhere.[28] The surviving evidence for Early Christian activity lies at the south end of the deserted township of Kiel near Port Mor, in the burial ground enclosed by a drystone wall.[29] The site itself is recorded as 'A'Chill' (Gaelic Cille 'chapel', also identified on neighbouring Canna and elsewhere on Early Christian sites), and appears to be of long standing, the name also being used to denote the township on that side of the island.

The burial enclosure itself may be the one denoted on the estate map of the island drawn up in 1809 (Fig 4.4), but is not depicted on the 1st edition OS 6-inch map or on any subsequent editions. Roughly oval in plan, measuring about 28m by 21m, much of the walling has been robbed, in places to little more than a scarp, and on the east side parts are missing altogether. On the westward side of the enclosure the ground is rough and uneven, possibly indicating that

the burial ground once extended across the adjacent part of the terrace on which it stands. Remains of a chapel lie in the south-east part of the burial enclosure, towards the leading edge of the terrace. This small structure is subrectangular (approximately 6m by 3m) with a faced rubble wall still standing to a height of around 1m. The configuration of a defined burial enclosure containing a small chapel or oratory has a long tradition reverting back to an era of Celtic monasticism (see also Eigg) and is a strong argument in favour of an early origin.

The 'Kiel' name for the township also reflects Early Christian importance and there is a knoll some 300m to the west known as Cnoc na Croise ('Mound of the Cross'). This symbolic focal point for denoting Christian activity is seen too on the adjacent islands of Canna and Eigg and, perhaps more significantly, on Iona from where Christian missions reached the Small Isles. Elsewhere on the island what may be the base for a cross or some form of marker is situated on a small headland to the east of the bay at Port Mor.[30] It comprises a roughly circular, steep-sided mound of stones with facetted edges. On the flat top there is a right-angled setting of stones bounding a depression that may be a socket. The 1809 estate map identifies the headland as 'Ru Cross', and the OS maps attribute the name Rubh' a' Chroisein ('Headland of the Cross(es)') to the rocky foreshore to the south. Local tradition maintains that a windmill once stood at roughly this location, but the remains are unconvincing for this interpretation, perhaps reinforced by MacDonald's early 19th century comment that there was no mill on the island.[31] The idea of a visible marker signalling a Christian centre to those approaching the island by sea, or as a symbolic prayer marker for a safe landing, is well attested elsewhere. It would have been particularly apposite here at Muck in view of the island's notoriously difficult access.

Further tangible evidence of an Early Christian origin comes from the presence of two carved memorial stones which formerly stood among the various grave markers packed within the enclosure. These markers include thirteen memorials of 19th century and later date (including two for sailors lost in the Second World War, and a tall pink granite pillar dedicated to islanders lost in a boating accident), over 100 undecorated markers, each comprising a water-rolled boulder or flat slab, mostly

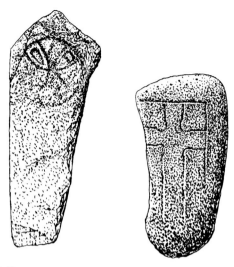

Fig 4.15 The two early Christian carved memorial stones now cared for in the local craft shop. HES SC406072, SC406073

arranged in rows, and several heaps of stones. Both of the carved memorial stones originally stood within these rows but were later moved to the nearby craft shop for safe keeping. One, a slab of grey flagstone, rectangular but with a slightly pointed top, is almost 1m in length and tapers upwards in thickness.[32] On one face there has been a cross-of-arcs within an incised circle. Although much of the surface of the cross has flaked off, there are clear indications of a small central sinking or compass-hole. The other is smaller and created from a round-ended igneous boulder, lacking the left edge. On the flat face is an outline Latin cross with curved armpits set within a partial rectangular frame. The cross-shaft has an open foot and the ends of the arms extend to the frame. The right edge of the frame terminates above the level of the foot of the shaft, presumably because the stone was intended to be set upright.[33] From an art-historical point of view, both can be attributed to the 7th to 9th centuries.

The dates at which these memorials may have been carved and set in the graveyard roughly coincide with the beginnings of Norse movement and raiding in the Western Isles, Iona being sacked in the late 8th century, and sporadically thereafter. Muck is remarkably void of Norse place-name evidence compared, for example, with Canna, but this

may in part be due to its lack of obvious landscape characteristics visible from the sea. That said, among the many grass-grown foundations scattered across the island there is at least one building, which, although overlain by lazy beds, displays structural features that strongly suggest an early date. It is situated on marginal land at Toaluinn, on the north-east coast of the island, with bow-sided walls 2.2m thick and an overall length of 13m. The walls survive as wide boulder-faced banks and in shape the building is more akin to Norse houses found elsewhere around the Atlantic fringe than the rectangular buildings of later date on Muck.[34] Its location on a former storm beach above the high water mark and adjacent to good quality land with easy access to fresh water is typical of a Norse settlement. Furthermore, the presence of a rock-cut slipway and the isolation of the site lend additional weight to the argument that the remains may represent a farmstead from the earlier phases of Norse settlement in the 9th or 10th century, perhaps the only example readily visible today within all of the Small Isles.

Figs 4.16 Survey work being carried out on the likely Norse house in 2002. HES SC1383838

Fig 4.17 Plan of the Norse house at Toaluinn showing the bow-sided walls and outshot. HES GV006117

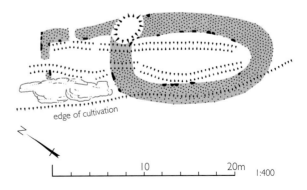

edge of cultivation

N

10   20m   1:400

Medieval and Post-Medieval Landscapes

The likelihood of identifying structural remains from the medieval period has been significantly lessened by the intensity of land use on Muck over the centuries. The relatively high population, persistent reuse and robbing of stone foundations, the rebuilding of huts and dwellings, and the construction of enclosures, pens and field boundaries have provided a landscape where change is manifest, but where any understanding of the absolute chronologies of early change remains undefined without the help of focused archaeological intervention. Seen today Muck is an eroded cacophony of grass-grown stone foundations testifying to generations of farmers, shepherds, and fishermen and their families who subsisted on the island, but whose place in time can at best be described as blurred.

However, in documented times we have some opportunity to map recorded population figures against changes on the landscape. Some of the best indications of early population density can be gleaned from McNeill's census of 1764/5 which identifies a population of 143 at that time divided into 28 families.[35] Unfortunately, and unlike his census for Rum and Eigg, McNeill was unable to divide these into named townships, although we can assume that seven or eight families might live in each. The subsequent population figures indicate a gradual rise in numbers towards the end of the 18th century, mostly resulting from the growth of the kelp industry. They also reflect an emigration that occurred in 1788–1790, which the writer of the *Statistical Account*, the Reverend Donald McLean, attributed to population pressure.[36] Some form of regeneration clearly occurred thereafter, and by 1821 the population peaked at over 300. After the collapse of the kelp market shortly afterwards the numbers dropped drastically. The *New Statistical Account* records a major emigration across the Atlantic in 1828,[37] and by the time of the census return in 1841 the number had declined further to a mere 68. Today, the island houses a small population around Gallanach which survives as the sole farm on the island, but the main focus of population (currently around 30) is located adjacent to the main harbour at Port Mor on the opposite south-east coast where the modern services including shop, school, community centre and ferry terminal are located.

Year	Population	Source
1764/5	143	McNeill (1764/5)
1768	172	Stat Acct (1796)
1786	253	Knox (1787)
1796	193	Stat Acct (1796)
1808	184	MacDonald (1811)
1821	321	Census
1841	68	Census
2011	27	Census

Fig 4.18 Recorded population figures for Muck.

Townships

The island landscape is complex, although the estate map drawn up by Chapman in 1809 (Fig 4.4) when Muck was under the ownership of the Clanranalds (1799–1814) is a useful guide to its understanding. The purpose was to provide land for those working in the kelp industry, which was a major employer from the late 18th century until the collapse of the market in the 1820s. It shows the settlement status quo at that time and gives some insight as to how earlier communities might have evolved. As mentioned earlier, this division into townships marks the first observable organisation of the landscape on the island. The map shows two boundaries, each running roughly north–south across the girth of the island, and almost certainly representing the boundaries of lands held by the earlier townships: Gallanach[38] on the west; Balmeanach[39] in the centre (later to merge with Gallanach and together comprising approximately two-thirds of the island), and Kiel[40] on the east comprising the other third. The line of the Gallanach/Balmeanach boundary can mostly be seen on the 1st edition OS 6-inch map surveyed in 1877, but the Balmeanach/Kiel boundary is not depicted. However, its line appears to be followed on the current series map suggesting some form of reinstatement following earlier lines. Today, both boundaries can still be traced on the ground, surviving as intermittent stretches of ruinous turf-and-stone walls, for the most part running along the floor of the glens below crags and ridges, or as maintained stone walling following parts of the original route.

Figs 4.19 Stone dykes of various dates are still visible running across the landscape. HES SC1383711

Alongside the boundaries, the map also shows the individual buildings of these townships, albeit schematically, some with adjacent yards and enclosures, as well as giving the areas of arable, pasture and moss. The western dyke is denoted as 'March betwixt Gallananch and Ballmeanach', and the eastern dyke 'Stone dyke the March between Balmeanachg and Kiel'. The origins of the three townships are obscure but it seems likely that the dense clusters of ruined stone foundations that can be partly seen today will have structural antecedents that are incorporated into, or may underlie them. Some may indeed date to medieval times.

Fig 4.20 The deserted township of Kiel contains the remains of at least 48 buildings. HES SC1383755

The deserted township of Kiel (*Sean Bhaile*) extends up a broad terrace to the north-west of the burial-ground at the head of Port Mor. It is by far the best preserved of the three townships and comprises the remains of at least 48 buildings, apparently scattered to either side of a trackway or street flanked by drystone walls. Closer inspection reveals that the construction of the walls delineating the trackway represents one of the latest active phases in the history of the township, both walls crossing an enclosure in the core of the township, and the north-east wall variously over-riding or incorporating no less than six buildings along its line. Indeed, at least 27 of the buildings are over-ridden by a system of small enclosures constructed amongst the ruins. Only one of these enclosures is shown on the 1st edition OS 6-inch map lying at

the south end of the township adjacent to the burial ground, and it is the only one containing visible traces of cultivation ridges (Fig 4.10). The earlier phases of the township appear to have lacked much in the way of infrastructure. According to Dr Johnson's account (second hand) there were very few trades there in the 1770s and the proprietor was obliged to import a smith and a tailor as necessary.[41]

The buildings are evidently multi-period, not only in the sense that so many of them predate the system of enclosures, but that in several locations they represent more than one phase of construction, ranging from the insertion of pens or partitions, to the reconstruction of the walls. In some cases, one building appears to have been butted against another, in a few others buildings have been superimposed on

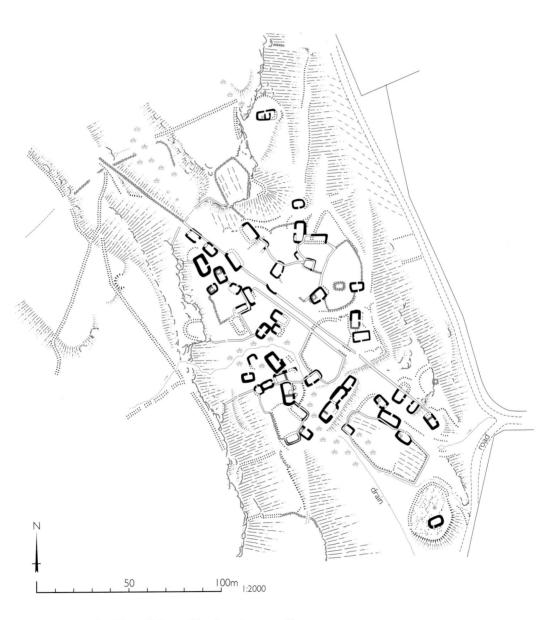

Fig 4.21 Different phases of building at Keil are evident from the survey. The burial ground and chapel lie towards the bottom of the plan. HES GV006118

Fig 4.22 This wide view of the Port Mor area shows different features of the built landscape – the harbour, quay and slipway (top left), the abandoned houses and burial ground at Keil (right) and the modern houses (left and centre). HES DP109111

earlier structures in an ad hoc manner. A row of three buildings immediately upslope from the southern-most enclosure, although now heavily robbed and disturbed, share their end walls in such a way that they cannot have been built as a single range. The expansion and density of the township shown by these buildings is a response, to some extent disordered, not only to demands of employment and subsistence, but also to the later movement of islanders driven from the land by the large-scale introduction of cattle (below) whose only option in avoiding emigration was to attempt a new life in what became the 'main' centre at Kiel.

Only three of the buildings are over 10m long, another seven are around 9m and the remainder fall between these and the smallest structure, which measures about 4m by 3m. Their stone-faced walls are generally turf-cored, and the corners are rounded internally and externally, with a single entrance in the middle of one side and no evidence of any windows. At least two buildings have kilns embedded in masonry behind an inserted wall at one end, and in one the mouth of the flue is visible. There is also a free-standing kiln at the top of the slope overlooking the track at the south-east end of the township. Two kiln-barns lie adjacent to each other at the north end of the township, one is heavily robbed but the other stands 1.5m high with the kiln bowl mostly intact. This and a neighbouring building with surviving walls almost 2m high are among the best preserved buildings in the township, and presumably are among the last to have been abandoned.

Fig 4.23 The ruined stone-built structures at Keil are some of the best preserved in the Small Isles. HES SC761115

Kiel is shown on Chapman's plan of 1809 but in a less busy manner and we can only assume that it evolved to its present complex state thereafter. This does question the extent to which it may have been settled prior to Chapman's map, particularly in the 1780s when the population was significantly higher, and what its medieval origins (if any) may have been. Assuming some accuracy of cartography and a degree of licence, it appears to have comprised only eight buildings and an enclosure at the time of Chapman's survey, but it is difficult to reconcile this depiction with the remains on the ground. If it is not the burial ground, the enclosure depicted probably lies towards

the southern end of the area occupied by the township where there are traces of an earlier enclosure beneath the southern-most of the later boundaries. In view of the well preserved character of some of the buildings at the northern end, it is likely that the township expanded northwards after the map was produced 1809, but the greater part of the system of enclosures is more recent still. With the exception of the southern-most enclosure, no trace of the walls of the system, nor those of the trackway appear on the 2nd edition of the OS 6-inch map published in 1903. They may, therefore, date from the early 20th century.

The township of Balmeanach takes in a narrow strip of ground that runs down the spine of the island, absorbing Druim Mor and Blar na Fionn-aird. Defined on the east and west by the boundaries marked on the 1809 plan of the island, this area has been extensively cultivated and plots of lazy beds

Fig 4.24 Remains of the Balmeanach township survive only in the form of a series of rectangular turf-covered foundations. HES SC1383834

survive in all but the improved fields from modern farming. On Druim Mor in particular, crags and natural terrace edges serve to subdivide the plots, and are on occasion supplemented by lengths of bank which effectively complete the sides of these fields. The township remains comprise at least nine subrectangular buildings, at least four enclosures and a pen, all located at the north-west end of Druim Mor immediately above the enclosed fields of Gallanach farm. Chapman's map shows a cluster of three buildings and four enclosures, but with a huddle of seven buildings lying off to the north (now in woodland) which makes it slightly larger than Kiel at the time of mapping. The stone walls of these fields cut across four of the buildings and one enclosure, and only faint swellings on the surface of the ground reveal their presence within the improved fields. Elsewhere, the buildings are mostly reduced to grass-grown footings with occasional facing stones, but two have been so heavily robbed that their walls are indicated only by robber trenches. These two are set on an area of flat ground overlooking the greater part of the township, and have traces of what are either adjoining enclosures or the remains of earlier buildings protruding from beneath them. One building, set at a lower level to the north-east, is the only one in which stretches of wall face still survive; it has a large pear-shaped enclosure appended to the south which is mirrored on Chapman's estate map. The township was probably abandoned by the mid 19th century and nothing at all is shown on the 1st edition of the OS 6-inch map surveyed in 1877.

At Gallanach the township remains are even less tangible. Five buildings and two enclosures annotated as yards are depicted on the 1809 map. The buildings are arranged in two groups, lying either side of a burn that drains an area of boggy ground. The three buildings on the west side are arranged in a U-shape with its open side to the north; these probably lie beneath the modern steading, as do their associated enclosures. Similarly, no trace of the two buildings and the enclosure depicted on the east side of the burn can now be found, but these too lie within the enclosed fields. Beyond the enclosed fields of the present farm there are large swathes of lazy bed cultivation which extend southwards along the ridge to Fionn Aird and north along the peninsula Aird nan Uan, tailing off to the west at Gleann Mhairten. Here the ground is higher and less fertile, and may have been used

as common grazing for all the townships until the beginning of the 19th century. This western end of the island is the only area where small huts have been recorded in any number, lending further weight to the possible seasonal use of this ground for shielings.

Shieling

The whole western area of the island, particularly Gleann Mhairten itself, is a useful indicator of the use of hill land. The Commission's survey work has identified over 30 huts in that western area alone, together with eight enclosures and a small number of pens both likely to be associated with shieling activity. The majority of the huts occur in ones and twos, each typically no more than 2m by 2m in size, although some are slightly larger with internal divisions. They are all of drystone rubble walling, presumably with an original turf superstructure, for example at Leam na Laraich,[42] the most westerly recorded site on the island which survives only as lines of rubble foundations. Patches of cultivation associated with these huts occur wherever the soil allows it, such as at Achadh na Creige.[43]

The majority of huts sit in isolation and presumably reflect the patterns of transhumance undertaken in the summer months which required temporary accommodation for herding, shepherding and for the processing of dairy produce, although there is a nagging concern as to why an island as small as Muck would need transhumance in the first place. In

Fig 4.25 Typical remains of a shieling hut with associated lazy beds on Gleann Mhairten. HES SC774884

Fig 4.26 Cultivation occurred on every available patch of soil, such as here in the narrow moorland gullies at Achadh na Creige overlooking Horse Island. HES SCI383808

Fig 4.27 Although only part of the stone base survives, the shieling at Leam na Laraich was probably a turf structure with a drystone rubble base. HES SCI383803

answering this, it is perhaps significant that a group of five huts has associated enclosures, field banks and surrounding lazy beds located on a level terrace towards the centre of the area. One hut is attached to a small enclosure set into the slope. There are also other enclosures and a mound with projecting stones which may represent an additional underlying structure. Several field banks are visible, partly enclosing an area of lazy beds. The whole cluster of features suggests organised activity at a level which is difficult to argue as being entirely temporary; it may reflect a more permanent movement of settlement away from the township centres in times of severe population density.

The same might be said for a group of eleven huts and two pens strung out along a natural terrace on the east flank of Fionn Aird at Leabaidh Dhonnchaidh on the south side of the island.[44] The terrace has been extensively cultivated in a patchwork of small plots of lazy beds, their extent and direction being largely defined by numerous rock outcrops and low ridges. A stony bank links up the local topographical features to form an enclosure taking in the greater part of the terrace itself. All but three of the huts lie among the plots of lazy bed cultivation at the rear of

Fig 4.28 Shielings adjacent to a sheltered terrace at Leabaidh Dhonnchaidh. HES SC1383828

the terrace. In instances where the relationship between a hut and the cultivation can be observed, the huts always appear to be the earlier. Four of the huts sit within grass-grown mounds and at least one of these mounds contains traces of another small hut or cell. The other huts in this cluster are more subrectangular and defined by stony banks, and it is not clear whether these remains are contemporary with the others. The same chronological difficulty applies to the three remaining huts which lie below the area of cultivation on the front of the terrace. At least

two of these overlie earlier features and reinforce the sense that this had been a long-standing area of activity, but exactly how long is another matter. In terms of individual size all these huts seem unlikely to represent anything other than temporary occupation, but the nature of their positioning around key locations, especially with the presence of lazy beds,

Fig 4.29 Horse Island, seen here from the tip of Aird nan Uan, was utilised for sheep after Captain Swinburne's purchase of Muck in 1854. HES SC1383727

continues to suggest a greater degree of permanency and careful utilisation of land than seen in the other three islands. It is always a possibility that these clusters and others like them, rather than reflecting transhumance activity, might represent 'work camps' occupied during the seasonal collection, drying and burning of kelp.

In the south-west end of the island, which has been least affected by agriculture, there is a series of field banks which do not appear to be associated with arable cultivation. They may instead reflect some measure of stock control, perhaps relating to use of this land as summer pasture. Elsewhere across the island, there are a number of large enclosures, which also appear to relate to stock management. The *Statistical Account* records that only cattle were reared on Muck at the end of the 18th century.[45] Sheep are not mentioned at all in the 1845 *Statistical Account*, arriving only in any number during the ownership of the island by Captain Swinburne from

1854. Their presence in large numbers will have necessitated the construction of a range of dykes, shelters and enclosures.[46] Sheep are also seen to be the reason for the construction of a series of stone walls across the narrow coastal gullies of Eilean nan Each (Horse Island), a small island lying off the north-west of Muck across a 'foul, rocky narrow channel, which frequently ebbs dry',[47] accessible mostly by boat and measuring barely 500m across. According to Monro, travelling in 1549, the islet was 'guid for horse and uther store',[48] and the purpose of the later walling would seem to have been to safeguard the limited grazing land by encouraging sheep to eat seaweed on the shore instead.

Farmsteads

Superimposed across the spreads of lazy beds are a series of straight boundaries that cut across the slopes. Where best preserved these take the form of drystone walls and are most visible in the east and south-east of the island. Their alignment and extent are comparable with the boundaries drawn on the 1809 plan (the second major landscape change) and it would seem that efforts were made at least in part to put in place the crofting scheme. In most places, however, it is apparent that this layout was never fully completed. In one instance, a long stretch of wall can be followed south-west on the ground from the crags north of Dun Ban as far as Blar na Fionn-aird, where it stops abruptly in open heather moorland. Adjacent to this end, there is a small pile of stones, presumably gathered to extend the line of the wall, but never used. The abandonment, or collapse, of this grand design may underlie the population movement into Keil, and partly explain the late increased level of building there.

No buildings are depicted on the plan of the proposed crofts due to its schematic nature, although on the ground there are the shells of over a dozen farmsteads that were presumably built as a result of this early 19th century land division. These too are to be found across the east and south-east of the island, and most are of drystone construction, comprising a range of buildings (typically two or three structures of which one was a dwelling) with adjoining yard. The farmsteads are represented on the 1st edition of the OS 6-inch map, although by this date of survey (1877) the buildings that are shown had all fallen out of use and are depicted as unroofed.

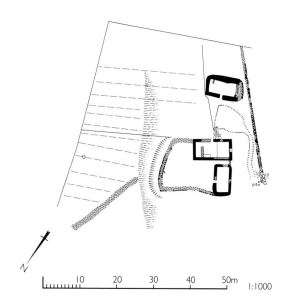

Fig 4.30 Plan of the Cnoc an Fheur Lochain farmstead. The central building with squared corners is probably the farmhouse, the other two being a byre and barn. HES GV006119

These farmsteads are quite distinctive from the buildings found among the earlier townships: they are isolated rather than clustered; the individual buildings themselves are larger, and there is often a discernible infrastructure within which individual functional elements such as dwelling, barn, byre and kiln can be identified. On a terrace at Cnoc an Fheur Lochain on the east coast the remains of a farmstead have been incorporated into a later sheepfold.[49] Some parts of the terrace are heavily improved, but an extensive field system of earlier banks and lazy beds still extends across the ridges to its east and west. The farmstead comprises three ruined buildings arranged along the terrace. The southern-most has been a byre, with a central drain in the interior and a midden scoop outside the entrance. At some stage the building has been reduced in length at its south-west end. The other two lie beyond the midden scoop and appear to form two sides of an enclosure or yard. The central building is the largest and of more distinctive quality, being

Fig 4.31 Buildings of the Cnoc an Fheur Lochain farmstead showing an extensive earlier system of banks and lazy beds. HES DP109112

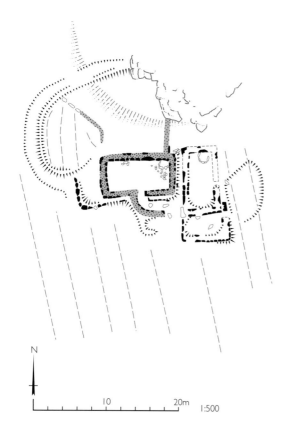

N

10   20m   1:500

Fig 4.32 Plan of the three buildings and enclosure at Blar na Fionn-Aird. The farmstead dwelling is probably the largest of the three. HES GV006120

constructed of coursed rubble walling and measuring over 9m by 4m internally. It is the only one of the three with squared corners and although used in more recent times as a sheepfold, the presence of a fireplace at one end indicates that it was originally built as a dwelling. The third building was probably a barn, and has what may be a winnowing hole in the base of the south-west side directly opposite the entrance.

Linked to the buildings are a number of field banks extending across the ridges to the east and south-west of the farmstead to form a series of small plots fringed by larger enclosures. To the east of the farmstead there are several conjoined plots, the field boundaries snaking their way along rock outcrops and ridges to create irregular fields, the largest of which measures about 60m by 50m. Extending in all directions from this core of small plots, larger fields drop down to the boggy ground to the east and become lost in the modern improvement. Lazy beds can be seen within the greater part of most of these plots, though at least one does not appear to have been cultivated. Elements of the regular division of ground depicted on the 1809 map can be seen riding across parts of the earlier field system, and include a ruined wall extending from the east coast of the island across the top of Carn Dearg to Port Mor.

Another farmstead (Fig 4.32) can be seen at Blar na Fionn-Aird which lies on the promontory to the west of Port Mor.[50] The old stone and turf dyke is clearly visible beyond it to the west, and the remains of a potentially

Fig 4.33 An old stone and turf dyke associated with the Blar na Fionn-Aird farmstead follows natural outcrops and runs down to the sea. John Hunter

Fig 4.34 Surviving walling from one of the Blar na Fionn-Aird farm buildings. HES SC1383820

Fig 4.35 The collapsed remains of the freestanding kiln barn at Druim Mor. Unusually, the flue lintels have remained in position. HES SC1383822

Fig 4.37 The turf-roofed Gallanach Cottage at Achadh na Creige is used today. HES SC1383841

older earth and stone dyke runs roughly parallel to the east, conjoining natural outcrops. The farmstead consists of three subrectangular buildings, an enclosure and a midden and lies at the rear of a grassy terrace below a nose of outcrop. The terrace has been cultivated extensively with lazy beds, but these are over-ridden by the widely spaced furrows of improved plough rigs which have also cut through part of the

Fig 4.36 Plan of the kiln barn at Achadh na Creige. HES GV006121

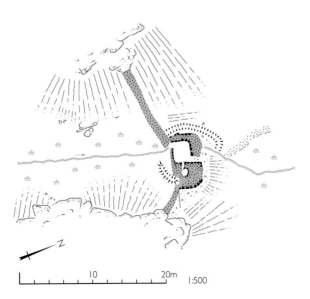

midden. The buildings are arranged in an L-shape on plan, with the enclosure off-set to the north-west of the largest building, probably the dwelling, which measures approximately 8.4m by 4m and is constructed of faced rubble walling. The entrance lies midway along one side and is protected by a baffle wall. To either side of the entrance there is a line of facing-stones belonging to an earlier structure; the enclosure also shows more than one phase of use. The two other buildings lie to the east; both are likely to have served an ancillary farming function, and both have cruder, boulder-faced walls.

Several corn-drying kilns appear to belong to this period. One of the best examples is at Achadh na Creige, near Gallanach where the kiln-barn lies at a slight distance from its parent farmstead which was probably constructed around the turn of the 20th century.[51] The unit comprises three buildings, a kiln-barn, enclosures and three pens, and is built at the back of a north-east facing terrace. There is also a cleared slipway in the inter-tidal zone to the north. One of the buildings (now known as Gallanach Cottage, and in occasional use) is still roofed with turfs and measures around 8m by 5m with rubble walls some 2m in height; the interior consists of a single room divided by a roughly constructed box bed. The walls are slightly battered and the central doorway is flanked by two windows. The kiln-barn (Fig 4.36) itself contains two compartments, one with a significantly higher floor level which contains the kiln. The kiln bowl, which is

Fig 4.38 Grubbing cabbages by traditional farming methods in the early 1960s – Muck was well known for producing high quality cabbages. © Scottish Life Archive. Licensor Scran

now choked with rubble, measures 1.2m in diameter, and the mouth of the flue has been built into the east wall of the compartment. There is also a freestanding kiln set against a low crag on the east side of a narrow gully at the south-east of Druim Mor.[52] This kiln is relatively well preserved, and the lintels covering the mouth of the flue are still in place.

Buildings such as these are relatively easy to interpret in terms of their use, but not all may have held a farming or dwelling function. A small structure lying on the east side of the island at Eilean Dubh is situated by a watercourse in a secluded location which requires some explanation.[53] The interior, which is thick with sediment and flag iris roots, measures around 4m by 2.5m, and is sunk below the level of the watercourse on the upstream side. Of the various interpretations proffered, that of an illicit still seems the most feasible and would be a rare discovery, as well as bringing some social colour to this lost community.

The key farming unit, however, undoubtedly belongs to Gallanach[54] at the north and consists of two complexes. The earlier is depicted on Chapman's 1809 map and the later, located some 100m to the east, appears on the 1st edition OS 6-inch map of 1880. Two large rubble stone byres have survived from the earlier complex and reflect the island's emphasis on cattle, denoted in both *Statistical Accounts*. Later rebuilding and additions, including a cobbled yard, date from the mid 19th century. This emphasis on cattle later became heightened under the proprietorship of Alexander Maclean from 1814,

the grazing demands of increased numbers of cattle playing no small part in the emigrations which occurred shortly afterwards. There were no enforced Clearances as such on Muck, but emigration was encouraged by the offer of assisted passage. Some took up the option, but the many who stayed moved away from the main pastures to the Kiel township by the harbour. Among the *émigrés* from the Small Isles to Canada MacDougall records one Hugh Campbell, 'a native of the Isle of Muck', who arrived in Pictou, Nova Scotia, in 1820. He established a farm inland and was joined later by his two brothers. Two years later six MacMillian brothers arrived from Muck, sailing from Tobermory on the ship *Commerce*.[55] Reference to the population numbers shows an island peak population of 321 souls in 1821 falling to a mere 68 twenty years later. The figures suggest not only a substantial emigration but also a relatively short-lived increase in building density in the township, and a relatively fast abandonment thereafter.

In 1854 Muck was sold to Captain Thomas Swinburne, who implemented a number of improvements (including the introduction of large scale sheep farming) and attempted to build up a fishing industry. Over the decades that followed, stone walls were built, areas of bog were drained and the road from Port Mor to Gallanach was formalised. The eastern farm complex at Gallanach had evolved to become the focal and 'industrial' heart of the island and additional byres for dairying were constructed. Gallanach effectively became the laird's residence

Fig 4.39 The earlier buildings and cobbled courtyard at the west of the Gallanach complex first appear on the Chapman estate map of 1809. John Hunter

Fig 4.40 The developed farmhouse and steading in the eastern part of the Gallanach complex, which continues to be the centre for farming on Muck. These initially feature on the 1st edition OS 6-inch map. HES SC1383867

Fig 4.41 The eastern (left) and western (right) parts of Gallanach farm overlook clear seas at the north coast of the island. The traces of fish traps can also be seen in the shallows. HES DP109117

and, at the end of the 19th century, the farmhouse was rebuilt by the new owner, Robert Thomson, who raised it to two storeys. The present arrangement now consists of the main house with an adjacent double byre, the majority of elements being whitewashed and slated. Thomson's rebuilding was part of a wider programme of farming innovation which saw the introduction of a new field system superimposed over earlier land divisions – the third significant landscape change noted above – although some of the boundaries evident on Chapman's map were utilised in this configuration. The landscape impact of this is demonstrated most clearly on the 2nd edition OS 6-inch map of 1903.

Maritime Remains

For an island that was historically well provided with fish, noted as early as the mid 16th century by Monro,[56] there are relatively few maritime remains surviving around the shores. Some fish may have been caught in-shore in traps and one example is visible at low tide at Bagh a' Ghallanaich below Gallanach on the north coast comprising a rickle of boulders extending in a gentle arc across the sandy beach between two rock outcrops. Others may have existed but none have been identified.[57] Remarkably, there is little tangible evidence relating to the kelping industry which was one of the underlying reasons for Muck's population boom. No kelp kilns or platforms are identifiable despite the intensity and importance of the kelping in the island's economy and population dynamic. Presumably ferrying occurred at the main landing place at Port Mor where modern concrete constructions have replaced earlier attempts to facilitate landing. A rough slipway some 47m long and over 5m wide cleared through the rocks littering the shore on the north side of the harbour, visible at low tide, may be all that survives.[58] An adjacent depression at the landward end, U-shaped and partly stone-lined with its open end facing the sea, is probably the remnants of a boat naust. The creation of nausts is relatively rare in the Small Isles. With strong Norse antecedents, in their simplest form nausts are little

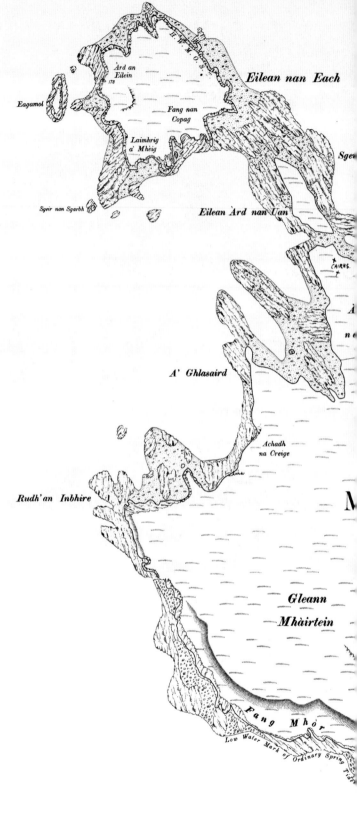

Fig 4.42 The alterations to the landscape following the reorganisation of the Gallanach farm are shown most clearly by the field boundaries on the 2nd edition OS map of 1903, especially when compared with Chapman's map of 1809 (Fig 4.4).

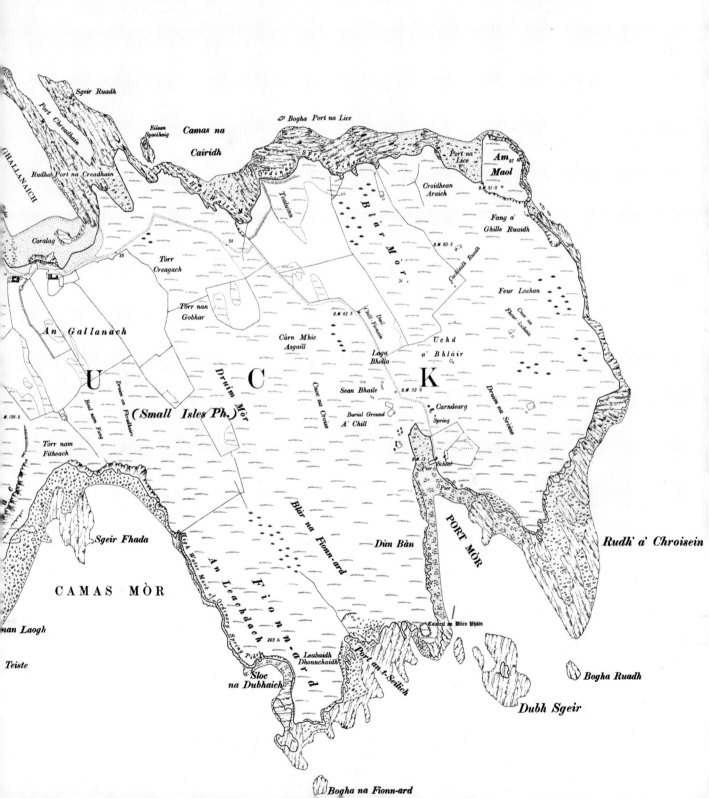

Gòdag

Sgeir Ruadh

Port Chreadhain

Eilean
Sgaothaig

CAMAS na
CAIRIDH

Bogha Port na Lice

Rudha Port na Creadhain

GHALLANAICH

Coralag

Port na
Lice

Am
Maol

B.M. 51·0 ⁰

Croidhean
Araich

B.M. 60·2 ⁰

Fang a'
Ghille Ruaidh

Cachladh Ruadh

Feur Lochan

Chuc na
Fheur lochan

Tòrr
Creagach

An Gallanach

Tòrr nan
Gobhar

Càrn Mhic
Asgaill

B.M. 62·5 ⁰

Dail
Chill Fionnain

U   C   K

Druim Mòr

(Small Isles Ph.)

Uchd
a' Bhlàir

Laga
Bholla

B.M. 32·6 ⁰

Druim na Sroine

M. 159·8 ⁰

Braid nam Fang

Sean Bhaile

Tòrr nam
Fitheach

Burial Ground
A' Chill

Carndearg
Spring

B.M. 13 ⁰

Pier

School

Sgeir Fhada

Blàr na Fionn-ard

Dùn Bàn

Pier

PORT MÒR

Rudh' a' Chroisein

CAMAS MÒR

High Water Mark of Ordinary Spring Tides

An Leachdach

An Fionn-ard

Caisteal an Dùin Bhàin

nan Laogh

203 △

Leabaidh
Dhonnchaidh

Teiste

Sloc
na Dubhaich

Port an t-Seilich

Bogha Ruadh

Dubh Sgeir

Bogha na Fionn-ard

Fig 4.43 A fish trap on Muck, visible at low tide at Bagh a' Ghallanaich. HES SC774888

Fig 4.44 Evidence of different eras of harbourage sit in close proximity to each other – the stone-built quay at Port Mor (centre), the cleared slipway curving to the head of the bay and the later concrete jetty (below). HES SC875632

more than scoops hollowed out of the foreshore just above the high water mark. They were used to shore boats when they were not required, especially during the winter months, and to protect them from rough weather. Some nausts are stone lined; some may have had wooden superstructures.

Port Mor boasts the only substantial jetty on the island, presumably the stone-built 'quay' built by the inhabitants alluded to in the 1845 *New Statistical Account*.[59] However, there are two structures denoted as a 'pier' on the 1st edition OS 6-inch map. The more southerly version may have been in existence (although not in is present concrete form) when Captain Swinburne took over the island in 1854 and began to develop the fishing industry there. The more northerly stone pier may have been of Swinburne's own making as he also built Pier House – a cottage located just above the pier for storing salt and gear for the boats; the upper floor was reached by a forestair (Fig 4.46). The cottage also became used as a school.[60]

Elsewhere in the vicinity there are other vestiges of maritime activity which almost certainly included fishing, for example at Leabaidh Dhonnchaidh on the east side of Fionn Aird where a slipway some 2.5m wide through a channel of cleared boulders can still be seen running down to the sea (Fig 4.47). The slipway belongs to a ruined farmstead which now survives in part as a restored holiday cottage (Fig 4.49).[61] There is a similar slipway connecting the old farmstead at Achadh na Creige to the sea on the northern side of the island (above).[62] The slipway at Port Mor was part of the harbour infrastructure that sheltered and serviced the boats exploiting the nearby ling and cod fishing grounds. It would have seen constant use as catches that were landed here were also prepared there before being sent off to the Clyde markets.

The *Statistical Account* notes that in the 1790s there were only 'a few creeks, which afford shelter to small boats; but no safe harbour for vessels'.[63] There is a slightly smaller slipway at Port nam Maol, a small bay on the north-west coast where the rocks have also been cleared,[64] and more substantial remains at Port Chreadhaih on the northerly coast in the form of two further slipways and a quay.[65] The quay appears on the 1809 estate map (Fig 4.4) but is not depicted on the 1st edition OS map. Presumably it was obsolete by this time, although it appears again on the current 1:10,000 map suggesting reuse. The walling is of rubble construction and has been extended along

Fig 4.45 The stone-built jetty, seen here at low tide, was constructed by Captain Swinburne and is recorded in the *New Statistical Account*. HES SCI383859

Fig 4.46 Pier House with its forestair, built by Captain Swinburne as part of the development of the fishing industry on Muck in the 1850s. HES SCI383860

the high water mark to the north-west with several metal mooring rings set into its upper surface. This extension may relate to the development of fishing by Captain Swinburne, whose ideas for increasing the wealth and security of crofters were outlined to the Napier Commission (Invernesshire) in 1883. Curiously, the evidence he gave pertained not to Muck, but to the island of Eilean Shona lying off the western mainland where he lived. He had owned Eilean Shona for approximately the same time as he had owned Muck and his philosophy on fishing investment, particularly with regard to establishing salt depots and using smacks (a traditional boat) capable of fishing out to Rockall, some 450km to the west in the North Atlantic, was presumably common to both. That said, it is strange that he never alludes to Muck, being the larger of the two, in his evidence at Arisaig,[66] or Edinburgh.[67] Perhaps his venture there was unsuccessful.

Swinburne was well aware of the best fishing grounds for cod and ling, and the types of vessel best suited to catch them. He lamented the need for markets, criticised the inadequacy of local boats (of 'fir skin and birch timbers') and gear available, and

Fig 4.47 The slipway at Leabaidh Dhonnchaidh, created by clearing rocks from the foreshore. HES SC1383844

Fig 4.48 Part of the ruined farmstead at Leabaidh Dhonnchaidh, to which the slipway belonged. HES SC1383817

Fig 4.49 One of the former farm buildings at Leabaidh Dhonnchaidh, now transformed into a holiday home. HES SC1383842

Fig 4.50 Low tide at Port Chreadhaih at the north of the island exposes an early stone-built jetty and the iron tramway from which boats were launched. *Cecily Cropper*

Fig 4.51 Sets of bogeys used for launching boats at Port Chreadhaih. The tramway system was an innovation of the owner Captain Thomas Swinburne. *Cecily Cropper*

pointed out the lack of good local harbours. He had successfully replaced the local Eilean Shona vessels with well-fitted boats and appropriate tackle before moving ultimately to larger deep-sea boats, and had a vision of a network of fishing stations for curing and shipping (including one on Canna). He also recommended designs of slipway for hauling up boats using 'a double line of tramway or a continuation of the slip forming an inclined plane.'[68] This design is perhaps mirrored in one of the Port Chreadhaih slipways, the longest on the island at 65m, which consists of I-section metal runners set on wooden sleepers and which can still be seen at irregular intervals, and where four of the wheeled bogey sets still survive. The other slipway at Port Chreadhaih lacks the ironwork and is much shorter; both are only visible at low tide. There is a third slipway, probably associated with the Gallenach township at Druim Mor where a cleared pathway extends for some 50m below the high water mark. The *Statistical Account* refers to two of the creeks that were used for harbourage (locations undefined) as being 'in an imperfect state', suggesting that decline may have already set in by that time in certain parts of the island,[69] but there is no later record of any resurgence under Swinburne's ownership.

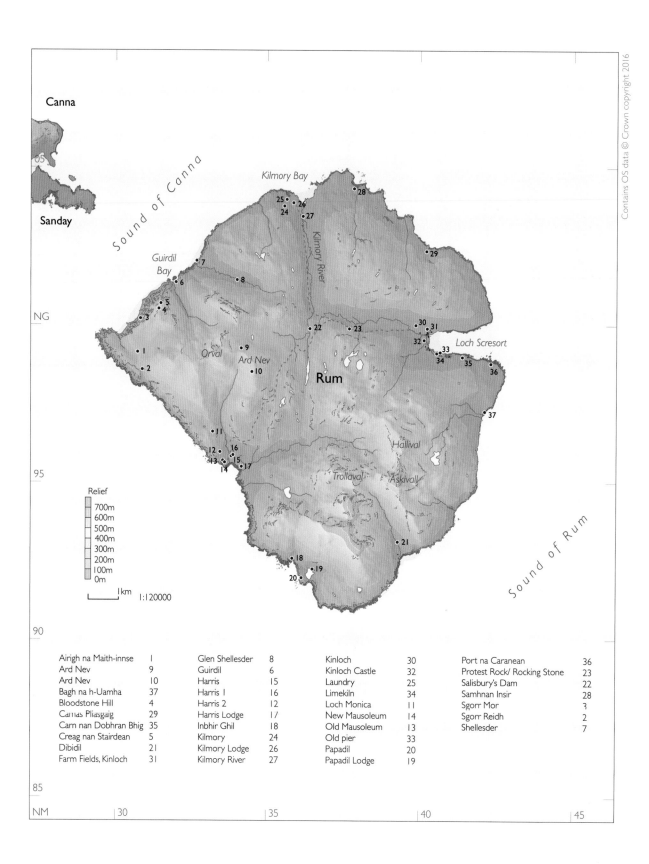

Canna

Sanday

Sound of Canna

Kilmory Bay

25 • 26
• 24
• 27

• 28

Guirdil Bay

• 7

• 6

• 8

Kilmory River

• 29

• 5
• 4
• 3

NG

• 22

• 23

30 • 31

• 32

Loch Scresort

33
34 • 35

36

Orval

• 9

Ard Nev

• 10

Rum

• 1

• 2

37

• 11

• 16
12 • 15
13 • 17
14

Hallival

Trollaval

Askival

95

Relief

700m
600m
500m
400m
300m
200m
100m
0m

1km
1:120000

• 21

Sound of Rum

• 18

• 19

• 20

90

Airigh na Maith-innse	1	Glen Shellesder	8	Kinloch	30	Port na Caranean	36
Ard Nev	9	Guirdil	6	Kinloch Castle	32	Protest Rock/ Rocking Stone	23
Ard Nev	10	Harris	15	Laundry	25	Salisbury's Dam	22
Bagh na h-Uamha	37	Harris 1	16	Limekiln	34	Samhnan Insir	28
Bloodstone Hill	4	Harris 2	12	Loch Monica	11	Sgorr Mor	3
Camas Pliasgaig	29	Harris Lodge	17	New Mausoleum	14	Sgorr Reidh	2
Carn nan Dobhran Bhig	35	Inbhir Ghil	18	Old Mausoleum	13	Shellesder	7
Creag nan Stairdean	5	Kilmory	24	Old pier	33		
Dibidil	21	Kilmory Lodge	26	Papadil	20		
Farm Fields, Kinloch	31	Kilmory River	27	Papadil Lodge	19		

NM   30   35   40   45

85

Contains OS data © Crown copyright 2016

Chapter Five
Rum

Rum is the largest of the four islands and by far the most visually dramatic and foreboding. It is hard not to be over-awed by the sheer size and hostility of the bare mountains and cliff faces that dominate its coastline. Rugged and unfriendly, Rum covers some 10,400ha (around 40 square miles) consisting mostly of volcanic slopes best suited only to upland grazing and deer, with a few patches of habitable green land in the river estuaries.[1] The name 'Rum' may have Gaelic origins, signifying 'roominess or capacity',[2] or possibly the Norse root *Rúm-oy* or variant meaning 'roomy island', both essentially referring to the island's relative size. However, despite the extent of the island's landscape, cultivation has always been limited to those few isolated coastal glens that reluctantly condescend to agriculture. Cultivation has always been small scale – so small, that in the mid 18th century ploughs were rarely used, and these 'little fields on the sea shore' were worked entirely by spade.[3] Balanced against a zenith population of 443 souls at the end of the 18th century (below) this low level of agriculture implies intense pressure on subsistence latterly and assumes a reliance on alternative resources. It also explains the ubiquity of lazy beds on every conceivable patch of useable soil, still evident on the landscape today.

Throughout history the wilderness nature of the landscape forced successive settlement into those same few areas of good land, either obscuring or eradicating those which went before. The surviving archaeological evidence is commensurately reduced. However, there is one feature of Rum for which settlement and the ability to cultivate was unimportant, and which was a major prehistoric asset – namely 'bloodstone', a hard hydrothermal rock which crops out in the mountains (Bloodstone Hill) at the west, and which can be worked in much the same way as flint. Small lithic artefacts could (and still can) be produced in a range of colours – cream, dark green and purple. It was a resource exploited from Mesolithic times onwards and may have done much to make Rum important even 10,000 years ago, irrespective of the island's awkward geography and difficult access by primitive boat.

From later periods of prehistory there is a possible group of hut-circles, but no evidence of standing stones, burial chambers or early landscapes, although little excavation has ever taken place. A few surviving cairns on the coastal edge and three coastal forts are the major physical testimony to Rum's prehistory. In later centuries the presence of early Christianity is shown by two carved crosses and a likely chapel site, and there are foundations of several groups of dwellings together with related shielings which may have their origins in the Middle Ages, and which are common elsewhere in the Highlands. However, among the Small Isles, Rum is unique in having deer traps – lengths of walling and adapted scree, covering vast tracts of mountainous landscape; these are almost certainly of medieval date, and give the island a distinctive historical identity.

In later medieval and pre-Clearance times settlement was confined predominantly to fertile areas, notably around Kinloch to the east, Kilmory at the north, Harris at the south-west, and Papadil at the south-east – four small oases in a volcanic desert –

Fig 5.1 Rum, showing locations mentioned in this chapter.
GV006122

Fig 5.2 The mountains of Rum – 'the wildest and most repulsive of all the islands', according to one traveller. HES DP094981

Fig 5.3 The distinctive peaks of the Rum Cuillin, once the roots of a volcano. HES DP094973

optimising the richer, but limited soils. The presence of hundreds of stone shieling huts scattered throughout the mountains points to a pastoral economy that was obliged to utilise every available source of grazing to fulfil domestic needs. These were the 'ancient habits' alluded to by James Macdonald on behalf of the Department of Agriculture, who criticised the islanders for failing to absorb a more modern approach to sheep farming.[4] The enforced Clearances which had occurred by 1828, and which are remembered in a number of emotive accounts, not only resulted in a calamitous exodus of population, but caused most of these shielings to become abandoned: the way of life to which they belonged had become obsolete. By the second half of the 19th century, after a period of unsuccessful sheep farming undertaken on an industrial scale, the island became used as a sporting estate. The great and the good arrived to catch fish and shoot deer, and many of the residual inhabitants became caught up in the estate infrastructure. A gentrified sporting landscape remains the dominant visual factor today through its scale, durability and bizarre character, not least being the dominance of Kinloch Castle constructed in the earlier

part of the 20th century. The perceived history of the island is inevitably an imbalanced one as a result.

Rum did not receive a great deal of attention from early travellers, partly through difficulty of access and partly through the hostile terrain where, like other islands in the group in the late 18th century, the roads were 'almost in a state of nature'.[5] At this time the largely untamed character of its landscape had also been encapsulated in an alternative name Riogachd na Forraiste Fiadhaich ('Kingdom of the Wild Forest'), although this was a name used only from the sea.[6] In 1824, one storm-bound visitor described Rum as 'the wildest and most repulsive of all the islands'.[7] Later still, the Reverend Donald McLean's 1845 description of the island noted that it had a 'rough, abrupt and craggy appearance' with a 'bold and wild' coastline, and with the south and west sides being surrounded by 'one continued rampart of rock'.[8]

There are similar descriptive passages in the writings of many who passed through, including Martin (in

1695),[9] Walker (in 1764),[10] Pennant (in 1772),[11] and Knox (in 1786),[12] and these have been discussed at length elsewhere.[13] Few visitors had anything good to say, key elements of distaste being the weather, local hygiene, and the midges; their works provide little more than a framework for understanding contemporary island life. One recorded story, no doubt containing some element of truth, relates to an islander who perpetrated some serious misdemeanour – he was consequently tied naked to the ground on the shore where he was bitten to death by the midges, and from where his groans are said still to be heard at night.[14] The visitor descriptions are otherwise mostly in keeping with the formulaic travel literature of the time; they have a museological flavour, treating the islanders and their culture as curiosities. However, some accounts offer the benefit of population figures (Fig 5.4) which, despite potential inaccuracies, can be used to demonstrate general trends and are tabulated with official census returns added for completeness. Together they show a population growing through the 18th century, peaking in the late 18th and early 19th centuries, followed by a catastrophic decline after the final Clearances of 1828.

Two early accounts stand out above the others, although these both belong to the 19th century: that of Edwin Waugh, a Lancastrian writer and poet who visited Rum for several months in 1882, and the geologist Hugh Miller who spent time studying the rock formations of the island from his yacht *The Betsey* in the 1840s. Waugh's volume *The Limping Pilgrim* (1883), written in the gentlemanly laid-back manner of his genre, provides detailed descriptions of the landscape, its people and their living conditions, and is unusually rich in social perception.[15] His work also cites a poignant eye-witness account of the Clearances on the island in 1826. By contrast, Miller's *Cruise of the Betsey* (1862) contains fewer items of cultural interest but is written with passioned intensity in describing the island's geology, geomorphology and lithology; it includes a chapter devoted almost exclusively to bloodstone.[16] There is a third, later, account – an autobiography by an islander called Archie Cameron who recounts his boyhood in Rum in the years before the First World War.[17] Perhaps not so much a history as a social commentary, it presents a vivid picture of island infrastructure and how resources were managed and exploited. But particularly, it lays bare the rigid class structure of islanders and gentry during the exotic years of Castle life in the early 20th century. The research of

Year	Population	Source
1764	304	McNeill (1764/5)
1768	302	Stat Acct (1796)
1772	325	Pennant (1776)
1786	300	Knox (1787)
1796	443	Stat Acct (1796)
1811	350	Macdonald (1811)
1821	394	Census
1831	134	Census
1841	124	Census
1851	161	Census
1861	161	Census
1871	81	Census
1881	130	Census
1882	70	Waugh (1883)

Fig 5.4 Recorded population figures for Rum.

John Love, a modern naturalist, also merits mention here: he lived on the island for many years and can be credited for much of our understanding of Rum's natural and historic environment,[18] not least the deer traps[19] and shielings,[20] which he studied and published in detail.

Early Prehistory

The earliest site in the whole of the Small Isles, and probably one of the earliest in Scotland, can be found at Farm Fields, Kinloch, at the head of Loch Scresort on the eastern side of the island. The site dates back to the 8th millennium BC and was discovered in 1983 from a scatter of stone flakes visible in the soil.[21] Subsequent excavation recovered over 100,000 such waste objects and cores, about half of them being of bloodstone brought across from the west of the island, and corresponding in shape to similar types of flint-working debris known from contemporary sites in both England and Scotland. This was an activity site where tools were fashioned or re-worked and used seasonally by nomadic peoples concerned primarily with hunting. Lines of stake holes in the ground associated with pits of unknown function can be interpreted as wind breaks or temporary shelters where the stone was worked. The location, at the head of the Loch, is well suited to people landing in small boats across from Skye and the mainland. Radiocarbon dating of hazelnuts on the site suggests that the site was used sporadically for up to four

thousand years, and into the Neolithic period, before it became overtaken by cultivation. The exploitation of bloodstone was undoubtedly Rum's attraction, and the distribution of bloodstone artefacts found in other parts of Scotland and almost certainly sourced to Rum promotes the island as a place of national rather than of local importance. Worked bloodstone has been recovered from archaeological sites up to 90km away on the mainland, Skye and Lewis and may indicate the scope of a prehistoric exchange network of materials current at the time.[22] This is an extraordinary piece of knowledge, given the paucity of other information available to us on Scotland's earliest inhabitants some ten thousand years ago.

Bloodstone could be exploited from two locations on the island, either from the main outcrop itself on the precipitous north face of Creag nan Stairdean (better known as Bloodstone Hill)[23] from where it could be taken in rough form and worked elsewhere; or less formally, from beach deposits. The principal outcrop is a solid band around 23cm thick not far from the summit, but pieces of bloodstone can also be procured in the scree below; there is a former

Fig 5.5 Bloodstone Hill from the south-west. The appeal of the bloodstone extracted from Rum during prehistoric times extended beyond the Small Isles. HES DP095090

Fig 5.6 Bloodstone is used today to make jewellery: these polished fragments show some of the colours and veining. The largest fragment shown is approximately 2cm in length. John Hunter

Fig 5.7 Survey work being carried out at Shellesder with Bloodstone Hill in the background. HES DP111083

quarry shown on the 1st edition OS 6-inch map surveyed in 1877, but this is no longer evident on the ground. Although the primary outcrop occurs in the mountains, fragments of bloodstone form a significant fraction of the beach pebbles in Guirdil Bay adjacent to the outcrop on the north-east. That part of the coastline (Sgorr Mor) was visited in 1797 by E D Clarke, Professor of Mineralogy at Cambridge, who described '… the most beautiful fossils I ever saw. In a few minutes we walked over a sufficient quality to supply half the museums in Europe.' He describes agates, jaspers, zeolites, crystals and spar, commenting specifically on the variety of colours.[24] Secondary deposits such as these may also have been a more easily accessible source of prehistoric supply and one approachable by boat as opposed to taking the tortuous trek through the mountains. In fact, there is every reason to believe that prehistoric activity was water – as opposed to

land – based. Other than Bloodstone Hill all the prehistoric remains are coastal, and the terrestrial resources, such as they were, lay concentrated in the few green estuaries around the island fringe. There was no need to travel further inland. That said, we have little understanding of the symbolic value attached to Bloodstone Hill itself, or whether bloodstone exploited from the mountain was considered to be of greater significance than bloodstone pebbles collected from the shore. We can only guess as to how 'ownership' of the outcrop may have been undertaken, whether exploitation of this exotic material was controlled, or the extent to which the mountain may have been revered. Given that flint was also available, bloodstone was clearly 'special' and its wide distribution suggests a more intrinsic value than simply that of pretty colours.

The continued exploitation of bloodstone at Farm Fields through the Neolithic gives some wider context to the three likely Neolithic burial cairns in different parts of the island, at Guirdil on the north-west coast,[25] at Kilmory at the north,[26] and at Harris at the south-west.[27] All have been eroded or damaged in some way by robbing. The Kilmory example is

Fig 5.8 The surviving burial cairn on the sea edge at Harris. A modern cairn has been constructed on top. HES DP234202

turf-covered and has a diameter of around 6.5m with obvious disturbance at the top, and the Guirdil cairn is larger but distorted by two small structures which have been built using the cairn stones, one structure being located on the edge of the cairn itself. The largest is the Harris cairn with a diameter of 12m. Two large disturbances in the surface suggest that this too has been heavily robbed. Some further continuity might be assumed from a group of three possible hut-circles of likely Bronze Age date located some 500m distant. Their outlines are unclear as a result of undergrowth and the construction of a later sheepfold built from the remains, but two of the huts were likely to have been around 10m in diameter and the third somewhat smaller. Possible traces of associated field systems in the form of lengths of dyke are located nearby. These are currently the only potential prehistoric settlement features on Rum but without excavation they remain, in the words of the Commission surveyors, 'unconvincing'.

Later Prehistory

Three monuments – at Shellesder, Papadil and Kilmory – have been interpreted as coastal forts, and all three are sited near places which were once populated. This would chime well with the theory that forts were defined areas of refuge for local communities under threat, but pre-supposes that the tradition of settlement stretched back to the Iron Age. Equally, the forts may be expressions of local wealth and standing, and constructed to impress rather than defend. In each case, the construction involved the modification and emphasis of a natural landscape promontory, their presence indicating an organised Iron Age society on Rum, probably in the latter half of the first millennium BC. All three forts stand at the edge of pre-Clearance townships, and while it may fairly be supposed that the Iron Age populations responsible for the construction of the forts and for whom they would have provided a place of refuge probably lived and farmed in much the same area, any surviving evidence has either been destroyed by or obscured beneath later settlement.

The Shellesder fort[28] is situated on a rocky promontory overlooking the Shellesder Burn, with a surface area of some 44m by 30m truncated by an

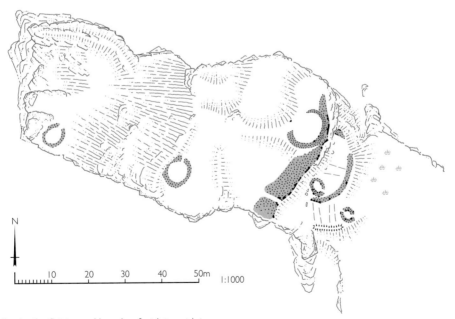

Fig 5.9–10 At Shellesder the flat-topped Iron Age fort juts out into the sea. The plan of the Shellesder fort shows the drystone walling across the promontory neck, three circular internal structures and further buildings on the outside. HES DP234199, GV006123

Fig 5.11 The fertile area of Papadil showing the ruined farmhouse at the mouth of the loch and the remains of the later Lodge adjacent to the plantation at the top. The fort, barely visible, sits on the uppermost terrace of the promontory at the bottom of the photograph. HES DP094980

arc of drystone walling cutting across the neck of the promontory. The wall is over 3m in thickness and still stands to a height of over 1m, with a narrow entrance at one end. Inside the enclosure (Fig 5.10) are two terraces containing the remains of three stone-walled huts: one oval, one circular, and the third visible only as a turf-covered spread of stones enclosing a roughly circular area. All three enclosed areas are approximately 6m to 8m in diameter, but it is not clear whether they relate to the original structure or not. On the landward side of the wall are the foundations of two small circular drystone huts. It is unclear how these might relate to the fort itself; they may more appropriately be associated with lazy beds in the vicinity.

The fort at Papadil[29] occupies the highest point of a rocky ridge, protected by sea cliffs on the western side, and by steep slopes at the east. Landward access is made along the spine of a ridge which rises in a series of terraces. The approach was once barred by a wall (now reduced to a band of rubble some 2m thick) with two possible entrances, one at the east, and one at the north-east corner. The irregular route of this wall results from the presence of natural rocky outcrops which were incorporated into the wall line, effectively joining them together. The enclosed area is substantial, roughly triangular in shape, with maximum dimensions of approximately 80m by 45m; it contains no obvious internal features. In the vicinity, at the north end of the nearby loch, the suggestion of Iron Age settlement is emphasised by the discovery of Iron Age pottery from within a natural cave which also contained rich midden deposits.[30] The final fort, at Kilmory[31] occupies a precipitous coastal promontory accessed across a narrow neck less than 10m wide, surmounted by a wall almost 4m thick built on natural rock (Fig 5.12). The enclosed area is relatively small at 25m by 12m and, like the fort at Papadil, is visually featureless inside.

Fig 5.12 The promontory fort at Kilmory, which uses Rum's north coast as a natural defence. HES DP234195

Early Christian and Viking

Early Christianity reached the islands on the western coast of Scotland from the Columban mission on Iona during the 6th century and its penetration into western Scotland, and into the Small Isles in particular, has been discussed in detail in a number of other works.[32] It is reasonable to assume that there was a Christian presence on Rum from around that time, probably following the Celtic model of monasticism. The significant place-name element in Kilmory (*Cille* – chapel) is of Gaelic origin and is relatively common throughout the Western Isles; it also occurs on neighbouring Canna (*A'Chill*) and Muck (*Kiel*). At Kilmory there is a raised irregularly shaped burial enclosure[33] measuring approximately 15m by 12m, revetted by a drystone wall (Fig 5.14), among the deserted buildings of the township which was evacuated in 1828. It contains a cross-marked pillar stone of the 7th or 8th century and may represent the ecclesiastical site denoted by Blaeu (after Pont) on his map (Fig 1.22) of the late 16th century (although confusingly Pont shows the island upside down, with Kilmory at the south). The carving is in shallow relief, on one face, with a long-shafted four-petalled 'marigold' cross surmounted by an incised Latin cross, and on the

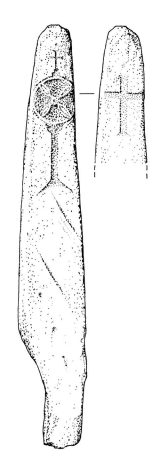

Fig 5.13 Drawings of the cross-marked pillar stone at Kilmory, showing the different design on each side. HES SC406083

Fig 5.14 The enclosed burial ground within the abandoned township of Kilmory, photographed in 1925. HES SC1467753

other face with a sunken Latin cross (Fig 5.13).[34] The two cross faces have been the source of some confusion: in the late 19th century T S Muir, a visiting antiquary interested in Early Christian activity, recorded 'a slender pillar incised with a plain cross',[35] but a visit by Commission staff almost 70 years later described it quite differently as 'a cross with expanding arms set saltire-wise',[36] implicitly dismissing Muir's description completely. It was not until relatively recently that it became apparent that Muir and the Commission had each been inspecting different sides of the same fallen cross, turning it over as they left to protect the carved surface and not noticing the other cross on the opposite face. A fuller account of this debacle has been detailed by Love.[37]

There are no visible remains of the associated chapel at Kilmory, although a chapel on Rum is mentioned by Martin at the end of the 17th century,[38] and 'the ruins of a church' (location unspecific) are recorded by Pennant.[39] An ecclesiastical building is shown at Kilmory on Langlands' map of 1810 (Fig 5.21); the OS survey for the first 6-inch edition identified a former burial ground there in 1877, and Muir describes 'a chapel, of which only some obscure traces remain' a few years later.[40] Neither chapel nor burial ground are depicted on later OS map editions. Waugh's visit of 1882 describes a church, but in Kinloch and built 'like a haystack with two windows'; it also doubled up as a school and was timber-built, and therefore presumably did not appear on any maps.[41] The modern school now sits on the same site.

A second pillar stone was discovered on the beach at Bagh na h-Uamha, on the south-east coast of the island in 1977. It was nearly 1.5m in height and depicted an incised equal-armed cross with forked terminals on a short pedestal.[42] It has tentatively been associated with Beccan of Rum, who is recorded as having died in 677 and who has been identified with the anchorite of the same name. Beccan was a prominent scholar and poet in the Columban community in the 630s.[43] The carving probably dates to the 7th century. Local legend asserts that a large rock known as 'The Priest's Stone' near the old pier in Loch Scresort is where Beccan tied up his boat when he landed for the first time. Possibly related to the pillar stone at Bagh na h-Uamha ('Bay of the Cave') is a nearby shallow cave which gives the bay its name and which contained exposed shell midden, a hearth, and a bone or ivory gaming piece, possibly of Norse

Fig 5.15 The early Christian pillar stone found at Bagh na h-Uamha. HES SC406082

character. The precise context of the gaming piece is unclear; some sources associate it with a nearby cist (unlocated), but the formal record states that 'it was found in a cave' and presented to the National Museum in 1943–4 by Lady Bullough.[44]

The place-name 'Papadil' belongs to a small group of locations in the Northern and Western Isles which contain the 'Papa' ('priest') prefix, here meaning 'priests valley', indicating the presence of holy men in a defined location. The word is of Norse origin, itself suggesting some element of Norse contact, although there is little archaeological evidence or documentation other than place-names to support a Norse presence on the island. The Norse place-names tend to be applied to the major features on Rum such as the mountain peaks of Hallival ('Mountain with Ledges'), Askival ('Spear-like Mountain') or Trollaval ('Mountain of the

Fig 5.16 Dibidil, Trollaval and the slopes of Askival. These Norse names suggest that the island's prominent features were familiar to Norse seafarers. HES DP094989

Trolls') and also to coastal glens such as Dibidil ('Deep Valley') which can be seen from the sea and may have been used as markers rather than as indicators of Norse settlement.

Research elsewhere indicated that groups of 'Papa' were often allocated specific areas of good quality land by secular overlords in order to facilitate monastic activities. The area around Papadil shows multi-period occupation, and the land is fertile. It may also be relevant that the loch and surrounds are almost invisible from the sea. The locality includes a coastal fort which might be seen as a defined parcel of land gifted to the Church for eremitic purposes – perhaps a gesture by the secular power of the day in order to boost personal prestige. There are a number of structural remains and other features on the ground, and these have hitherto been interpreted as secular; there is no evidence of a burial ground. None of the early maps, including the 1st edition OS map surveyed in 1877, depict ecclesiastical activity. This would suggest that any Early Christian community there may have been eremitic, with a relatively short life, whereas the community at Kilmory, a 'main' settlement on the island, may have been home to a number of monks or holy men dedicated to conversion in the surrounding area, later flourishing as a settlement in its own right.

Medieval and Post-Medieval Landscapes
Deer Hunting

On the western side of the island there are three substantial landscape features two of which at least might be interpreted as deer traps. Of all the Small Isles, Rum with its extensive landscape of mountains was the only one sufficiently large to have supported a permanent stock of deer. Despite their inaccessibility, these supposed deer traps have merited some antiquarian interest and have been the subject of specific island comment,[45] as well as having been discussed within the wider context of medieval hunting.[46]

Descending to the foot of the scree slopes below and to the south-west of the summit of Orval are the remains of the best example.[47] This comprises an area of cleared ground defined by two dykes of loose rubble that converge as they head down slope to the south-east. The dykes funnel firstly into an oblong enclosure and then drop down into an oval enclosure as the ground flattens out (Figs 5.17, 5.18). This is a vast monument: the funnel runs down for several hundred metres; it survives sporadically over that distance and appears to

Fig 5.17 Survey work on the loosely piled stones that constituted the enclosure end of the deer trap. HES DP165369

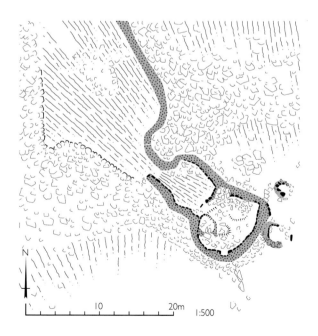

Fig 5.18 This plan of the Orval deer trap shows how the deer were forced into stone enclosures from which they were unable to escape. HES GV006124

Fig 5.19 Looking down the funnel into the Orval Deer trap
HES DP234204

incorporate patches of scree as it drops downhill. This method of hunting involved driving the deer along the top of Orval, then down the slope into the funnel which became progressively narrower as it descended. Patches of scree may have acted as part of the funnel edge on the basis that deer are reluctant to move over loose stones.

At the bottom the deer were forced through a gap barely a metre wide, where the two walls were pinched together, and entered an oblong enclosure measuring some 8m by 5m. The inside of this has a vertical face, in places still surviving to a height of 1.7m, with a loose rubble spread packed on the outside. From here the deer could be manoeuvred into the slightly larger oval enclosure which was of similar construction, but surviving to a height of 2m in places, through a narrow gap in the wall. A hut has been inserted into one corner of the enclosure, and there are traces of at least three further huts amongst the scree and stone litter outside.

Once trapped in the high-walled enclosures the deer were unable to escape; the narrow entrances allowed only one animal through at a time. This not only made a return into the funnel more easily preventable, but also made them easier to kill in a confined space.

It is unclear how the system operated in detail, but the upper, oblong, enclosure may have been used as a secure holding area, and the lower, oval space one into which the animals could be individually driven and slaughtered. The adjacent huts may have been associated with the slaughtering process, or used to hold equipment.

This method of hunting is well described in the late 18th century *Statistical Account*:

> On each side of a glen, formed by two mountains, stone dykes were begun pretty high in the mountains, and carried to the lower part of the valley, always drawing nearer, till within 3 or 4 feet of each other. From this narrow pass, a circular space was enclosed by a stone wall, of a height sufficient to confine the deer; to this place they were pursued and destroyed.

The writer, the Reverend Donald McLean, noted that one of these traps still survived, implying that there were others known on the island,[48] an observation continued in the subsequent *New Statistical Account* of 1845.[49] The tradition appears to have been of long standing. Martin Martin refers to 'hundreds of deer' on the mountains in the late 17th century,[50] but the earliest reference to this type of deer hunting (known as the tinchell) belongs to the account of Monro (who additionally refers to a similar example on Jura); he also comments on the 'abundant deer' on the high mountains in 1549.[51] This mid 16th century date of writing suggests that this local method of hunting goes back to medieval times at least, although it was a method that would appear to have been outmoded by the use of firearms. Under the constrained circumstances of deer capture, the use of firearms would seem to have been considered both unnecessary and rather unsporting, although when Edward Clarke was taken to Orval in 1797 he was told that men with muskets shot the deer as they entered the 'pit'.[52]

It was also a method of hunting which required considerable manpower, as endorsed by Taylor's account in his *Penniless Pilgrim* written in 1618, which describes a tinchell on the Earl of Mar's estate on the Scottish mainland.[53] This required 'five or six hundred men' spread out over an area of up to 10 miles in order to round up the deer. The deer were

then chased down the glen with the help of hounds in order for the 'lords and gentlemen' to lie in wait in order to slay them at the valley bottom. The Rum enterprise was undoubtedly on a smaller scale, but it would, nonetheless, have required a significant active population in order for the hunt to be effective. It must have been a well-planned operation since the site is a good two hours' walk from the nearest (modern) track. Given the suggestion in the *Statistical Accounts* that the methods were no longer in use on the island at a time when the contemporary population stood between approximately 400 and 500 (figures which also include women and children), and that the recorded (or estimated) population of the island (Fig 5.4) before that time was significantly lower, it would seem probable that the traps are unlikely to have been used since the 16th century at the very latest. One of the earliest references to the island, from the late 16th century, seems to suggest that it was 'commodious only for hunting of deer' rather than anything else.[54]

Another example on Rum, and one which may also have been known to McLean, is situated on the north flank of Ard Nev,[55] only 1km north-east of the Orval trap. Here, it is possible to interpret a similar

Fig 5.20 The question remains as to whether the long walling and associated chambers along the coastline at Sgorr Reidh constitute a deer trap, or hold some other function. HES DP234198

configuration, albeit partial, with two lengths of low dyke discernible in the scree leading down to two sets of trap, of different constructional phases, at the bottom. Parts of the scree appear to have been cleared and piled up on either side in lieu of more formal walling. Neither dyke presents an obstacle on the uphill side, presumably on the basis that the deer would be reluctant to move from cleared ground on to the scree. At the bottom the later (eastern) trap comprises a funnel about 40m long which narrows down from 20m to 8m in width between lines of scattered or loosely piled stones. At the lower end, the ground drops sharply over a slight revetment into two small enclosures, only half the size of those at Orval. The earlier (western) trap is of similar construction but with fragments of only one enclosure surviving at its lower end. Much of the end of the original 'funnel' has been destroyed by the later trap.

Another possible contender is located to the west, on the steep cliff top at Sgorr Reidh overlying Wreck Bay.[56] This is a more unusual in that it consists of a stone dyke running parallel with the cliff edge for several hundred metres, interspersed with at least seventeen small roughly circular drystone cells set at intervals along its length. It is difficult to credit the need for such an edifice in one of the most remote and dangerous locations on the island, although there is an abundant supply of suitable building materials available. The cells were corbelled and with sunken floors; their circular form may have been a response to their elevated and exposed situation. It is hard to envisage this being used for herding deer as it could only result in them being forced over the cliff and into the sea some 300m below. This idea has little to commend it, although it has been suggested that the raised beach at the foot of the cliff, accessed by a gully, would allow the recovery of carcasses.[57] The idea that the cells were built as hides (*settis*) for the hunters to shoot the deer as they rushed past is equally far-fetched. More plausible, but still not entirely satisfactory given the sure-footed nature of the livestock, is Love's interpretation of the dyke being designed to prevent domestic stock from falling to their death in the search for good grazing during the summer months;[58] this might go some way to explain the function of the cells as shielings. His view that the lack of mounding below the cells and the relatively high level of preservation might indicate a relatively recent construction is worth bearing in mind.[59]

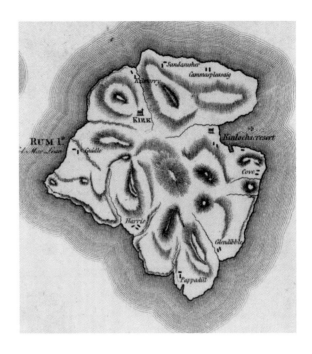

Fig 5.21 Langlands' 1801 map illustrates the clusters of buildings on Rum's compact areas of arable land. © National Library of Scotland. Licensor Scran

Townships

The Clearances on Rum took place between 1826 and 1828, and while some monuments and features firmly belong to a period later than this, the majority of sites are not precisely datable and could easily straddle this important social boundary. Shieling huts, for example, which on Rum numbered almost 400,[60] are notoriously difficult to date. Black cattle and sheep were a key part of the domestic subsistence economy well before the Clearances, and several hut sites which display a depth of chronology could easily have their roots in the medieval period or earlier. Like the stone dwellings in townships, they were subject to change and rebuilding during their lifetimes. Some useful information can be gleaned from visitor accounts but, like the *Statistical Account*, most of these sources belong to the 18th century, and to the latter part at that. The Clearances may have left behind little more than the foundations of abandoned dwellings, and Waugh could only trace 'the faint outlines of these ruined habitations, here and there, overgrown with grass and moss, and wild lichens'.[61] These presumably represent the type of dwelling described by Pennant a century earlier. He alluded specifically to Kinloch,[62] but the structures are likely to be typical of those elsewhere on the island 'built in a singular manner, with walls very thick and low, with the roofs or thatch reaching little beyond the inner edge, so that they serve as benches for the lazy inhabitants'. One, he noted, had a chimney and windows which distinguished it from the others.[63]

A number of clusters of structural remains have been recorded on various parts of the Rum landscape; these represent the small communities or townships which may have had their origins in medieval times and which survived through, and in some cases beyond, the traumas of the Clearances. Macfarlane's *Geographical Collections* (Mitchell 1907) includes a reference, probably from around the 1630s, which refers to 'two tounes' at that time, one at Kilmore (Kilmory)[64] and one at Glenhairie (Harris).[65] McNeill's 1764/5 census later identifies seven settlement centres and gives population figures for each: at Kilmory (84 persons in 17 families); Sandyness (Samhnan Insir, 43 persons in 7 families);[66] Loch (Kinloch, 46 persons in 8 families); Harress (Harris, 74 persons in 15 families); Papadil (12 persons in 3 families); Guirdhil (Guirdil, 22 persons in 5 families),[67] and Cove (unidentified but likely to be Bagh na h-Uamha on the east coast, 20 persons in 3 families)[68] indicating that the township dominance of Kilmory and Harris had continued into the later 18th century. Langlands' 1801 map of Argyllshire depicts a number of small clusters of houses spread throughout the island together with a kirk and large (laird's) house located at Kinloch. It includes locations other than those mentioned in the 1764/5 census suggesting the development of occasional settlement away from the main townships. In addition, field survey has located a small number of individual farmsteads which can still be identified on the ground, often with associated outbuildings, enclosures and cultivation strips. These are of unknown date, and are not recorded by Langlands. Many, however, appear on the 1st edition OS 6-inch map and are likely to be later and associated with the sheep rather than with earlier townships.

Some of the clusters depicted by Langlands may represent the 'little hamlets' seen by Pennant in 1772, but there may have been smaller settlements in addition to house the population of over 300 divided into the 59 families that Pennant describes.[69] There is evidence from other islands (below) that groups of shielings might eventually evolve into more permanent forms of settlement to absorb population increases and land shortage. All but one of Langlands' settlements can be roughly located on the ground. The foundations of six rectangular buildings adjacent to an area of cultivation strips are evident at Bagh na h-Uamha on the east coast and probably represent the settlement at 'Cove' depicted by Langlands. At Camas Pliasgaig ('Cammaspleasaig')[70] on the north-east coast are the remains of eight rectangular buildings, also with associated cultivation strips, and at Dibidil ('Glendibble')[71] on the south-east coast are the remains of two heavily robbed rectangular buildings (Fig 5.16) adjacent to the stream accessing the limited resources around the mouth of the river. There are a series of ruinous buildings and a later shepherd's cottage at Guirdil ('Guidle') (Fig 5.22) on the north-west coast where, in 1797, Clarke wrote of 'A few huts, with a small boat or two, drawn up upon the beach',[72] and at Samhnan Insir ('Sandanisher') at the north of the island (Fig 5.23) there are at least four buildings, all partly buried in sand, as well as later occupation, all typically lying within a location severely constrained by a mountainous landscape.

Langlands' three remaining sites are at Papadil, Harris and Kilmory, the three 'main' settlement sites recorded later lying in the few available green coastal glens. Of these, evidence for the early township at Papadil ('Pappadill') is all but lost. Over half a century after the Clearances, in 1882, Waugh refers to it as 'a lonely spot' where 'James Chisholm and his family dwell in solitude by the side of a little lake'; this says much for the catastrophic effect of the earlier Clearances on the population.[73] Other than by boat Papadil (Fig 5.11) is probably the least accessible, yet seems to have been important in both the Iron Age and Early Christian periods. Former structures may have been dismantled to build the extant sheep dyke and the later farmstead; the latter sits at the mouth of the loch and comprises the remains of two buildings set on a terrace, both roofed at the time of the 1877 OS survey. The scattered remains of a single structure survive to the west, surrounded by lazy beds, and it is tempting to believe this may have been the chapel site implied by the 'Papa' place-name.

Fig 5.22 The 'few huts' recorded at Guirdil in 1797 may lie partly visible within the ruins of a later farmstead and enclosure.
HES DP165356

Fig 5.23 The area of Samhnan Insir, hemmed in by the mountains and the sea, was home to seven families in 1764. HES DP094857

Fig 5.24 Foundation remains of the two Harris settlements can be seen on terraces separated by the river valleys.
HES DP094977

Fig 5.25 John Love's notes and measured drawings provide an invaluable record of earlier landscapes on Rum. This pair of drawings outline the field systems at Harris (top), and the township buildings and enclosures (bottom). © John Love

The settlement at Harris can be divided into several discrete areas of which two are of particular note, both taking advantage of the low-lying, but limited fertile land on the coastal fringe. The first (known as Harris 1) comprises some 37 buildings, the majority measuring 5m to 10m in length and 2.5m to 4m in width between thick rubble-cored drystone walls, with associated dykes and lazy beds. Love's plans of the Harris settlement show a complex of dwelling houses with associated outbuildings (mostly byres), and associated enclosures sitting within an equally

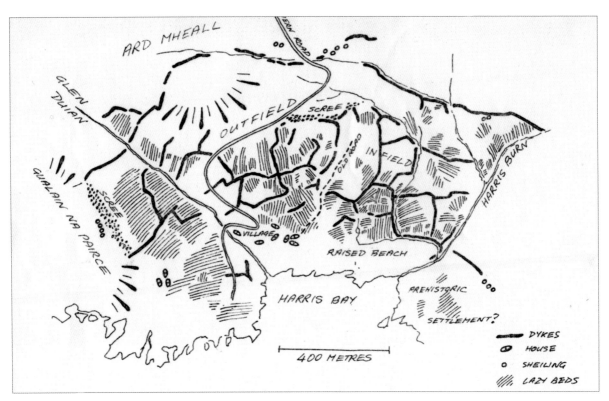

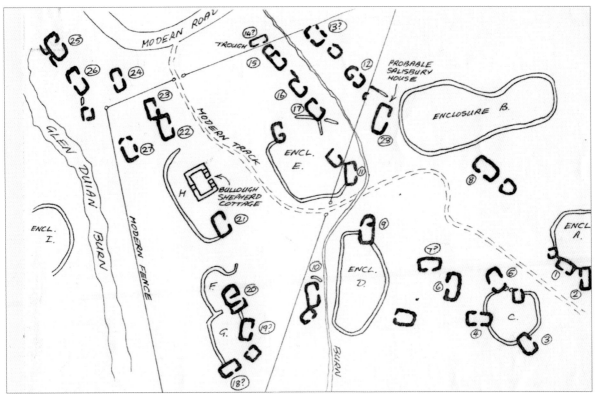

Fig 5.26 The 37 structures which comprise the Harris 1 township are spread across the lower terrace. HES DP234201

Fig 5.27 Survey plan of a small complex of buildings and an enclosure outlying the settlement at Harris 1. HES GV006125

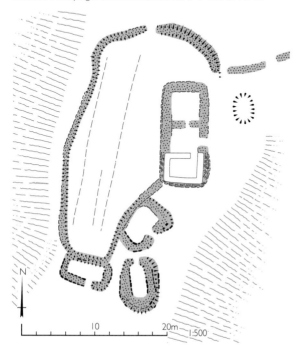

complex system of cultivation strips and field dykes.[74] These cultivation strips around the township are largely undisturbed by later activity; the township itself survives as rough turf-covered foundations (Fig 5.26) and cultivation strips. While many of the buildings probably relate to the immediately pre-Clearance period, at least five are earlier forms, and a small number probably later. One obvious group of buildings lies on a grass-grown ridge some 50m from the main concentration; it consists of a main structure with three ancillary buildings and an enclosure. The large building measures approximately 14m by 6.5m and has rounded corners with battered sides (Fig 5.27).

The second concentration of settlement (known as Harris 2) lies on a higher terrace and has been mutilated by later cultivation activity. There are at least ten buildings, one with an adjoining yard, with buildings ranging in size from 16.1m by 6.5m to 3.8m by 3.1m. In some instances collapse of the grass-grown foundations shows the presence of turf- or earthen-cored walls, quite different from those seen elsewhere, and possibly indicative of earlier construction. The range of building sizes here and at Kilmory (below) suggests different uses rather than simple variations of dwelling capacity, possibly a reflection of communal infrastructure. Only two

Fig 5.28 The grass-covered ruins and lazy beds at Harris, once housing over 70 islanders. HES DP234200

Fig 5.29 Survey plan of the Harris 2 settlement showing the density of cultivation lines, some overlying ruined dwellings to use all available land. HES GV006126

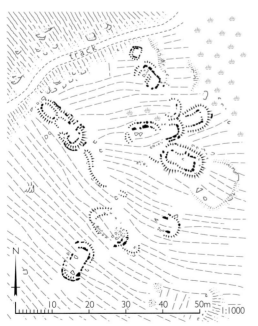

roofed buildings are shown at Harris on the 1st edition OS 6-inch map.

The final township, at Kilmory ('Kilmorry') comprises the remains of sixteen buildings and a burial ground ranged along the west side of the Kilmory River, staggered along a sunken road. The buildings are rectangular and vary in size from 10.5m by 3.5m to 3.5m by 2.7m with thick drystone walls, and with scattered cultivation strips in association. This is likely to be one of the earlier settlements: it features on Pont's mid 17th century map and may also have been a focus of Early Christian activity (above). None of the buildings in the main cluster of settlement are shown as roofed in the OS 1877 survey.

The *Statistical Account* notes a population in these townships peaking at around 440 at the end of the 18th century,[75] on an island 'much fitter for pasture than for crop'.[76] Pennant, writing at roughly the same time, presents a picture of a society of prehistoric character, if his detailed descriptions of threshing and grinding are anything to go by.[77] His observation that the islanders only produced about a quarter of their consumption of oats and bere (a type of barley) suggests that much was imported.[78] Compensation for this may have been in organised trade: there was a regular sale of peat to supply Canna and Muck; black

Fig 5.30 The remains of the Kilmory township lie mostly on the upper (west) side of the Kilmory River. The strangely shaped burial enclosure is in the centre of the image. HES DP094965

Fig 5.31 Part of the ruined township and burial ground at Kilmory. HES DP234203

cattle and horses were exported; goat hair was sent to Glasgow in order to make wigs that were shipped to America,[79] and the wool from the native sheep on Rum was recorded as being of exceptional quality and worth up to twice as much as wool from other sources at the markets near Inverness.[80] At this time the number of deer seems to have declined considerably, a phenomenon ascribed to the presence of eagles by Pennant,[81] and by the writer of the *Statistical Account*, who also blamed the loss of woodland shelter for the animals.[82] A main contributing factor, however, was probably the relatively large population needing to supplement local food sources, when venison was still both plentiful and accessible.

Any significant maritime trade was carried out through the only natural harbour on the island at the mouth of Loch Scresort where, according to a late 18th century account, a pier had been started but not yet finished,[83] although exactly when it was started is unclear. Elsewhere, the hostile shoreline limited the collection of kelp, but one possible site lies at Inbhir Ghil on the south-west coast of the island where the remains of an oval hut and other structural remains have been identified.[84] Local subsistence fishing

presumably occurred, and there is some evidence of organised commercial activity particularly with regard to herring, although it was noted that 'the inhabitants were ill-provided with fishing materials'.[85] This was an observation previously made by Knox, who records in 1786 how the inhabitants were packing herrings, although 'more might have been cured, if they had been provided with salt'.[86] Waugh records fish traps at Kinloch a century later, and other examples have been mooted at Kilmory,[87] but the dates of these are unknown. At Kinloch, the remains of a trap can be seen from the air showing an incomplete arc, broken in the centre below the water line at the north-west side of the bay (Fig 5.32);[88] there is also an artificial tidal pond in front of the school formed by an arc of low rubble walling on the south-west side. It may well be that either of these is the 'barrier of stones' noted by Cameron as he crossed the beach as a boy, and which was a (failed) attempt to create an oyster bed during the time of the castle.[89]

Shieling

More tangible remains of island life, but equally obscure in terms of their origins, are the shieling-huts which can be found scattered throughout the island. Love's study of these identified nearly 400 examples; more have been identified since, and his research and recording of these monuments is probably unequalled in the Highlands.[90] His notes and sketch plans from fieldwork (Fig 5.33) depict a range of configurations, set against an ecological background which allows them to be viewed not only in terms of their morphology, but also of their altitude, vegetation and degree of shelter. They typically lie around the 100m contour on the less steep slopes on the northern and western side of the island. The practice of transhumance which is shown by these small structures is suited to small communities and reflects the supervised grazing of domestic livestock on higher ground during the summer months. Many of the clusters of huts can be associated with specific townships; few of them lie more than two and a half miles from their settlement focus.[91] The large number of shielings on Rum is a response to the island's topography, one which is less acute on Eigg, Muck

Fig 5.32 The surviving stone walling of a fish trap can be seen projecting from the shore under the water in Scresort Bay.
HES DP094946

and Canna where the landfalls are less demanding. Rum was an island 'best calculated for rearing sheep, being wholly covered with hills and high mountains',[92] but the impact of sheep farming on an industrial scale introduced by the Clearances effectively made obsolete the system of domestic grazing represented by shielings. As such the majority of shielings can be confidently dated to pre-19th century times, although a small number may have continued as temporary shelters, or have even been built later. By the turn of the 20th century their use survived in memory only: Cameron recalls how, as a boy, his mother regaled him with stories of the 'wonderful life' at the shieling in her own childhood in Lewis when the cattle were taken to graze on the hills all summer. Boys from the various crofts looked after the herds while the girls undertook the milking and made the butter and cheese.[93]

The surviving shielings are all stone built and Love has been able to provide a coarse division into

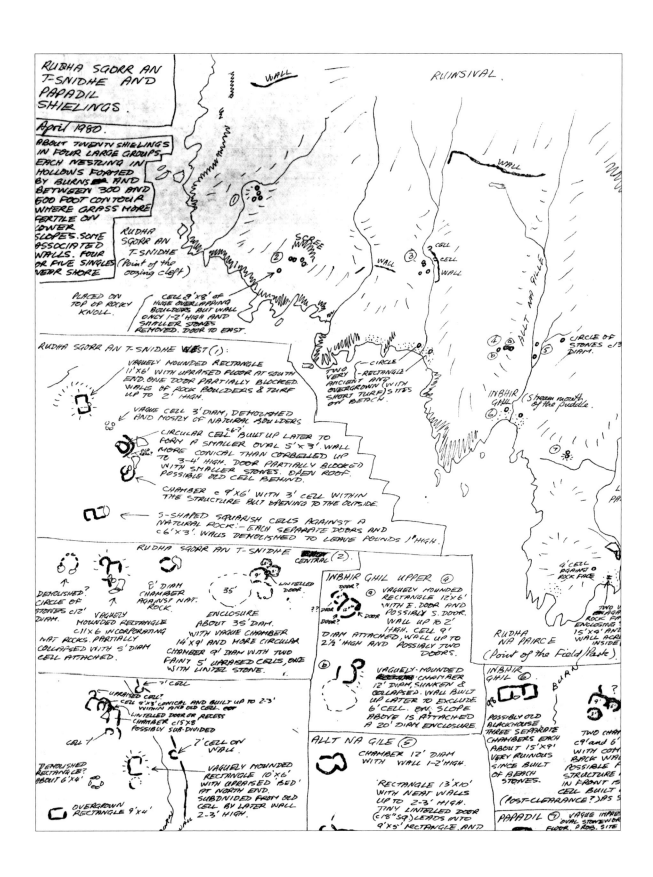

three constructional types: those which are cellular; those which are chambered, and those which are rectangular;[94] there is some evidence to suggest that this is also a chronological order, based according to the level of mounding below the surviving walls. Mounding reflects the persistent accumulation of organic materials, either from human midden, from animal waste, or collapsed organic building materials and is some indicator of longevity. Moreover, shielings tended to be constructed where supplies of stone were convenient, typically scree slopes or where natural rock outcrops could be utilised as part-walling. They might also utilise, or adapt, the walling of existing structures such as hut-circles, parts of which may still lie below the mounding and which push the origin of a site back into prehistory. This itself might explain why there are relatively few identifiable prehistoric monuments, particularly hut-circles, on the island.

All shielings were either stone-built throughout, notably the cellular examples several of which exhibited corbelling, or had stone foundations with a

Fig 5.34 The mounding of earth under shieling huts, such as here on Rum, can often reflect lengthy periods of use spanning many generations. HES DP234205

Fig 5.35 Survey plan of Harris shielings sheltered under an outcrop. HES GV006127

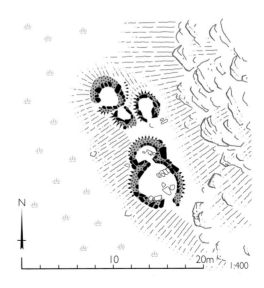

Fig 5.33 Part of a page of John Love's notebook showing his annotated plan of shielings at the south of the island, a few of the many he located. © John Love

mixture of stone and timber superstructures with a turf covering. In the latter the major timber components were subject to storm damage during the winter months and the beams taken back to the settlement for safe-keeping. Some shielings may also have been totally turf-built and not have survived at all between one year and the next, nor for later record; other stone versions may have vanished, being a convenient resource for dyke building.

Love identified four main concentrations of shielings, each broadly associated with a known township: at Kilmory (103 huts); Papadil (35 huts); Harris (124 huts), and Guirdil (114 huts) mostly running along the upper slopes of the river glens.[95] There are also huts on the north side of Kinloch, but only a single hut appears to be associated with settlement at the south and this itself may reflect on the nature of activities in that township. The shielings tend to cluster in groups of three to eight, with good examples near Harris[96] or nearby Loch Monica[97] where one corbelled example retained its roof until recently, but there are at least 80 huts which occur either singly or in pairs. The largest cluster is at Airigh na Maith-innse at the very west of the island and consists of 22 ruins.[98]

Fig 5.36 Shielings in Glen Shellesder utilised fallen rocks and exposed rock faces in their construction. HES DP234208

Fig 5.37 As is clear in this survey plan of shieling huts at Glen Shellesder, the buildings could take on many forms and configurations. HES GV006128

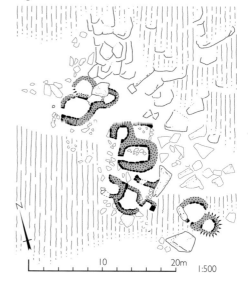

Fig 5.38 Looking out towards Scresort Bay, this rock may have been rolled and wedged into its present position as a protest against enforced emigration. © Sylvia Beaton

Detailed survey has taken place along the burn at Glen Shellesder on the north-west of the island where a group of at least sixteen scattered huts has been recorded extending across an area measuring 155m by 80m.[99] Most are to be found sheltered below rocky crags, utilising natural contours or rock faces. They are of drystone construction, built from stone acquired locally, and all but one stand to the north of a footpath that runs along the glen. Surviving heights vary, with the tallest over 1.5m. The huts range in shape and size: three are rectangular; six are subrectangular, and seven are oval. Almost half have adjoining cells and at least two are divided into sections. Configurations are presumably a reflection of function, with the cells or divisions more likely to be associated with the storage of dairy produce. Some that exhibit internal kerbing or division may represent bedding areas which might be filled with heather. Miller's enlightening visit to a shieling hut on Eigg in the 1880s is recounted in Chapter 1, but it makes the point that, even at that time, and well after the Clearances, shielings could still be a functioning part of the domestic economy in the Small Isles.

The Clearances

There are numerous historical accounts which attest to the catastrophic nature of the Clearances on Rum which took place between 1826 and 1828, and these have been thoroughly discussed by others.[100] The Clearances saw the island virtually depopulated to allow for the introduction of some 8,000 black-faced sheep. Less than two decades later the *New Statistical Account* recorded how 'the old and the young, the feeble and the strong, were all united in this general emigration.'[101] The main departure was to 'the distant wilds' of America leaving, according to the *Statistical Account*, only one family remaining behind. This was the time when the islanders were said to have rolled the huge stone known as the 'Protest Rock' (Fig 5.38) into a prominent position as an unmarked memorial to the centuries of traditions and memories that vanished from the island that day. It was made secure by wedging stones under the base. There is a conundrum here, however, in that this is also referred to as the 'Rocking Stone' which may have a quite different connotation and folklore background.[102] Rocking stones are regarded by some as being of ancient origin and synonymous with judgement by which the accused was made to touch the rock to determine guilt or innocence. Guilt was determined if the rock 'rocked' as a result. The names carved into a rock-face further up the glen are said to be those of the émigrés, but the earliest date shown is 1914, far too late for the Clearance events and more likely to belong to road builders whose work started in 1909 during the Bullough era. If there was such a thing as a protest rock it presumably lies lower in the glen by the old track used earlier in the 19th century.[103] That said, Archie Cameron carved his own name on the list, dated 14 July 1920, on his own expulsion from the island, and he added subsequent dates on his occasional visits.[104] Perhaps he was perpetuating some tradition that this was the place where enforced emigration was recorded.

Over 50 years later Waugh recorded a conversation with a shepherd who witnessed the emigration, although the shepherd's claim that 750 folk left the island that day is likely to have been rather exaggerated:

Fig 5.39 On Rum Archie Cameron is remembered in stone as well as in literature. © Sylvia Beaton

> *… on that day, when the people of the island were carried off in one mass, for ever, from the sea-girt spot where they had been born and bred, and where the bones of their forefathers were laid in the ancient graveyard of Kilmory … the wild outcries of the men, and the heart-breaking wails of the women and their children filled all the air between the mountainous shores of the bay; and that the whole scene was of such a distressful description that he should never be able to forget it to his dying day. But they went away wailing across the stormy sea; and the wild hills of their native isle will see them no more for ever …*[105]

The arrival of one such boat load of émigrés for Canada has been recorded by MacDougall as part of a wider demographic study: he lists by name 208 islanders arriving from Rum on the ship *St Lawrence* in 1828.[106] He also gives their ages, which range from infants to the elderly – the oldest male being 89 years of age (Alan McLean) and the oldest female 88 years of age (Marion McMillan) – describing them as 'a large portion of the whole island of Rum', and adding, rather ungraciously, that they landed in 'one promiscuous lump'.[107] Most

of those families he was able to trace appear to have dispersed, settled on farms and become absorbed into the local communities, although there are problems in establishing the exact numbers.[108]

On Rum, the emigration partly backfired in that it largely erased the island's already fragile subsistence infrastructure. The newly introduced sheep breed required attention and shepherds needed to be brought across from Skye; artisans including weavers, boat-builders, smiths, tailors and a shoemaker later followed, eventually leading to a population recorded as being around 100–130.[109] But even by the middle of the 19th century Miller was still able to record 'a landscape without figures',[110] – a phrase which Love later used as a title for his book on the island in 2001 – and a sentiment with which Waugh commiserated in 1882, there being 'no inn, no shop, no magistrate, no lawyer, no policeman, no doctor, except one or two wild-eyed Celtic herdsmen'.[111] Some dwellings continued in the traditional hubs, notably 'in the solitary nooks of the isle' at Kilmory, Harris and Papadil, with the rest being 'scattered about the shore of the [Scresort] bay'.[112]

Waugh's visit undertaken over half a century after the Clearances is of some interest here. His descriptions are both detailed and vivid, and he makes much store of local personalities. A cursory reading of his movements on Rum give the impression that he visited much of the island, but closer scrutiny of his rather illogical text suggests that he ventured little further than the southern part of Loch Scresort itself and avoided hills. He was not a well man. Recalling his route, he followed 'a wandering slip of road, about half a mile long, which led from the rude pier on the south side of Scresort Bay, through a straggling cluster of eight or ten thatched cottages'. He refers repeatedly to a 'town' in the area of the modern campsite in Kinloch and records a 'cluster of huts … like one another as peas', almost certainly the area of the modern campsite where foundations are still visible.[113] These are also evident from the OS survey of 1877. Waugh's description is worth citing in some detail:

They are all strongly built of fragments of basaltic rock; and they look as if they had been built a long time, for they all are more or less moss-grown, especially near the ground, where grass as well as moss has crept up the walls. They are little and low, although they look strong; and their thatched roofs are crossed and re-crossed with ropes, from the ends of which heavy stones are slung, to keep the thatch on in stormy weather. Only two of them have each a little rude chimney, which have evidently been added a long time after the cottages were first built; from the rest, the smoke escapes by a hole in the roof, or by the doorway … Each thatched roof is more or less covered with a pretty wild growth of grass and field flowers, which makes them look, at a distance, as if they were part of the natural landscape around.[114]

Waugh's romanticisation of the Kinloch dwellings was immediately dispelled on entering the hut of one Etty Russell, an elderly lady of the village:

The inhabitants of these dingy buildings seem to keep out the blessèd light and the pure air as carefully as possible; and just as carefully they seem to keep in everything that it is desirable to part with. I am told that this smoke is a powerful disinfectant. I can only say that, if it be a disinfectant, it finds plenty to do in those gloomy highland huts, however powerful it may be. Any stranger to the way of life in the Hebridean isles, entering one of these cots at early morning when the turf fire is new lighted upon the hearth, would start back from the dense smoke which met him at the doorway, effectually concealing every object within.[115]

It may have been this experience that prompted him to compare the Rum dwellings with those Hebridean houses described by Dr Johnson over a century earlier,

Fig 5.40 Apart from the windows and chimney, this blackhouse, photographed near Kinloch in the 1920s, would have been little different to those visited by Waugh in 1882. HES SC1081101

Fig 5.41–2 Later buildings were built at Carn nan Dobhran Bhig on land formerly owned by Kenneth MacLean. Among other building are the remains of an abandoned dwelling and street (above), and an agricultural building with wall alcoves (below). HES DP038827, DP038836

Fig 5.43 One of the ruined farmsteads at Port na Caranean built by immigrants from Skye shortly after the Clearances.
HES DP234194

noting that they were 'much the same'.[116] Traditions changed only slowly: a typical dwelling, photographed near Kinloch at the turn of the 20th century shows a stone-built structure with window and chimney – features considered exceptional at the time of Waugh's visit 20 years earlier – but still with the traditional thatched roof 'crossed and re-crossed with ropes'.

A further group of buildings lies eastwards along the southern shore of the loch at Carn nan Dobhran Bhig ('Cairn of the Little Otter') where several ruins are partly hidden within the trees together with a dyke and trackway.[117] The dyke appears to be partly functioning as a lade for some 150m, deliberately stone-faced on the upper side, less so on the lower, channelling water across the face of the hillside from one stream to another. At the lower (south) end it appears to run through a small rectangular structure measuring approximately 4m by 3m, appropriate to a mill or washing area. The whole arrangement is unusual and carefully constructed; the positioning of the buildings appears to be significant and has an 'industrial' feel, but there are no records regarding function and the word

'mill' does not appear on either of the first two editions of the OS 6-inch survey where all the structures are still shown as roofed. Within the group, the largest building measures approximately 10m by 4m within a wall 1m thick and 1.6m high; two more, much smaller, appear to have been rebuilt and there are further small structures in the vicinity. Three roofed, four unroofed buildings and a head dyke are depicted on the 1st edition of the OS 6-inch map resulting from survey in 1877. Nearby is a simple grave, unmarked, with a plain headstone.

The grave almost certainly belongs to Catharin MacLean, who died in 1863 having suffered all her life from tuberculosis. In common with many paupers elsewhere in Scotland she was denied burial or a named headstone in a formal burial ground; her grave is the only recognised example of this on Rum. The site of the grave here is on land then owned by her close cousin Kenneth MacLean, whose eldest son Hector may be represented by the inscribed initials 'HMcL' next to one of the doorways.[118] Kenneth was a character well known to Waugh, who refers to him as 'Old Kenneth' and with whom he discussed island history at length. Watching him at work, Waugh once remarked that it seemed to be a custom of the island that he should take 'a long time to do very little' but accepted that it was a

mutually agreeable arrangement between employer and employee.[119]

Further east along the coast the settlement at Port na Caranean, cleared in 1826, became resettled a few years later by a group of families from Skye.[120] Nine buildings are grouped into four small units, set in a rough line and spaced about 50m apart (Fig 5.43). Each farmstead comprises a house facing the shore, and one or two smaller buildings. In front of one, in the centre of the settlement, a slipway has been cleared through the rocks below high water. In three cases there is also a small yard attached to the rear of the house. The buildings are rectangular, with rounded external corners but square internal corners. There is a pronounced batter to the outer wall faces giving the impression that the walls are leaning inwards. Many of the buildings still survive to wall-head height, and most appear to have been hip-roofed. One of the houses still has a stone lintel over the doorway, two have internal partitions, and two have visible fireplaces (one with a mortared chimney). There is also a head dyke of drystone construction which can be traced for at least 300m, running behind the farmsteads and roughly parallel to the shore. Behind the dyke there are several piles and spreads of stone, presumably resulting from ground clearance evidenced by patches of cultivation. There are also remains of five further buildings but these are likely to be earlier: two of them have been incorporated into the head dyke which changes alignment in order to utilise their stonework,

and the remaining two survive only in fragmentary state in dense bracken. The 1st edition of the OS 6-inch map depicts nine buildings there (six roofless) and six enclosures, and this depiction remains unchanged on the 2nd edition map published in 1903. It shows a persistent, if reduced, level of occupation surviving into the 20th century and into the subsequent change of island fortunes when Rum became a sporting estate.

The reoccupation of Port na Caranean is less evident elsewhere, but with sporadic occurrences, for example at Papadil (Fig 5.11) at the south of the island where there are two ruined buildings of similar construction type to those at Port na Caranean. The larger of the two has a central door flanked by a pair of windows, and the interior is subdivided; one of the divisions inside has a fireplace and a chimney.[121] Love notes that one of the shepherds and his family lived at Papadil in the mid 19th century,[122] and that a house there was rebuilt in 1847. On the 1903 OS map both are depicted roofless. Papadil finally had become deserted. The remains of a similar post-Clearance farmstead (Fig 5.22) with enclosure can be seen at the far west of the island at Guirdil,[123] and the ruined foundations of structures can be found sheltered among the trees (Fig 5.44) by the side of the track leading down to Kilmory Bay.[124]

Sporting Estates

Shortly before the Clearances, the construction of a substantial house on the island by the tacksman Dr Lachlan Maclean, cousin of the owner Maclean of Coll, set the scene that would allow the island to offer hospitality for guests to enjoy sporting activities. It was 'a good dwelling house, with splendid offices' for which no expense was spared and was located in its own grounds for Maclean's personal comfort,[125] This house (originally called Tigh Mor but later Kinloch House), which served as the principal island residence until 1901, stood on a site to the north-east of the present castle, the construction and landscaping of which no doubt hastened its demise. It is still shown roofed on the 2nd edition OS 6-inch map published in 1903, with landscaped gardens and with the castle standing behind. Only the gates still survive, one still *in situ*, together with a stone bench and line of gateposts. Some of the 'splendid offices' which served the residence, possibly including the former post office on the island,[126] are still evident, albeit modernised

Fig 5.45–6 Little of Kinloch House survives apart from a few resilient reminders in the grounds. A surviving gate can still be seen (top) This c1910 photograph (bottom) shows it in its early ornamental setting. HES DP039725, SC1081018

and no longer serving their original purpose. The exact configuration of Kinloch House is unclear, but a contemporary description by Waugh in 1883 records it as being 'a plain strongly-built stone house, with a steep roof, and with a porch, and with a small wing at each end, one of which is used as a gun room and the other as a kitchen'.[127] When Maclean's sheep-farming enterprise was eventually abandoned, the island was sold to the Marquis of Salisbury in 1845.

Salisbury's purchase of the island had a new motivation, and little to do with sheep. Under his ownership Rum was transformed into an immense sporting estate, essentially for deer, in many senses recreating previous island hunting traditions. His initiative in transforming the island into a shooting estate possessed an irony that Miller was quick to observe; he summed up eight thousand years of island history in a perceptive, if florid, way:

> Uninhabited originally save by wild animals, it [Rum] became at an early period a home of men, who, as the gray wall on the hillside testified, derived, in part at least, their sustenance from the chase. They broke in from the waste the furrowed patches on the slopes of the valleys,— they reared herds of cattle and flocks of sheep,— their number increased to nearly five hundred souls ... then came the change of system so general in the Highlands; and the island lost all its original inhabitants, on a wool and mutton speculation ... and now yet another change was on the eve of ensuing, and the island was to return to its original state, as a home of wild animals, where a few hunters from the mainland might enjoy the chase for a month or two every twelvemonth, but which could form no permanent place of human abode. Once more, a strange and surely most melancholy cycle![128]

Salisbury's sporting vision necessitated improvement of the island's infrastructure, including the construction of trackways for which labour from Eigg was utilised, consolidation of the rubble jetty[129] mentioned in the *Statistical Account* (the 'rude pier' to which Waugh later alluded), and the building of a circular structure argued to have been a limekiln measuring some 3.8m in diameter and still standing

Fig 5.47 The pier at Kinloch, restored under Lord Salisbury's ownership. HES DP038807

to a height of over 3m located on the southern shore of Loch Scresort.[130] Hunting and fishing were dominant pursuits of Kinloch House guests, and Waugh presents a vivid account of the extent to which it dominated daily activities during the final years of the house's hospitality:

> When the sportsmen started from Kinloch House in a morning, clad in their shooting gear, with their guns, and their gillies, and their deer-stalkers, and their dogs bounding around them, wild with delight, those who were not going to the hills used to follow them to the edge of this wood at the rear of the house, to 'see them off,' and to bid them 'good morning,' and to wish them 'good luck,' and such like; and I was generally one of those who lingered behind ...[131]

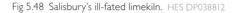

Fig 5.48 Salisbury's ill-fated limekiln. HES DP038812

Fig 5.49 The collapsed wall of the disastrous Salisbury Dam, an unsuccessful attempt to improve the fishing on Rum. HES DP234207

Fig 5.50 This impressive rock-cut lade was part of Salisbury's failed hydro-engineering venture. HES DP234206

There is no mention of the use, or indeed of the presence, of deer traps in his extensive descriptions.

Salisbury restocked the island's deer population and was also concerned with improving the salmon fishing. In the late 1840s, he had built a massive structure known as the Salisbury Dam (Fig 5.49)[132] in order to divert the headwaters of the Kilmory River through a lade into the Kinloch River. The curving dam was formed by two battered drystone walls enclosing an earth core; it was over 10m in thickness at the base and stood almost 6m in height. More than half of the original 60m length still survives. The lade ran for some 300m and included a rock-cut section up to 7m

Residence Isle of Rum. N.B

for George Bullough Esq.

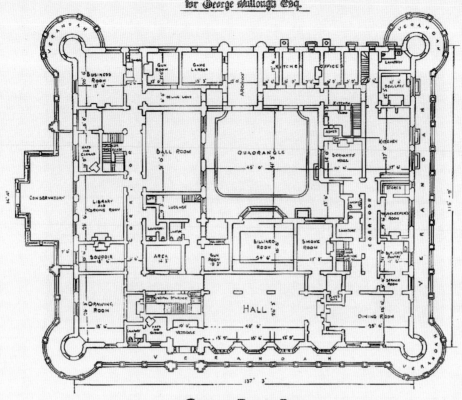

— GROUND FLOOR PLAN —

Residence Isle of Rum N.B

for George Bullough Esq

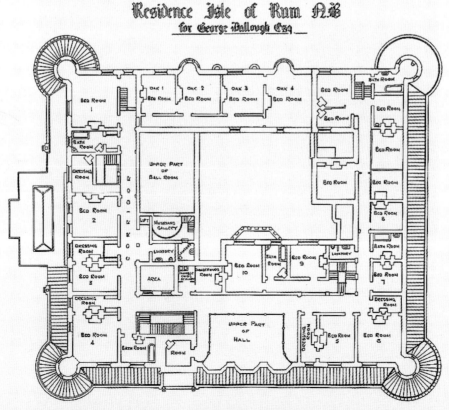

— FIRST FLOOR PLAN —

5.52 This aerial photograph reveals the courtyard design of the castle and the extravagance of the crenellated covered walkway and turrets. HES DP039608

wide and 4m deep. Unfortunately, it was breached at the north-west a few days after the reservoir was filled and was never repaired. The limekiln (Fig 5.48) also seems to have been ill-designed: Waugh noted during his visit that it had been abandoned 'because it was found that the stones of which it was built would not stand fire'.[133] Like the dam, this seems to have been an extraordinarily incompetent piece of design but, given that one ton of limestone (not available on Rum) or shell sand needed to be used to produce half a ton of quicklime, and that local fuel is limited, it would have been an extraordinarily inefficient process too.[134] Waugh is the first to refer to it as a limekiln, but its

5.51 The lavish original plans for Kinloch Castle, completed in 1897. The building was later modified after Sir George's wedding. HES SC731170

real purpose might be seriously questioned, although it appears of the 1st edition OS map as a 'limekiln' as opposed to an 'old limekiln' which suggests it was in use at that time.[135] Other possible functions for this circular stone-built edifice include kelp burning which largely died out in the 1820s, but kelping sites known in the islands tend to be rectangular and without formal superstructure.

In 1888 John Bullough, an extremely wealthy Lancastrian textile machinery manufacturer, bought the island, which he had rented for a number of years from a Campbell owner. He died three years later, bequeathing Rum to his eldest son George, who built the present Kinloch Castle.[136] The life of the Bullough family, with its relatively humble origins in Accrington, its marriages, divorces, intrigues, world travel and general ostentation has been well researched, and Rum is pivotal to much of its story.[137] George appears to have been uncomfortable with the title of his new inheritance: he was known as 'Rum' in the highland tradition of ownership and, believing that he would become ridiculed, attempted to change it to 'Rhum' – a resurrection of a perceived

Fig 5.53 The approach to Kinloch Castle c1910 at the height of its opulence. HES SC1085600

former Gaelic name for the island, but one of dubious linguistic correctness.[138] George's efforts were only partly successful – the new name appears to have been used sporadically, causing confusion to some writers and cartographers ever since. A cursory view of the references at the end of this volume show how the variation has unfortunately persisted. The Laird of Muck had similar issues with his own title, but was less successful in resolving them (Chapter 4).

The architects commissioned to build the castle, the firm Leeming and Leeming, had already won the Glasgow Municipal Buildings Competition in 1881 and had also designed the extension to the Admiralty on Horse Guards Parade in London. The castle was completed in 1897. The new building was on a par with Mar Lodge, the Earl of Fife's shooting lodge in Aberdeenshire, but took the form of an extensive

5.54 The castle sits at the head of the bay amid its own plantations and surrounded by mountains. HES DP094939

5.55 Kinloch Castle was designed to be the heart of an exclusive hunting estate, socially distinct from the rest of island life. HES DP094949

5.56 Sir George Bullough kept many of his acquisitions from foreign travel in part of the grounds' outer wall – an hexagonal gazebo. HES DP039693

regency villa with baronial overtones built using Arran
sandstone and with elaborate crenellations. It lacked
perhaps the 'taste and judgement' of Kinloch House,
the castle's predecessor, and has been described,
not entirely unfairly, as 'being reminiscent of a
metropolitan railway station' in view of its imposing
covered walkway,[139] with proportions that were
'self-consciously awkward'.[140] In short, few people
find it aesthetically stimulating. Its situation, among
earlier plantations, was convenient and sheltered
rather than romantic, hemmed in by mountains and
moorland on the landward sides. There appears to
be a sharp difference between a landscape of 'wild
forests' alluded to in the *Statistical Account* and the
seemingly treeless environment inherited by MacLean
one century later when the creation of plantations was
implemented. The newly designed landscape featured
an octagonal gazebo (Fig 5.56)[141] overlooking the
harbour as part of the crenellated outer wall as well

as a service infrastructure including small dwellings,
extensive steading[142] and stables,[143] a dairy,[144] kennels,[145]
icehouse,[146] and a garden nursery which has the
appearance of a Nissen hut.[147] The castle's maintenance
was heavily labour intensive. Archie Cameron, who was
a boy at the time, records a permanent outdoor staff
of 40–50 on the island, plus about another 30 during
the 'season'. The two populations, the islanders and the
castle staff, were socially separate.[148]

Kinloch Castle was designed as one of the ultimate
shooting lodges in Scotland and furnished with
commensurate opulence. The ground plan (Fig 5.51)
was of paramount importance, providing a large living
hall from which separate male and female domains
radiated. It was built for a wealthy bachelor in his late
twenties (and of playboy inclination) and for partying;
prominence was given to the male spheres of a galleried
living hall, dining room, smoking room and, of course,
billiard room. There were also two gun rooms and

a business room. The ladies were confined to a drawing room, boudoir and morning room leading into a conservatory. The building was very efficiently planned around a central service courtyard with the service accommodation at the north-west corner. Much of the furniture was supplied by Shoolbred & Co., a London firm, of which the partner Walter Shoolbred was a sailing and shooting friend of the owner. In keeping with the social needs of himself and his guests, George Bullough incorporated the most modern of Edwardian technologies. He was one of the first in Scotland to use electricity; he installed central heating, an internal telephone system, a novel 'Orchestrion' (a type of electric organ), and the latest in decorated toilet and bathroom wares.

George Bullough's mode of transport was the vast Clyde-built steamer, the *Rhouma*, which was said to be the length of the castle itself, in which his guests were transported to and from the island via a smaller tender which berthed at the stone-built pier still visible today. He was knighted in 1901 for having it fitted out as a hospital ship during the Boer War and, now with title as well as wealth, became extremely eligible, marrying into society through Monica de la Pasture (formerly Mrs Monica Charrington – by a previous marriage – of the brewing family) two years later. His marriage and the subsequent introduction of a female presence in the Castle impacted on the partial redesign of the layout. In 1906 Leeming and Leeming were recommissioned and prepared plans for an extension to the castle, providing two new suites of bedroom and dressing room, with servants' rooms above, on the west side above the courtyard entrance. This relatively modest addition was combined with an extensive programme of redecoration doubtless under the influence and guidance of Lady Monica herself: the drawing room and boudoir were joined together; the dark Jacobean panelling was painted white; new Adam-style fireplaces were installed, and loose covers were used to disguise the wooden furniture. The morning room became Lady Monica's sitting room (or the Napoleon Room on the basis of

Fig 5.60–1 The billiard room and dining room both reflect the strong male influence in much of the castle's design and furnishings. HES SC420143, SC420149

Fig 5.62–3 Even the decorated lavatory cistern and bowl reflect Sir George's insistence on the latest in technology and design. HES SC1506296, SC1506297

her unconfirmed connection to Napoleon's sister) and was furnished with French neo-classical furniture. The ballroom appears also to have been 'feminised' at this time.

When first built the principal bedroom suite appears to have been above the dining room in this bachelor house, and this is the only suite with direct access to the service wing. Lady Monica, however, chose the south-east corner for her suite. The new principal bedroom suite was created by combining two bedrooms and an adjoining bathroom. New Adam-style fireplaces were installed. The two new bedroom suites, now known as the oak rooms, were decorated with 'antique' salvaged panelling, some of which is said to have come from Wandsworth Palace.

Although architecturally hardly of the first flight, the great glory and unique feature of Kinloch is the survival of its original contents. Although many items have been moved internally, the lavish contents remained largely complete when Lady Monica passed Rum to the Nature Conservancy Council (now Scottish Natural Heritage) in 1957. Sir George died playing golf in France in 1939 and her visits to the castle were sporadic thereafter. She also presented a small number of items to the National

Museums Scotland including a set of 17th century Brussels tapestries, a Japanese bronze of a cockerel and chickens, a four-poster bed said to belong to Marie Antoinette (which had to be burnt because of woodworm) and a magnificent ivory eagle.

The lavishness of the interior was matched in the gardens. A formal garden[149] was created for Lady Monica on the former site of Kinloch House, entered through elegant decorated wrought iron gates bearing her initials and the beehive element from the Bullough coat of arms (Fig 5.65).[150] The Bullough arms consisted of a knight's helmet surmounted by a beehive with bees around the base and on the crest, the bees presumably representing industry.[151] Cameron often refers to the castle itself as a 'beehive', with Lady Monica as the Queen Bee. A Japanese water garden was also

Fig 5.65 The beehive symbol of the Bullough family tops the wrought-iron gateposts leading into Lady Monica's garden. HES DP039724

Fig 5.68 At Kilmory the old laundry building is now used as a deer research storage area. HES SCI088755

established around the burn to the south, complete with bridge (Fig 5.64).[152] It is reported that half a million tons of Ayrshire soil were imported to encourage the garden and make the castle as self-sufficient as possible. A walled garden was laid out, and extensive glasshouses erected for the production of exotic fruits. Even the castle's central heating was adapted to heat tanks for alligators and turtles, the latter to provide real turtle soup beloved of the Edwardians. There was also a squash court. A network of metalled roads provided vehicular access to other parts of the island including the castle laundry at Kilmory[153] – a facility deliberately located at a discrete 5 miles distance from the castle and its guests, and which now serves as a storage area for antlers for the Cambridge Kilmory deer study.

Small shooting lodges were also erected at Harris,[154] Kilmory[155] and Papadil, the last being especially favoured by Lady Monica and most easily accessible by sea; the servants went ahead overland by pony to

Fig 5.66–7 Comparative photographs of the Japanese water garden taken in 2015 (top) and around 1910 (bottom) in its more formal state. HES DP039022, SCI081098

prepare for the guests. It presumably also provided a source of fresh fish to supplement local salmon. There is little documentation for fishing during Bullough's time, but there is a well-recorded story of how two seasoned and well-respected island fisherman, taking time off from scrubbing the decks of the *Rhouma*, encountered a 'large sea serpent' which reared up in three loops each of which the boat could have passed through, complete with hoisted sail. Interestingly, neither man ever fished again, nor were they ever ridiculed by the older boatmen.[156]

The Harris Lodge (Fig 5.69) stands above the shore towards the west end of Harris Bay on the south-west coast. It still stands today and remains in occasional use by research teams, consisting of a main single-storey block of four rooms with a slate roof, harling, and with an outshot to the rear. It is recorded as being constructed in 1889.[157] The Papadil Lodge (Fig 5.70) was probably similar. It can still be seen as a roofless shell within an overgrown plantation on the shore

Fig 5.69 The bland but functional Harris Lodge. HES SC1088745

Fig 5.70 The roofless remains of Papadil Lodge in the shelter of the plantation. HES DP234197

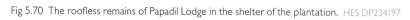

Fig 5.71 Remains of the original mausoleum at Harris which was eventually blown up. HES SCI522811

of the loch next to the ruined farmstead. The walls, which are of mortared rubble with a cement render, are now densely overgrown with rhododendron, but still stand to wall-head height. In plan it is closely similar to the Harris Lodge with a main block facing the loch and with an outshot to the rear. There are no internal partitions surviving, but two stone chimneys aligned across the centre of the house, each with a fireplace on both sides, suggest that there were also four principal rooms. By contrast the Kilmory Lodge was much smaller and survives only as ruined foundations. Probably contemporary with these lodges, built in the last decade of the 19th century, is an estate-built three-bay shepherd's cottage, also at Harris.[158] This is not shown on the first OS survey of 1877, but appears on the later revised 1903 edition. A similar shepherd's cottage was also established at Kilmory[159]

A partially subterranean mausoleum (Fig 5.71)[160] was erected at Harris on the south-west side of the island for Sir George's father, John Bullough. It was of similar grandeur to the rest of Sir George's ideas, with a canted neo-classical entrance leading into a colourful, if gaudy, mosaic-lined chamber. The style was not to everyone's taste: one of Lady Monica's friends is reported to have inspired a newspaper report comparing it to lavatories in the London Underground. It was subsequently blown up, possibly as a result of this comment, but not before John Bullough's body had been removed to

Fig 5.72 Detail of the mausoleum's vibrant ceramic design. HES SCI522812

Fig 5.74 The corroded chassis of Sir George's car is still visible at low tide at Scresort Bay. John Hunter

a new location. Fragments of mosaic can still be seen scattered around the site and on the surviving back wall against the hillside. The extravagance of the new mausoleum (Fig 5.73)[161] completely surpassed that of the original and is a stunning epitaph of cultural mismatch. It was constructed in the form of a Doric-style temple built of sandstone on a concrete plinth with a pitched roof supported by eighteen columns, probably the most bizarre and unexpected landscape feature anywhere in the Scottish islands. Apart from presenting a stark image of the ancient Mediterranean world in a completely incongruous setting, it also stands as a reflection of the rather pretentious nature of the family who had it built. Although much survives of this flamboyant era, much has also been lost: the gardens are overgrown, many of the outbuildings lie derelict and many items are recorded as having been disposed of in the sea after Sir George's death, notably his collection of tribal weapons from his world travels, some of which were kept in the gazebo together with military souvenirs.[162] One of his motor cars, a Glasgow-made Albion Shooting Brake, met a similar

fate – it can still be seen at low tide languishing on the rocks on the north side of Loch Scresort, chassis intact and the four wheels still retaining their spokes and solid rubber tyres after 75 years of twice daily tidal immersion.[163]

John Bullough's body was encased in a sandstone table tomb in the new mausoleum, later flanked by Sir George's and Lady Monica's pink granite table tombs on their respective deaths. Together with Kinloch Castle the mausoleum survives as a dominant and somewhat biased testimony to Rum's history, derived from a single generation of affluence and vulgarity. As a result, the previous 10,000 years of islanders' struggle against a hostile environment have become visually overwhelmed on the landscape and all but forgotten.

Fig 5.73 The later mausoleum at Harris, built by Sir George in a discordant classical style. HES DP165364

Chapter Six
Epilogue

Between them the Small Isles contain a rare collection of monuments of all types and from all periods. There can be few places so geographically concentrated that provide such a vivid illustration of Scotland's past from prehistory to the 20th century. From earliest times the four islands offer lithic workings, burial mounds, prehistoric hut-circles and field systems, coastal forts indicative of an elite presence, and Early Christian monuments constructed during the Age of the Saints. From later times survive the jumble of successive building foundations of townships, farmsteads and outbuildings, and a landscape peppered with shielings for use in the summer months. Then, finally, there is the inescapable and dominant presence of the modern landed gentry, their sporting estates and the sometimes lavish homes and farms they built. Some of these still stand and are occupied, such as Eigg Lodge, Kinloch Castle on Rum, and the modified farm at Gallanach on Muck. But we can only identify the activities and dwellings of the majority of islanders, the 'everyday folk', through what is left, typically lengths of walling, foundations, grass-covered ruins, natural features altered to suit some particular purpose, earthworks and cultivation lines. The monuments possess an anonymity, a type of clinical detachedness, which is hard to square with the heavily peopled landscape in which they once played a part.

Some of these monuments can be brought to life by the descriptions written by travellers such as Thomas Pennant or Edwin Waugh in the 18th and 19th

centuries. They spoke to people who lived and worked in buildings that are still recognisable on the ground, but are now ruinous. They allow us to picture a living landscape rather than a dead one, in the way that Hugh Miller's inadvertent meeting with dairy girls in a remote part of Eigg adds colour to the hundreds of grass-grown hut foundations scattered throughout the islands. The township ruins seen on all four islands speak only of desertion, but the full social impact of the Clearances that brought about their abandonment is difficult to appreciate without the eyewitness laments recorded by Waugh, or the listing of names and ages compiled by MacDougall as the émigrés arrived in Nova Scotia. Even a little knowledge about the people who lived there makes the ruins of the old townships less impersonal.

This patchwork of archaeological and historical evidence for the Small Isles flags up various questions: now that the sites have been described and discussed in the preceding chapters, are we able to identify gaps in our knowledge? How might we look to the future in terms of finding out more? And how might we best safeguard what we feel to be important and present it to others in the future?

In the many centuries before the written accounts we can only guess or imagine how the landscape may have looked, and how it was populated. Where did people live? How were they organised? How did they use the land? Unfortunately, the raw material needed for answering these questions usually consists of partially hidden, distorted fragments of what was originally there. Many of the sites discussed here can only be interpreted in the vaguest of terms, or in levels

Kilmory Glen, Rum SC1341245

of uncertainty which might perhaps be improved by archaeological intervention. And those discussed are just the visually obvious sites (in fact the minority), the ones that with reasonable degrees of knowledge we can classify as specific *types* of site. But what about the sites of which we know less – the ones that are too ephemeral or too disturbed to allow more definitive description? These are the ones denoted under the general headings of 'foundations', 'huts', 'enclosures' or 'cairns' and fill the pages of Canmore, the national database for the historic environment. Most are too uncertain in type and date to be included here, but they represent the majority of sites recorded during field survey. The text in this book probably includes no more than about 10% of the sites recorded for the Small Isles in Canmore. The remainder, were we able to understand them more, would flesh out a landscape that we tend only to see in terms of individual monuments rather than an island with a dynamic infrastructure. All our recognised hut-circles, forts, shielings and townships were part of a wider landscape, joined together by people in a social context.

Of course, people have different views as to what might be important, or where research should take us next. Ten archaeologists asked what important questions about the Small Isles should be resolved by further work might well give ten different answers, each backed up by a strong rationale and sound academic argument. Which should have priority? As a possible aid to answer this we might refer to the overarching archaeological research strategy for all of Scotland known as the Scottish Archaeological Research Framework (SCARF) which was developed between 2008 and 2102. This was drawn up by archaeologists in different walks of archaeological life throughout the country and presents a national picture which covers all the periods and themes evident in the four islands. Although too detailed to enter into here, some of the areas of interest flagged up nationally in SCARF certainly have much in common with questions we might ask locally. That said, there are also local priorities and questions about the Small Isles that would never feature in a national strategy.

There are a number of options for further research in the Small Isles that might be pursued: additional field survey work, for which there will always be potential; the use of remote sensing with its advancing technologies and, finally, archaeological intervention. As far as the first is concerned, there are certainly gaps we might fill in the existing record. Comprehensive though the field survey has been over the years, there are always places and monuments that can be investigated further, or surveyed in greater detail. Some may never have been investigated thoroughly by reason of access, logistics, or available resources. There are some standing buildings, particularly on Muck, which would benefit from a detailed record of their structural development, and there are some potential sites which are still unexplored such as the caves and rock shelters, particularly on Eigg and Rum, where there may be evidence of Mesolithic activity. Also on Eigg, in the hill loch known as Loch nam Ban Mora adjacent to the Sgurr, is a small island dun which has been described only from the shore, supported by early accounts – a site begging for more direct attention and survey.

The increased deployment of non-destructive remote sensing techniques can play a significant archaeological role, typically involving the use of aerial methods, including lidar (a developing system that allows the terrain to be modelled showing even the slightest of contour changes), and geophysical survey. Nature is often destructive, with the power to cause abandoned buildings to decay and collapse, hiding them beneath vegetation. Many of these obscured monuments on the islands were first identified through aerial photography, but their discovery depends on angle of light, vegetation growth and a range of climatic factors. Some sites are visible from the air on certain days but not on others, some are never visible at all. As climatic conditions vary there is always the potential to identify new sites (although no technique will necessarily prove what they are) and there is the opportunity to enhance our knowledge of existing sites by showing further detail or their physical extent. Aerial reconnaissance of any type has the advantage too of facilitating the mapping of large, complex monuments that spill across the landscape, such as the field systems on Canna and Eigg, and the deer traps on Rum.

On the ground itself geophysical survey is a technique better suited to specific targets than to broad overviews. Available methods differ, but all are based on an examination of the shallow subsurface and offer the potential to identify features below the ground which may not be evident, or are unclear, on the surface or from the air. The techniques do not discriminate between cultural periods or even depth in the ground; they simply respond to what is there and the extent to which the particular technique used – magnetic, electrical or electro-magnetic – is likely to detect it. It would probably not be worthwhile using geophysics in the core of a township, such would be the lack of discrimination between walling and rubble of all periods, but it could be more effective in better determining the extent and shape of partly buried hut-circles, particularly on Rum and Muck, and their possible junctions with field boundaries on Canna. It might be a way to determine whether several of the curious features on Canna are kelp kilns or burials, or perhaps to clarify the nature of structures within the coastal forts on Eigg, or to give us a better idea of the extent and internal arrangements of the postulated Norse dwelling on Muck. It many cases it may not help, but it takes us a step further in understanding what may be there as a prerequisite to any excavation. Geophysics also has a role to play in identifying sites which are mooted but not yet located, for example on Rum where the small fertile area of Papadil was once the site of postulated Early Christian activity and, later, supported a small township containing at least three families. Nothing is visible on the modern landscape, and there is a clear role for systematic geophysical survey to be undertaken over wide areas. The technique might be equally useful in exploring the vicinity where the wooden boat stems were found at Laig on Eigg to detect any associated structures or slipways.

Archaeological excavation is a final option and is destructive. Little in the way of excavation has been undertaken to date in the Small Isles, but the knowledge gained has been immense. Without excavation we would know little of the exploitation and distribution of bloodstone from Rum in the Mesolithic. Now the data from those excavations give us the opportunity to ask new questions about access, control and distribution of both raw and worked material. Thanks to other excavations, we can also take a fresh look at peripatetic metalworkers in the Bronze Age on Eigg, or Early Christian activity on Canna. Research questions likely to be resolved by excavation might be broadly based, or specific to time and place. For the former, one key area of interest must be a greater understanding of the palaeoenvironment by the use of pollen cores, as well as the investigation of domestic middens to clarify climatic change, land use over the centuries, and how terrestrial and

marine resources were exploited by the islanders. Useful by-products of this might be the modelling of environmental data reflecting the Clearances for application elsewhere, or the identification of deep sea and coastal fishing practices over time by using excavated fish bone remains.

More specific themes for which excavation might provide some answers include research into the origins and longevity of certain shielings on Rum, the methodology of kelp burning on Canna, or the nature of the later chapel at A'Chill, also on Canna. We can use archaeological intervention to resolve specific problems, for example whether a particular type of site is a kelp kiln or a burial, because excavation can give us an increased level of knowledge. But it is unlikely to tell us whether a 'fort' has been used for fighting or not, or whether a stone 'beehive' hut has been used by a dairymaid or a monk. While we might be justified, for example, in arguing the case for excavation work on the two interesting Iron Age monuments on Canna (the souterrain to determine details about the associated chamber, and the postulated Atlantic roundhouse to establish its exact purpose), we may not reach solid conclusions. Excavation does not provide an absolute 'truth'; it merely provides more evidence for interpretation, and different interpretations can be made by different people based on the same evidence. T C Lethbridge interpreted the findings from his early 20th century sondages on Canna one way, and the Commission staff interpreted them differently. Both used the same data. Neither can definitively be said to have been 'right' as such.

Another, more major, pressing question that might be resolved by excavation involves the investigation of township remains, for example at Port Mor on Muck where the concentrated settlement remains span an undefined period of time. The population tables for the four islands demonstrate roughly parallel rises in the 18th century and catastrophic falls from peak densities in the 19th. However, before the 18th century there is little on which to base population numbers. This is no different from elsewhere in the Western Highlands, but because we are dealing with islands where the land mass is small and tightly defined by the sea, we can only assume that the optimum places to live were taken up first and used over and over again through time. We believe that Iron Age society must have been highly organised for the forts to have been constructed, but how large was this island population, where did the community live, and how? And did their successors in the Middle Ages live in the same places because those were still the most suitable? Were their dwellings the same, or different? Does this mean that the ruined foundations of deserted townships at Port Mor (Muck), Five Pennies (Eigg) and at Harris (Rum) are just the latest layer in a settlement evolution in that place, stretching back some 2,500 years? Clearly, the only way to find out, and to understand how the township itself developed through time, is by relatively large-scale excavation. Would the knowledge gained justify the level of destruction required? If so, which township should be chosen, and on what grounds?

There is always the opinion that there are some sites which should not be excavated at all, because to excavate them, even in part, would be to destroy their visual and historic integrity, such as the possible nunnery at Sgorr nam Ban-Naomha on Canna. There may be questions we would like to answer about the site but perhaps they are insufficiently urgent to merit destructive intervention. This is a site that can be still be seen and largely understood in its surviving state after over 1,300 years. Its importance is not so much what it represents as an Early Christian community, but the fact that it seems to have lain undisturbed since its abandonment. Perhaps we can apply a slightly different argument for preserving the integrity of the 'ritual' site lying on the remote Struidh on Eigg. This is a site that begs for greater understanding, but would excavation really answer the questions as to what it represents, or how it was used? Its position in relation to the rock strata and associated cave gives it a remarkable resonance, and the location was undoubtedly chosen specifically. There is an argument, although not an academic one, to suggest it should remain unexplained and left alone. That to identify it as 'special' is enough, but to find out any more might be to risk its demystification.

One of the characteristics of the built past is that its character or atmosphere can be enjoyed on a number of levels. When this writer was a boy, he was taken on holidays in the 1950s and 1960s by a father keen on history. Visiting monuments was a high priority – usually castles, monasteries and monumental earthworks – but they were all stereotypical. The memories are of closely manicured grass with neatly cut edges, standing walling with sharp pointing and gravel pathways. It was a clinical and wholly artificial excursion into the past, presented for the combined

purposes of education and preservation for perpetuity. Should there have been some form of compromise that allowed character or authenticity to be enjoyed too?

The deer traps on Rum, some of the few examples surviving in Scotland as a whole, have never been formally maintained in the several centuries since they were constructed. There has been some collapse and erosion, but they have survived as a result of their durability. They have not been a focus of visitor interest, other than by the few hardy souls who have made the difficult trek out to see them, and there is something intrinsically authentic about them which would be lost if they were to be restored physically. The history of deer on Rum reverts to medieval times, and the deer traps at Ard Nev and Orval are part of the long history of deer 'management' on the island, now vested as part of the breeding and research programme carried out under the auspices of Scottish Natural Heritage (SNH), the current owners. Because of their location, they remain a remarkable but hidden asset. Attempts to make the traps more accessible, or to increase visitor footfall there, would arguably be at odds with retaining a natural environment free from human interference. Perhaps they could be recorded digitally to produce a virtual reconstruction to be made available to a wider audience? That too would be a compromise. These sites exemplify the need to bear in mind that there are sometimes constraints in how we manage and present the past.

By contrast, one of the most accessible and visible sites, also on Rum, is the cluster of buildings known locally as 'Old Kenneth's'. The complex consists of a series of structural shells, all roofless, hidden together in a small wood near the modern ferry terminal on the south side of Loch Scresort. Together the buildings stand as a monument to a specific age, and indeed to a named person, Kenneth MacLean, who lived there and who claimed eleven generations of his family lived there before him. The place requires some clearance of undergrowth (as opposed to excavation) to make it more visible, but little else in addition. The whole complex is more poignant and real with its moss and tree growth than it would be through any formal restoration that might aid its place in perpetuity. It survives as nature has allowed it to survive; it speaks of a lost culture, but one which is tangible and authentic.

There is never likely to be a strategy for investigating, preserving and presenting the archaeology and landscapes of the Small Isles that will be to everyone's satisfaction. There are too many differing views and interests as to what might be important, not to mention other management issues such as farming or conservation where the agendas may be in conflict. But the character of all four islands is undeniably moulded by their past and is to be witnessed in its many surviving forms. Most of the sites and monuments lie beyond the roads and trackways; some are hard to find, surviving as nature has left them. Discovering the sites often requires lengthy walks across beautiful and isolated landscapes where it is hard to imagine the density and complexity of the communities that existed there, and which have inspired so many curious visitors and travellers over the centuries. It is a past to be shared and enjoyed, even if not always fully understood.

Editorial Notes

References
Every chapter includes a series of end notes which refer to primary and secondary sources. These are fully expanded in a reference list at the rear of the volume. Recourse has also been had to material that is usually not publically available within the administrative archive of Historic Environment Scotland, but applications can be made to view these items.

The end notes also include the unique reference number of each of the sites mentioned in the text in bold type. By entering this number as a search, it is possible to access specific information from Canmore, the online catalogue of Scotland's historic environment: www.canmore.org.uk.

Canmore holds descriptive notes prepared by archaeologists of the Ordnance Survey Archaeology Division and HES investigators during more than a century of recording, as well as information derived from a wide range of other organisations and individuals. It also provides access to material held within the HES, including manuscripts, drawings and photographs.

Copyright
Unless otherwise specified, the contents of this volume are Crown Copyright. Copies of HES photographs, maps and plans are available to view and purchase online at www.canmore.org.uk. Vertical aerial photographs can be viewed and purchased through the National Collection of Aerial Photography (www.ncap.org.uk). In addition, a wide range of historic images from a variety of collections can be viewed at www.scran.ac.uk.

Photographs
Each photograph is accompanied by a caption that includes, when known, the collection from which the image is sourced and a unique identification number. Items held in the HES Collection can be identified by the prefixes DP (digital photograph) and SC (scanned image).

Maps
Unless otherwise stated each is aligned to Grid North, and the National Grid is marked along the margin. All maps are based on information derived from the Ordnance Survey and are reproduced with their permission © Crown Copyright 2016 License Number 100057073.

Plans
All of the original drawings are available to view in person at Historic Environment Scotland, John Sinclair House, 16 Bernard Terrace, Edinburgh, EH8 9NX and on the Canmore website.

Conventional Representations on Maps and Plans

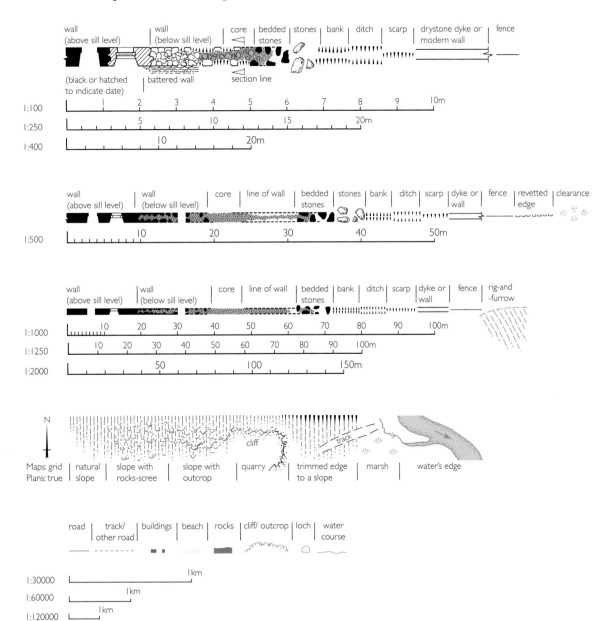

End Notes
Chapter One

1 Emeleus 1987; 1997
2 Ball 1987
3 Hirons & Edwards 1990
4 Flenley & Pearson 1967
5 Gilbertson *et al* 1996
6 Stat Acct 1796, 286
7 Ball 1987, figure 4.1
8 Otter 1825, 336
9 Stat Acct 1796, 283
10 Cowie 2002
11 For example, see Crawford 2002
12 Campbell 2002, 33–5
13 Love 1980
14 Love 1981, 59
15 Miller 1862,100
16 *Stat Acct* 1796, 274
17 Forsythe 2006
18 Otter 1825, 340
19 Walker & McGregor 2000
20 After Rixson 2001, 172, with amendments
21 Hill 2003
22 These are derived solely from Whittaker 1998
23 Miller 1862 and Otter 1825 respectively
24 Muir 1885
25 Withers & Munro 1999
26 Murray 1810
27 Stat Acct 1796; NSA
28 Munby 2007
29 McKay 1980
30 Cited in full in Campbell 2002, 121–126

31 MacDougall 1922, 305
32 Rackwitz 2007; Rixson 2004
33 Ayton & Daniell 1978, 75, 77
34 For example, see https://canmore.org.uk/collection/1176358
35 Cameron 1988
36 These are increasingly available online. See http://www.scotlandsplaces.gov.uk/digital-volumes/ordnance-survey-name-books
37 Campbell 2002, Appendix IX
38 Campbell 2002
39 Dressler 1998; Wade Martins 2004
40 Love 2001
41 Scott 2011
42 Sabbagh 2001
43 Pullar 2014
44 Dobson & Hodgetts 1985–95
45 SNH 1999
46 Clutton-Brock & Ball 1987
47 For example, Banks 1977; Haswell-Smith 2004; Miers 2008; Rixson 2001
48 MacPherson 1878
49 RCAHMS 1928
50 Campbell 2002, 234
51 Miller 1967
52 Love 1981
53 Wickham-Jones 1990
54 RCAHMS 1999
55 Campbell 2002
56 RCAHMS 2003
57 Munby 2000
58 HAS 2005

Chapter Two

1	Stat Acct 1796, 283; Martin refers to it as 'Tarsin'
2	Miers 2008
3	Withers & Munro 2002, 167
4	Campbell 2002, 10
5	NSA 149
6	Withers and Munro 1999, 167. Interestingly, Pennant, writing around a century later found his compass needle settling due west (1776, 316)
7	Campbell 2002, 74; **10709**
8	Stat Acct 1796, 286
9	*Ibid*, 273
10	NSA, 149
11	Mitchell & Clark (eds) 1907, 177
12	Pennant 1776, 311
13	RCAHMS 1999
14	Spearman 1994
15	Lethbridge 1925; **10759**
16	Campbell 2002
17	Hunter and Roberts 1994; **10698**
18	Harden 2006, 2007; **10716**
19	**141642**
20	**141639**
21	**141587**
22	**141586**
23	**141617**
24	**142479**
25	**141568**
26	**142470**
27	**142489**
28	**142496**
29	**10769**
30	**10768**
31	**10721**
32	**137806**
33	For example **141750**
34	**137797**
35	**137751**
36	**137752**
37	**142342**
38	Lethbridge 1925, 238; **10759**
39	**10710**
40	Spearman 1994
41	Armit 1999
42	**10726**
43	**10764**
44	**10738**
45	**10767**
46	**10709**
47	**10741**
48	**10735**
49	Campbell 2002, 5
50	Reeves 1988, 123
51	*Ibid*, 66
52	Cited in Campbell 2002, 19f
53	Withers & Munro 1999, 318
54	Blundell 1917, 121
55	Withers & Munro 1999, 167
56	Pennant 1776, 316
57	Cited in Campbell 2002, 123
58	Alexander *et al* 2013, figs 8 and 9
59	Muir 1885, 32
60	**10708**
61	Hunter & Roberts 1994, 3–5
62	Cited in Campbell 2002, 160f
63	NSA, 153
64	Muir 1885, 32
65	Fisher 2001, 96–101
66	**10698**
67	Alexander & Connor 2013; **10698**
68	**319390, 319888 & 319889**
69	**319886**
70	**319892**
71	**319391**
72	**319885**
73	**319887**
74	**319893**
75	**319890**
76	**319891**
77	**319894**
78	Interesting early stylised (and simplified) drawings have been made by Stuart (1867, plates L and LI) and by Muir 1885, 32; **10705**
79	Blundell, 1917, 200; **10766**
80	**319397**
81	**319395**
82	**319396**

83	Campbell 2002, Appendix IX	116	**142360**
84	Cited in Campbell 2002, 234	117	**142488**
85	Spearman 1994	118	**142509**
86	Cited in Campbell 2002, 235	119	**142507**
87	Alcock 1983, 294	120	**142436**
88	**10733**	121	MacCulloch 1824, 30
89	**10771**	122	Pennant 1776, 313
90	Pennant 1776, 316; **10709**	123	*Ibid*, 311
91	Stat Acct 1836, 152	124	Stat Acct 1796, 278
92	Skene [1577–95] 1890, 434	125	Otter 1825, 340
93	Cited in Campbell 2002, 123	126	Both reports are cited in full in Campbell 2002, 119–127
94	**137739**	127	Stat Acct 1796, 291
95	**142446**	128	Rixson 2001, 8
96	**10706**	129	Buchanan 1793, 158
97	Stat Acct 1796, opposite p 272	130	Hunter & Roberts 1994, 7–8; **10740**
98	**10730**	131	**10742**
99	**141559**	132	**10763**
100	**141514**	133	**10744**
101	**10724**	134	Forsythe 2006
102	**10756**	135	**10751**
103	**137767**	136	**141504**
104	**137750**	137	**76047**
105	**10714**	138	**76046**
106	For instance **10734**	139	**137814**
107	**10695**	140	Cited in Campbell 2002, 121
108	**10696**	141	*Ibid*, 122
109	**10720**	142	**76045**
110	**142386**	143	Fisher 2001, 97
111	**10753**	144	RCAHMS 1928, 216
112	**10752**	145	Alexander *et al* 2013, 9–12
113	**141556**	146	**76044**
114	**141565**	147	**76049**
115	Letter to J N G Ritchie at the Commission on 17 October 1968; **10695**		

Chapter Three

1	MacDonald 1811, 737	40	Withers & Munro 1999, 167
2	Stat Acct 1796, 281	41	Mitchell & Clark 1907, 175–6
3	**81906**	42	Miller 1862, 41
4	Withers & Munro 1999, 169	43	For early descriptions see Blundell 1913; **22148**
5	**106067**	44	Mitchell & Clark (eds) 1907, 176
6	Stat Acct 1796, 272	45	**202968**
7	Jameson 1800, 47	46	**255793**
8	MacDonald 1811, 739	47	**269299**
9	Miller 1862, 54	48	**22171**
10	Stat Acct 1796, 289	49	**22177**
11	*Ibid,* 286	50	**240681**
12	*Ibid*	51	I am grateful to Camille Dressler for this information.
13	RCAHMS 2003	52	**255803**
14	**149414**	53	Withers & Munro 1999, 319; **22152**
15	For detailed descriptions see Calder 1952, Calder 1963 and Calder 1965; for comparisons, see Whittle *et al* 1986	54	Stat Acct 1796, 286
16	Whittle *et al* 1986	55	Steer & Bannerman 1977, 34–6
17	Simpson *et al* 2006	56	Dressler 1998, fig 1, following p 53
18	**236660 & 301461**	57	Fisher 2001, 92–4; **22158**
19	**297983 & 297986**	58	*Ibid,* 93
20	**22143, 22162, 22167 & 22168**	59	Argued by Professor T. Clancy in his lecture 'St. Donnan of Eigg: Context and Cult' at St. Donnan's seminar, Isle of Eigg 2015.
21	**22174**	60	Gondek & Jeffrey 2003
22	**215188**	61	The sources are summarised and discussed by Anderson 1990, 142–5
23	Cowie 2002 and pers comm. I am grateful to Trevor Cowie for allowing me sight of his unpublished text prior to publication.	62	*Ibid*
24	Parker Pearson *et al* 2000	63	Withers & Munro 1999, 69
25	**22010**	64	MacPherson 1878, 584–6, drawing 585
26	**301135 & 301136**	65	Stat Acct 1796, 287
27	**240682**	66	Hunter 2012
28	MacPherson 1878	67	Anderson 1990, 221
29	**22147**	68	Smyth 1984, 108
30	MacPherson 1878, 593–4	69	Anderson 1990, 241
31	Clough & Cummins 1988, 236	70	Rixson 2001, 37f; **22160**
32	Schmidt & Burgess 1981, 224, no. 1368	71	**22181**
33	MacSween 2012, 37	72	**22187**
34	MacPherson 1878, 593	73	**22165**
35	**22188**	74	**22159**
36	**22176**	75	**22142**
37	**22189**	76	Withers & Munro 1999, 169
38	**22166**	77	**202978**
39	MacPherson 1878, 597; **22175**	78	MacPherson 1878, 586 and plate opposite; **22155**
		79	*Ibid,* 589; **22182**

80	**22163**	118	**118027**
81	MacPherson 1878, 594	119	**22160**
82	**22183**	120	**118022 & 301136**
83	Skene [1577–95] 1890, 433	121	**297181, 297982, 297984, 297985 & 297986**
84	Stat Acct 1796, 289	122	**22144**
85	NSA, 147	123	**301461**
86	Miller 1862, 38	124	**22210**
87	Information from R. Gourlay, Inverness Museum, 7 September 1979	125	**301153**
88	Campbell 2002, 40f. See also Campbell's footnote p 55	126	Clanranald Papers, cited in Dressler 1998, 62
89	Stat Acct 1796, 274	127	**301169**
90	Munby 2007	128	**301147**
91	**118019**	129	**236659**
92	**22191** (Upper Grulin); **22170** (Lower Grulin)	130	**305903 & 305953**
93	**106205 & 295401** (present farmhouse and steading)	131	Stat Acct 1796, 277
94	**106157**	132	Mitchell & Clark 1907, 176
95	NGR NM 478 899 – later part of Five Pennies	133	Buchanan 1794, Chapter XII
96	**118020**	134	**106132**
97	**287393 & 295449** (present farmhouse and steading)	135	NSA, 148
98	**255800**	136	**255802**
99	**108857 & 253799** (present farmhouse and steading)	137	**240683**
100	NM 476 890	138	NM 487 848; Dressler 1998, 56
101	**301589**	139	**301170**
102	**22178**	140	Blundell 1917, 195
103	**108858**	141	**288495**
104	**106075**	142	Blundell 1917, 199
105	MacDonald 1811, 737	143	*Ibid*, 198
106	Dressler 1998, 37	144	**106200**
107	**147832 & 118030** (former farmhouse & steading)	145	**253802**
108	MacDougall 1922, 42	146	**81906**
109	*Ibid*, 205	147	**108866**
110	Stat Acct 1796, 281	148	NSA, 154
111	Miller 1862, 33	149	**191970**
112	Withers & Munro 1999, 168	150	**106067**
113	Blundell 1917, 195	151	**305951**
114	Miller 1862, 63	152	**295451**
115	*Ibid*, 100	153	**295450**
116	**300634, 300640, 300643 & 301146**	154	**220915**
117	**22193**	155	Simpson & Brown Architects 1988

Chapter Four

1 Stat Acct 1796, 273
2 Levi 1984, 82
3 NSA, 148
4 Withers & Monro 1999, 319
5 Stat Acct 1796, 286
6 *Ibid*, 289
7 MacDonald 1811, 736
8 NSA, 148
9 Stat Acct 1796, 286
10 Miers 2008, 1553
11 NSA, 150
12 **291519**
13 **291678**
14 **22196**
15 **291328**
16 **291887**
17 **291856**
18 **22140**
19 **22138**
20 **22194**
21 **291664**
22 **22139**
23 **22137**
24 Mitchell & Clark 1907, 175
25 **21858**
26 **NGR NM 4039 8036**
27 **291670 & 291671**
28 Levi 1984, 294
29 **22136**
30 **291353**
31 MacDonald 1811, 736
32 Fisher 2001, 92: B1
33 *Ibid*, 92: C2
34 **269277**
35 Munby 2007

36 Stat Acct 1796, 281
37 NSA, 153
38 **291346**
39 **278654**
40 **73961**
41 Levi 1984, 83
42 **291698**
43 **21860**
44 **278662**
45 Stat Acct 1796, 274
46 Walker & McGregor 2000
47 Stat Acct 1796, 273
48 Withers & Munro 1999, 319
49 **118008**
50 **278625**
51 **108861**
52 **278646**
53 **291518**
54 **108348**
55 MacDougall 1922, 511–2
56 Withers & Munro 1999, 319
57 **291347**
58 **291506**
59 NSA, 148
60 **292256**
61 **118031**
62 **108861**
63 Stat Acct 1796, 279
64 **291403**
65 **291342**
66 Napier Commission, evidence taken for Invernesshire at Arisaig, August 1883
67 *Ibid*, Appendix LXXXIX, evidence taken at Edinburgh, October 1883
68 *Ibid*
69 Stat Acct 1796, 279

Chapter Five

1   Emeleus 1987

2   NSA, 148

3   McKay 1980, 195

4   MacDonald 1811, 741f

5   Stat Acct 1796, 292

6   *Ibid*, 283

7   MacCulloch 1824, 60

8   NSA, 148–9

9   Withers & Munro 1999

10 McKay 1980

11 Pennant 1776

12 Knox 1787

13 For example, Love 2001

14 Waugh 1883, Ch II; Cameron 1988, 116 (with variation between tying to a post, or pinned to the ground)

15 Waugh 1883

16 Miller 1862

17 Cameron 1988

18 Love 2001

19 Love 1980

20 Love 1981

21 Wickham-Jones 1990; **22202**

22 I am grateful to Torben Ballin for providing me with this information

23 **11014**

24 Otter 1825, 322f

25 **11015**

26 **10979**

27 **21911**

28 **10995**

29 **21950**

30 Wickham-Jones 1994

31 **10990**

32 For example, Love 2001, 27–31

33 **10946**

34 Fisher 2001, 95

35 Muir 1885, 33

36 RCAHMS 1928, 220

37 Love 2001, 29–30

38 Withers & Munro 1999, 166

39 Pennant 1776, 323

40 Muir 1885, 33

41 Waugh 1883, Ch II

42 Fisher 2001, 95. John Love (pers. comm.) re-erected it *in situ* in order to prevent it becoming lost; **22201**

43 Anderson 1990, 184; **22197**

44 Anon 1944, 139, no.4

45 Love 1980

46 Rixson 2001, 99–112

47 **21940**

48 Stat Acct 1796, 275

49 NSA, 152

50 Withers & Munro 1999, 166

51 *Ibid*, 318

52 Otter 1825, 330

53 Taylor 1618, 27

54 Skene [1577–95] 1890, Appendix III, 434

55 **21939**

56 **21933**

57 Miller 1967, 212, note

58 Love 1980, 131

59 Handwritten notes in Love's records

60 Love 1981, 29

61 Waugh 1883, Ch II

62 **118018**

63 Pennant 1776, 317

64 **10993**

65 Mitchell & Clark 1907, 176; **21948 & 21949**

66 **10955 & 10956**

67 **11019**

68 **22033**

69 Pennant 1776, 318

70 **11220**

71 **21958**

72 Otter 1825, 321

73 Waugh 1883, VII

74 Love 2001, 87

75 Stat Acct 1796, 281–1

76 *Ibid*, 283

77 Pennant 1776, 321–2

78 *Ibid*, 319

79 McKay 1980, 195–9

80 Stat Acct 1796, 274

81 Pennant 1776, 320

82 Stat Acct 1796, 274–5

83 *Ibid*, 278

84 **21952**

85 Stat Acct 1796, 275

86 Knox 1787, 88

87 Rixson 2001, 8

88 **338661**

89 Cameron 1988, 77

90 Love 1981; for detailed discussion see also Love 2001, Ch 7

91 *Ibid*, 43

92 Stat Acct 1796, 274

93 Cameron 1988, 50

94 Love 1981, 59

95 *Ibid*, 44–5

96 **21967**

97 **21927**

98 Love 1981, 43; **21890, 21891, 21938**

99 **10971, 10974, 10995, 10999–11004**

100 Love 2001, Ch 10

101 NSA, 152

102 See also Love 2001, 126 for a fuller account

103 I am grateful to Sylvia Beaton for researching this information

104 John Love pers. comm.

105 Waugh 1883, Ch III

106 The passenger list is also documented by Love 2001, Appendix III

107 MacDougall 1922, 126–131

108 I am grateful to personal comments from John Love here. There is some discrepancy between the numbers recorded as arriving from Rum and those from Muck – a difference also noted by John Lorne Campbell. Some of the surnames do not quite square with those known from Rum at the time.

109 NSA, 153

110 Miller 1862, 154

111 Waugh 1883, Ch II

112 *Ibid*, Ch III

113 **118017 and 118018**

114 Waugh 1883, Ch III

115 *Ibid*, Ch VI

116 *Ibid*, Ch VIII

117 **22204**

118 I am grateful to Sylvia Beaton for researching this information

119 Waugh 1883, Ch V

120 Love 2001, 142–3; **349813**

121 **21961**

122 Love 2001, 143–5

123 **11019**

124 **10949**

125 NSA, 152

126 **107929**

127 Waugh 1883, Ch XIII

128 Miller 1862, 155

129 **107923**

130 **108863**

131 Waugh 1883, Ch XII

132 **21880**

133 Waugh 1883, Ch VII

134 I am grateful to Professor Paul Bishop for giving me these details

135 Bishop & Thomson 2013

136 **22200**

137 Scott 2011

138 Campbell (2002, 35, note) is very dismissive of the authenticity of this. Campbell also reported (John Love pers. comm.) that Sir George bullied the Post Office to have the 'Rhum' version put on the postmark.

139 Miers 2008, 150

140 Scott 2011, 123

141 **107913**

142 **276850**

143 **276849**

144 **276872**

145 **276874**

146 **276875**

147 **293197**

148 Cameron 1988, 10

149 **200218**

150 **293236**

151 Scott 2011, 54

152 **290356**

153 **10988**

154 **200219**

155 **136717**

156 Scott 2011, 63

157 Love 2001, 228

158 **312587**

159 **312587**

160 **200220**

161 **21945**

162 John Love, pers. comm.; also Cameron 1988, 66

163 There has been some difficulty in identifying the make of vehicle in the sea and I have relied on Sylvia Beaton's own research which has involved examining chassis types and local records.

References

Alcock, L 1983
The supposed Viking burials on the islands of Canna and Sanday, Small Isles, in O'Connor & Clarke (eds) 1983, 293–309

Alexander, D & Connor, S 2013
'Small Isles, A'Chill', *Discovery Excavation Scot*, New Series 13, 113

Alexander, D, Ahlers, M & Connor, S 2013
A'Chill Graveyard Survey, Canna. Data Structure Report, Glasgow: National Trust for Scotland

Anderson, A O 1990
Early Sources of Scottish History AD 500 to 1286, Vol. 1, Stamford: Paul Watkins

Anon 1944
Donations to and purchases for the Museum 1943–44, *Proc Soc Antiq Scot* 78 (1943–4), 139

Armit, I 1999
The abandonment of souterrains: evolution, catastrophe or dislocation, *Proc Soc Antiq Scot* 129 (1999), 577–96

Ayton, R & Daniell, W 1978
A Voyage Round Great Britain. Revised edition of 1813–1823 text and images, Ilkley: Scolar Press

Bald, W 1805
Map of Canna and Sanday, Small Isles. Inscribed: 'Canna. The property of Ranald George M'Donald of Clanranald. Surveyed by Wm Bald, 1805'.

Bald, W 1806
Map of the Island of Eigg commissioned by the Chiefs of Clanranald.

Ball, M E 1987
Botany, woodland, and forestry' in Clutton-Brock & Ball (eds) 1987, 43–62

Banks, N 1977
Six Inner Hebrides, London: David and Charles

Bishop, P & Thomson, G 2013
How OS depicted limekilns in Scotland's Central Belt, *Sheetlines* 98, 19–31

Blaeu, J c1635
Scotia Regnum cum insulis ajacentibus / Robertus Gordonius a Straloch descripsit, Map of Scotland, imprint: Amsterdam 1654

Blundell, O 1913
Further notes on artificial islands in the Highland area, *Proc Soc Antiq Scot* 47 (1912–13), 292

Blundell, O 1917
The Catholic Highlands of Scotland: The Western Highlands and Islands, Edinburgh: Sands & Co

Buchanan, J L 1793
Travels in the Western Hebrides from 1782 – 1790, London

Buchanan, J L 1794
A General View of the Fishery of Great Britain, London

Calder, C S T 1952
Report on the excavation of a Neolithic Temple in the parish of Standsting, Shetland, *Proc Soc Antiq Scot* 84 (1949–50), 185–205

Calder, C S T 1963
Excavations in Whalsay, Shetland 1954–5, *Proc Soc Antiq Scot* 94 (1960–61), 28–46

Calder, C S T 1965
Cairns, Neolithic houses and burnt mounds in Shetland, *Proc Soc Antiq Scot* 96 (1962–3), 37–86

Cameron, A 1988
Bare Feet and Tackety Boots. Edinburgh: Luath Press

Campbell, J L 2002
Canna: The Story of a Hebridean Island , 2nd edn, Edinburgh: National Trust for Scotland

Chapman, J 1809
Plan of the Island of Muck as surveyed and divided into lots in spring 1809 by JA Chapman

Clough, T H McK & Cummins, W A 1988
Lists of identifications, in Clough, T H McK & Cummins, W A (eds) *Stone Axe Studies, Volume 2: The Petrology of Prehistoric Stone Implements from the British Isles,* London: Council for British Archaeology Research Report no. 67, 141–264

Clutton-Brock, T H & Ball, M E (eds) 1987
Rhum: the Natural History of an Island, Edinburgh: Edinburgh University Press

Cowie, T 2002
'Galmisdale, Isle of Eigg, Highland (Small Isles parish), late Bronze Age metalworking debris, *Discovery Excavation Scot*, 3, 78

Crawford, B E (ed) 2002
The Papar in the North Atlantic: Environment and History, St Andrews University: St John's House Papers No 10

Dobson, R M & Hodgetts, N G 1985–95
Ten papers on the natural history of Muck, *The Glasgow Naturalist*

Dressler, C 1998
Eigg: The Story of an Island, Edinburgh: Polygon

Emeleus, C H 1987
The Rhum Volcano in Clutton-Brock, T H and Ball, ME (eds) 1987, 11–26

Emeleus, C H (ed) 1997
Geology of Rum and Adjoining Islands, Memoirs of the British Geological Survey, Sheets 60, 61 and 71 (Scotland), British Geological Society

Fisher, I 2001
Early Medieval Sculpture in the West Highlands and Islands, Royal Commission on the Ancient and Historical Monuments of Scotland and the Society of Antiquaries of Scotland, Monograph Series 1, Edinburgh

Flenley, J R & Pearson, M C 1967
Pollen analysis of a peat from the island of Canna (Inner Hebrides), *New Phytologist* 66, 299–306

Forsythe, W 2006
The archaeology of the kelp industry in the Northern Isles of Ireland, *International Journal of Nautical Archaeology* 35:2, 218–29

Gilbertson, D, Kent, M & Grattan, J (ed) 1996
The Outer Hebrides. The Last 14,000 Years. Sheffield: Sheffield Academic Press

Gondek, M M & Jeffrey, S 2003
The re-use of a figurative panel from Eigg, *Medieval Archaeology* 47, 178–85

Harden, J 2006
Beinn Tighe, Canna *Discovery Excavation Scot,* New Series 7, 101

Harden, J 2007
Beinn Tighe, Canna *Discovery Excavation Scot,* New Series 8, 123

HAS (Highland Archaeology Services Ltd) 2005
Archaeological Development Plan for the Small Isles, Report no. HAS051202, Inverness: Highland Archaeological Services

Haswell-Smith, H 2004
The Scottish Isles, Edinburgh: Canongate

Hill, P 2003
Stargazing: Memoirs of a Young Lighthouse Keeper, Edinburgh: Canongate

Hirons, K R & Edwards, K J 1990
Pollen and related studies at Kinloch, Isle of Rhum, Scotland, with particular reference to possible early human impact on vegetation, *New Phytologist* 116, 715–27

Hunter, J R 2012
Excavations at Kildonnan, Eigg, 2012. Eigg: Isle of Eigg Historical Society (archived on Eigg and at the Royal Commission on the Ancient and Historical Monuments of Scotland, Edinburgh)

Hunter, J R & Roberts, C A 1994
Archaeological Fieldwork on the Islands of Canna and Sanday, Inner Hebrides, Summer 1994. Interim Report, Bradford: Bradford University Department of Archaeological Sciences

Jameson, R 1800
Mineralogy of the Scottish Isles, Vol II, Edinburgh

Knox, J 1787
A Tour through the Highlands of Scotland and the Hebride Isles in 1786, London

Langlands, G 1801
This map of Argyllshire: Taken from Actual Survey, George Langlands and Son: Campbeltown

Leslie, T 1824
Map of the Island of Eigg, Robertson & Ballantyne Lithography, Edinburgh

Lethbridge, T C 1925
Exploration of a cairn on Canna, *Proc Soc Antiq Scot* 59 (1924–5), 238–9 (notes)

Levi, P (ed) 1984
Samuel Johnson and James Boswell: A Journey to the Western Isles of Scotland and *The Journal of a Tour to the Hebrides,* London: Penguin

Love, J A 1980
Deer traps on the Isle of Rum, *Deer* 5:3, 131–2

Love, J A 1981
Shielings of the Isle of Rum, *Scottish Studies* 25, 39–63

Love, J A 2001
Rum: A Landscape without Figures, Edinburgh: Birlinn

MacCulloch, J 1824
The Highlands and Western Isles of Scotland (Vol 4), London: Longman

MacDonald, J 1811
General View of the Agriculture of the Hebrides, Edinburgh: Board of Agriculture

MacDougall, J L 1922
History of Inverness County, Nova Scotia, Belleville, Ontario

McKay, M M (ed) 1980
The Rev. Dr. John Walker's Report on the Hebrides of 1764 and 1771, Edinburgh: John Donald

MacPherson, N 1878
Notes on antiquities from the island of Eigg, *Proc Soc Antiq Scot*, 12 (1876–78), 577–97.

MacSween, A 2012
'Pottery Report' in Hunter 2012, 37–40.

Miers, M 2008
The Western Seaboard: an illustrated architectural guide, Edinburgh: Rutland Press

Miller, H 1862
The Cruise of the Betsey, Boston

Miller, R 1967
Land-use by summer shielings, *Scottish Studies* 11:2, 193–221

Mitchell, A & Clark, J T (eds) 1907
MacFarlane's Geographical Collections – Geographical Collections relating to Scotland Made by Walter Macfarlane, Vol. III, Edinburgh: Scottish History Society

Muir, T S 1885
Ecclesiological Notes on some of the Islands of Scotland, Edinburgh: David Douglas

Munby, J 2000
Isle of Muck, Small Isles Parish, Highland Region, Scotland: An Archaeological Survey of the Historic Landscape, Oxford: privately printed

Munby, J 2007
Lost Ancestors. Island families in 1765 on Eigg, Muck, Rum and Canna: (An edition of Neill McNeill's Census of Small Isles Parish, Inner Hebrides in 1764/5), Oxford: privately printed

Murray, S 1810
A Companion and Useful Guide to the beauties of Scotland, to the lakes of Westmoreland, Cumberland and Lancashire; and to the curiosities of the district of Craven, etc. (A Companion and useful guide to the beauties in the Western Highlands of Scotland and in the Hebrides, 3rd edn, London

NSA 1845
The New Statistical Account of Scotland was commissioned by the Committee of the Society for the Sons and Daughters of the Clergy and was published by Blackwood and Sons, Edinburgh, in fifteen volumes between 1834 and 1845. The entry for the Small Isles, written by the Reverend Mr Donald McLean in 1836, is included in volume 14, 145–54.

Otter, W 1825
The Life and Remains of Rev. Edward Daniel Clarke, Vol. 1, London: Cowie & Co

Owen, T M (ed) 2000
From Corrib to Cultra: Folklife Essays in Honour of Alan Gailey, Belfast: Institute of Irish Studies

Parker Pearson, M, Marshall, P, Mulville, J, Smith, H & Ingrem, C 2000
Cladh Hallan: Excavation of a Late Bronze Age to Early Iron Age settlement. August–September 2000, University of Sheffield

Pennant, T 1776
A Tour in Scotland and Voyage to the Hebrides, 1772, London

Pullar, P 2014
A Drop in the Ocean, Edinburgh: Birlinn

Rackwitz, M 2007
Travels to Terra Incognita, Berlin: Waxman

RCAHMS 1928
Ninth Report with Inventory of Monuments and Constructions in the Outer Hebrides, Skye and the Small Isles, Edinburgh: His Majesty's Stationary Office

RCAHMS 1999
RCAHMS Broadsheet 5, Canna, the Archaeology of a Hebridean Landscape, Edinburgh: RCAHMS and NTS

RCAHMS 2003
RCAHMS Broadsheet 12, Eigg, the Archaeology of a Hebridean Landscape, Edinburgh: RCAHMS

Reeves, W (ed) 1988
Adamnan: Life of Saint Columba. Facsimile reprint from 1874, Lampeter: Llanerch Enterprises

Rixson, D 2001
The Small Isles: Canna, Rum, Eigg and Muck, Edinburgh: Birlinn

Rixson, D 2004
The Hebridean Traveller, Edinburgh: Birlinn

Sabbagh, K 2001
A Rum Affair, Boston: Da Capo Press

Schmidt, P K & Burgess, C B 1981
The axes of Scotland and Northern England, Prahistorische Bronzefunde, 9:7. Munchen: Beck

Scott, A 2011
Eccentric Wealth: the Bulloughs of Rum, Edinburgh: Birlinn

Simpson, D D A, Murphy, E M & Gregory, R A 2006
Excavations at Northton, Isle of Harris, Oxford: BAR British Series 408

Simpson and Brown Architects 1988
The Lodge: Isle of Eigg. Conditions Report and Options Appraisal, Edinburgh

Skene, W F [1577–95] 1890
Celtic Scotland: A History of Ancient Alban, Vol. III, Land and People, 2nd edn, Appendix III, Edinburgh: David Douglas,

Smyth, A P 1984
Warlords and Holy Men, Guildford: Arnold

SNH (Scottish Natural Heritage) 1999
Rum: Island Place-Names, Inverness: Scottish Natural Heritage

Spearman, R M 1994
Portable Antiquities from the Islands of Canna and Sanday, Unpublished manuscript, National Museums Scotland

Stat Acct 1796
The Statistical Account of Scotland was edited by Sir John Sinclair of Ulbster and published in twenty-one volumes by William Creech, Edinburgh, between 1791 and 1799. The entry for the Small Isles, written by the Reverend Mr Donald McLean in 1796, is included in volume 17, 272–94

Steer, K A & Bannerman, J W M 1977
Late medieval Monumental Sculpture in the West Highlands, Edinburgh: Royal Commission on the Ancient and Historical Monuments of Scotland

Stuart, J 1867
Sculptured Stones of Scotland, Vol II, Aberdeen: Spalding Club

Taylor, J 1618
The Penniless Pilgrim (1876 edition), London

Wade Martins, S 2004
Eigg – An Island Landscape, 3rd edn, Hunstanton: PWM Heritage Management

Walker, B & McGregor, C 2000
Buildings associated with post-Clearance sheep roumes in Lochaber, Lochalsh, Skye and the Small Islands, in Owen (ed) 2000, 95–121

Waugh, E 1883
The Limping Pilgrim, Manchester: John Heywood

Whittaker, I G 1998
Off Scotland: A Comprehensive Record of Maritime and Aviation Losses in Scottish Waters, Edinburgh: C-Anne Publishing

Whittle, A, Keith-Lucas, M, Milles, A, Noddle, B, Rees, S & Romans, J C C 1986
Scord of Brouster: An Early Agricultural Settlement in Shetland, Oxford: Oxford University Committee for Archaeology, Monograph 9

Wickham-Jones, C R 1990
Rhum: Mesolithic and later sites at Kinloch. Excavations 1984–86, Edinburgh: Society of Antiquaries of Scotland Monograph Series 7

Wickham-Jones, C R 1994
A round bottomed vessel from a new archaeological site at Papadil, Rum, *Glasgow Archaeological Journal* 18, 73–5

Withers, C W J & Munro D (eds) 1999
A Description of the Western Islands of Scotland circa 1695: a voyage to St Kilda by Martin Martin, with A Description of the Occidental i.e. Western Islands of Scotland by Donald Monro written in 1549, Edinburgh: Birlinn

Glossary

Anchorite
A Christian who withdraws from secular society, having taken vows to lead a life devoted to prayer, characterised by strict self-discipline and abstention from all forms of indulgence.

Baffle Wall
A short length of wall projecting from the face of a building and designed to protect the external face of a window or door from the natural elements.

Bank Barn
A dwelling set into a natural slope so as to provide easy access to the second storey from ground level.

Barrow (Tumulus)
A mound of earth, or earth and stone, raised over one or more burials.

Bloodstone
A natural mineral that has similar flaking properties to flint. Rum is the only British source of bloodstone.

Cairn
A heap of stones raised over one or more burials; also a geographical marker or a commemorative monument.

Cist
A grave, the ends, sides and cover of which are formed from slabs or boulders.

Corbelled
A method of spanning a void with projecting courses of well-anchored, overlapping stone slabs.

Crannog
A small artificial island constructed of timber, earth and boulders, and originally supporting a timber or stone dwelling.

Earth-fast
Usually used of stone firmly rooted in the ground.

Edge-set
Usually used of a stone set upright in the ground.

Facing-stone
The outer stones of a wall, commonly with a central core made of earth, rubble, or turf.

Eremitic
A solitary and reclusive way of life, often for religious contemplation.

Field bank
A linear feature constructed of a variety of materials, including earth, stone and turf, often defining an enclosure or otherwise delimiting a piece of ground.

Glebe
A parcel of land the income from which supported a parish priest or minister.

Head-dyke
A wall or bank that separating the arable lands of a township from the rough grazing.

Horse Gin
A device comprising shafts and gearing usually attached to the outside of a barn and used to harness the power of a horse to drive machinery, such as a threshing machine, located within the barn.

Hut-circle
A low, roughly circular, bank of earth, turf or stone, representing the degraded remains of the wall of a prehistoric circular building.

Isthmus
A narrow strip of ground, with the sea or a loch to either side, which links two larger areas of land.

Kelp Kiln
A stone-lined pit in which seaweed was burned to produce soda and iodine.

Lade
An artificial channel conveying water from a stream or river to a water mill.

Lazy beds
Spade-dug linear cultivation ridges, often used for growing potatoes.

Lithic Tool
Prehistoric stone tool.

Naust
A roughly boat-shaped hollow, sometimes lined with stone, which was usually sited on, or above a shoreline and used for the temporary storage of vessels.

Orthostatic Wall
A wall constructed of individual stone slabs or boulders set upright adjacent to one another.

Promontory
A headland jutting into the sea.

Revetment
A wall retaining a bank of earth.

Scree
An expanse of loose stone usually on the lower reaches of a slope.

Shieling
Typically, an upland area set aside for summer grazing. A shieling hut is a small temporary dwelling of turf or stone occupied by those tending livestock.

Sound
A narrow stretch of water connecting two larger bodies of water.

Souterrain
A subterranean, stone-lined and slab-roofed passage or chamber often associated with a surface dwelling and usually dating to the Iron Age.

Subrectangular
Of roughly rectangular shape.

Tacksman
A principal tenant who sub-let the land of a Clan Chief (to whom he was sometimes related), who also oversaw its management and collected rents on his behalf.

Tinchell
The body of hunters that would drive deer into a trap.

Transhumance
The practice of moving livestock seasonally from one grazing to another.

Turf, Earth, or Rubble Core-Wall
A wall that comprises two stone faces separated by a core of turf, earth or rubble.

Unstan Ware
Round-bottomed, early Neolithic pottery vessels identified originally in Orkney, but also found in the Western Isles.

Whetstone
A rubbing stone for sharpening metal tools.

Winnow
The act of separating the chaff from the grain after threshing.

Acknowledgements

Between 1994 and 2012 staff from what was then the Royal Commission on the Ancient and Historical Monuments of Scotland (RCAHMS), now part of Historic Environment Scotland (HES), undertook a number of field surveys in the Small Isles (Canna, Eigg, Muck and Rum) in order to update the rather patchy and out of date record of sites and monuments made and published in the inter-war years. This renewed fieldwork, undertaken in various stages, resulted in written descriptions, site photographs, scale drawings and aerial images. In drawing together these various records I have been very conscious of using, sometimes wholesale, the text and interpretation of the Commission surveyors. Some of this is derived from their primary records and field-notes, others from secondary texts produced by Commission staff, for example from excursion guide notes, or from published broadsheets. Numerous individuals were involved in the surveys that provided this content and this book relies heavily on the survey and writing of project managers Eve Boyle and Angela Gannon, together with contributions, including illustrations and aerial imagery, from Robert Adam, John Borland, Georgina Brown, Julie Candy, Dave Cowley, Piers Dixon, Tahra Duncan-Clark, Andrew Dutton, Ian Fisher, Dorothy Graves McEwan, George Geddes, Simon Gilmour, Simon Green, Alex Hale, Strat Halliday, Rebecca Jones, Angus Lamb, Alan Leith, Amy Mack, Jim Mackie, Leanne McCafferty, Alison McCaig, Peter McKeague, Kevin McLeod, Bob Mowat, Ian Parker, Matthew Ritchie, Ian Scott, Sam Scott, Rob Shaw, John Sherriff, Ian Smith, Clare Sorensen, Jack Stevenson, John Stevenson, Stephen Thompson and Adam Welfare. The publication project was managed by John Sherriff and the original text edited into acceptable shape by Robin Turner; the layout and design are by Alasdair Burns and the final editing was undertaken by Christine Wilson. Jamie Crawford managed its transition into printed form. I am grateful to them all for efficiently creating the final product.

I have also relied on some unpublished material, and I am particularly grateful to Trevor Cowie for allowing me to use data from his excavations on Eigg.

I am also immeasurably grateful to have received helpful advice and suggestions from people who are far more familiar with the respective island landscapes and history than I ever will be. Derek Alexander (Canna), John A Love (Rum), Julian Munby (Muck), Susanna and Peter Wade Martins (Eigg) and Camille Dressler (Eigg) all kindly took time to read and comment on the respective chapters. I am indebted to them for their knowledge and for tactfully putting me straight on a number of counts. In addition, Camille Dressler provided essential access to the Eigg Archive; Susanna Wade Martins kindly loaned her hand-copied version of Bald's map of Eigg, as well as helping me through the history of Eigg Lodge, and John A Love generously allowed his sketches and notes to be used for publication. Their support has been invaluable throughout.

On Rum I was fortunate to be helped by Sylvia Beaton, who undertook much fieldwork on my behalf and I have relied heavily on some of her research, as well as her local knowledge and enthusiasm. Cecily Cropper helped me search for particular sites on Eigg, Muck and Rum, often trekking into obscure parts of a midge-infested landscape, and in pouring rain; I am indebted to her persistent support and good humour.

The content of this volume is, therefore, largely other people's: my role has been to pull the various elements together, to supplement, omit or to prune as I felt appropriate, and to provide the necessary threads of argument and balance. I hope I have presented the efforts of their work and expertise in a manner they find acceptable.

Index

Page numbers in *italics* refer to captions.